IMAGES
of America

THE ELKS OPERA HOUSE

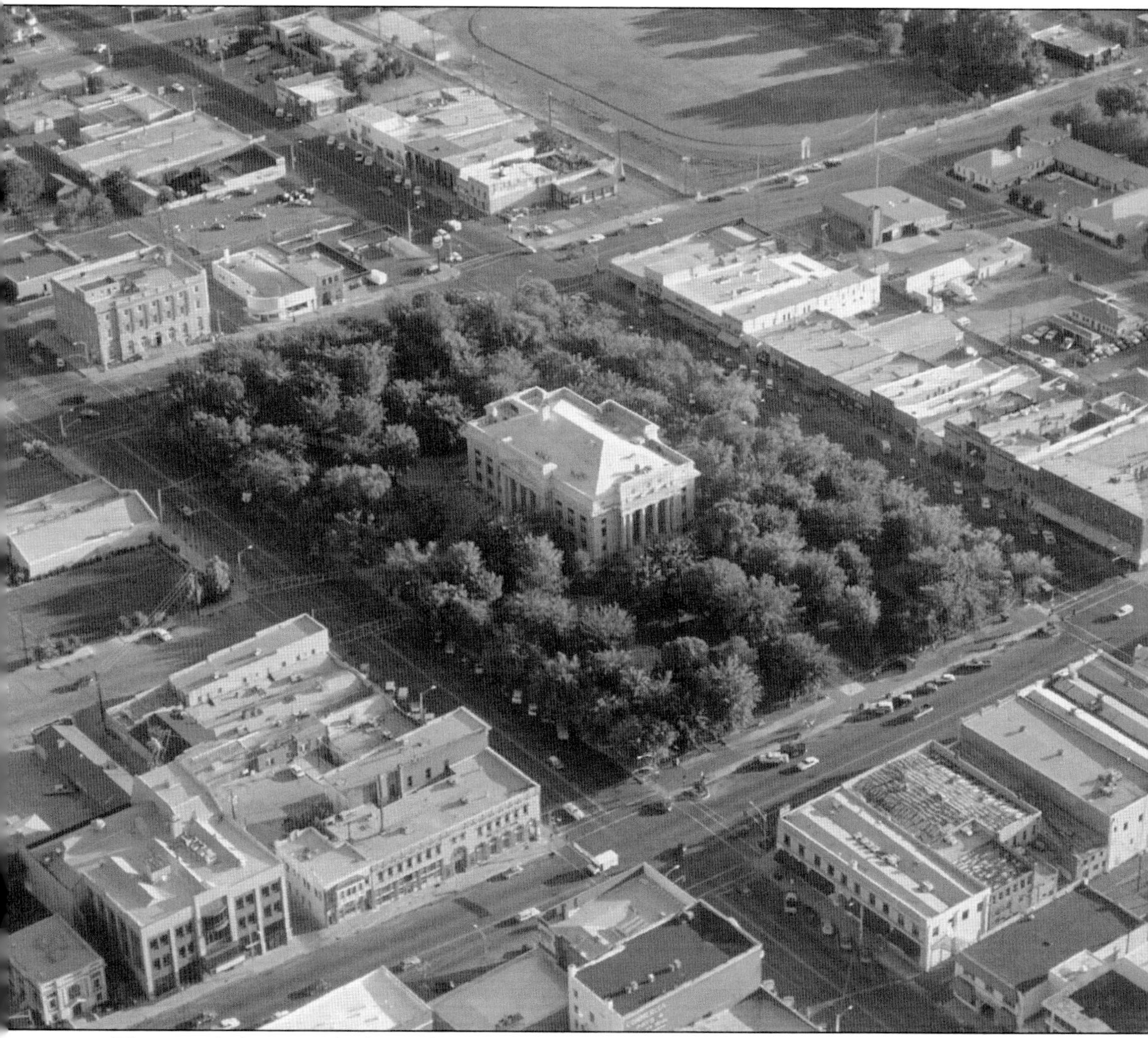

This aerial photograph shows downtown Prescott in 2010 with the historic Courthouse Plaza as the center of attraction and the Elks Opera House only one block away. The opera house is the three-story building in the lower left and can be distinguished by its marquee, which is facing Gurley Street. (Photograph by William Otwell.)

On the Cover: Florence Roberts was one of the most prominent touring actresses on the road in her day. She and her troupe opened the Elks Opera House on February 20, 1905, with the acclaimed Spanish Catalan play *Marta of the Lowlands* by Angel Guimera. This undated photograph shows Miss Roberts, probably in San Francisco where she lived, in her most famous role as Zaza in a play of the same name. (Parker Anderson collection.)

IMAGES
of America

THE ELKS OPERA HOUSE

Parker Anderson and Elisabeth Ruffner

ARCADIA
PUBLISHING

ISBN 978-0-7385-8542-0

Published by Arcadia Publishing
Charleston, South Carolina

Printed in the United States of America

Library of Congress Control Number: 2011940758

For all general information, please contact Arcadia Publishing:
Telephone 843-853-2070
Fax 843-853-0044
E-mail sales@arcadiapublishing.com
For customer service and orders:
Toll-Free 1-888-313-2665

Visit us on the Internet at www.arcadiapublishing.com

This book is dedicated to everyone who has contributed to and made possible the Elks Opera House's triumph over time, extending for more than 100 years.

Contents

ACKNOWLEDGMENTS

The authors thank the architects and artisans who conceived the restoration and the construction contractors and workmen who brought the beauty back. We also thank the many generous donors who contributed both their time and money, thereby making the restoration a reality.

We further thank Sharlot Hall Museum Library and Archives, the Prescott City Council and staff, the *Daily Courier*, the Elks Opera House Guild, and the Elks Opera House Foundation and Board for their assistance in the production of this book.

Finally, we thank Terry Berrett, an Elks Opera House Foundation board member, for his preparation of the photographs for publication and for performing many other graphic-arts production activities. The creation of this book was greatly enhanced by his help and involvement.

INTRODUCTION

Prescott, Arizona, became the first capital of the Territory of Arizona with the arrival of a governor's party and military escort in the spring of 1864. As the Yavapai County seat, Prescott grew and over the years and became the business center for mining, banking, and agriculture in the Territory of Arizona.

With growth in commerce and population came a desire by the residents for entertainment. This resulted in the first local performing-art houses in a variety of venues, ranging from crude stages in log cabins to wooden and, later, brick buildings. Plays were written, and performances were given by both local actors and musicians as well as by traveling performance companies. While this provided some degree of entertainment, it was insufficient for the growing need.

In 1904, the Prescott Lodge of the Benevolent and Protective Order of Elks (BPOE) no. 330 considered adding a world-class opera house as an addition to their new lodge building. The cost (in dollars of the day) was estimated at $15,000. As many of Prescott's then 3,000 residents were from the East and were used to top-notch entertainment, community support was overwhelming. The necessary funds were raised, and noted architect John R. Minor was engaged for design. With great fanfare and in front of a large crowd, the cornerstone was laid on April 3, 1904. Less than a year later, construction was complete.

Little expense was spared in its design and construction, and upon completion, Prescott arguably had the finest opera house between St. Louis and San Francisco. Private boxes, gold-leaf columns, stenciled decorations, plaster elk heads, and unique stage backings were only a few of the features that set this theater apart from others throughout the West. A copper elk was placed upon the roof, where it contentedly watched over Prescott and its increasing population. All of these characteristics attracted the best talent to Prescott, with the first performance given by famed San Francisco artist Florence Roberts on February 20, 1905. Building upon this successful start, New York Metropolitan Opera performers, composers, concert pianists and violinists, and other noted artists of the day graced the stage in a series of ongoing popular performances.

With the advent of moving pictures, the Elks Opera House catered to the public's desire to see these new silent films and, later, the "talking pictures." While live performances were a stalwart of the theater, moving pictures were shown more frequently, and a number of films that have become classics were seen at the Elks Opera House during their original theater release.

Over the years, changes were made to the theater that reflected shifts in the public's taste and a lack of capital for needed renovations and improvements. The marquee and entrance were altered to present a more modern appearance. The opera boxes were removed for the installation of wood panels that enhanced the showing of movies on the large screen installed over the stage. When interior maintenance was required, it was done with cost considerations taking priority over historic preservation. Rather than being replaced, the original plaster and stencil decorations were painted over, covered with outer board, or just removed. Father Time took his toll on the original tin ceiling tiles, which fell into various stages of disrepair. As time went on, the theater looked less and less like it did during its inaugural performance.

In addition to physical changes in the theater, there were ownership and management changes as well. BPOE no. 330 eventually sold the building, and the copper elk was removed. The last movie performance was in 1982, and Yavapai College and Prescott College took over the management of performances from 1982 through 1999. Showing great foresight by realizing that the opera house was a tremendous local asset that needed to be saved, the City of Prescott purchased the building from the Arizona Community Foundation in 2001. In 2002, the Elks Opera House Foundation was formed with a mission to restore the theater to its original 1905 grandeur.

With support from Mayor Sam Steiger and the Prescott City Council, a large, generous donation from the James Family Trust, and numerous private donations, the foundation undertook the project. Award-winning Prescott architect William Otwell, AIA, and his associates were hired to oversee the renovation process. Working with Haley Construction, Evergreene Architectural Arts, E&M Rigging, Inc., Custom Service Innovations, Paul Lester, and others, the project commenced after the final stage performance in 2009. Working diligently with the goal of reconstructing the theater to its original 1905 appearance, the various teams successfully completed the project with a reopening of the theater on July 24, 2010. Even the copper elk was restored to its home above the theater. The theater today is essentially the same as one would have seen it in 1905.

The following pages contain a collage of photographs, newspaper clippings, advertisements, playbills, and other pieces of nostalgia that attempt to tell the story of the Elks Opera House. We hope that you too will realize what a treasure this historical theater is to the city and residents of Prescott.

—Terry Berrett, Elisabeth Ruffner, and Parker Anderson

One

An Opera House for Prescott

By 1896, the small mining town of Prescott, once the territorial capital of Arizona, had branches of all the major fraternal organizations in the world except for the Benevolent and Protective Order of Elks (BPOE). It changed that year when Prescott Lodge no. 330 was installed and the first members initiated.

For a number of years, the Elks rented meeting space throughout Prescott but desired to build a lodge hall of their own. As plans for this went forward, they began to consider adding an opera house to their new building as many lodges across America had done in those days. Blueprints were drawn up for a three-story building with an opera house auditorium, lodge rooms upstairs, and rental storefronts on the street. In 1904, the cornerstone to the new building was laid amid much fanfare, and work proceeded full steam.

The Elks Opera House opened on February 20, 1905. The village of Prescott was very proud of this new addition to the downtown and believed it would change the area for generations to come. The Elks Opera House has served Prescott for more than 100 years.

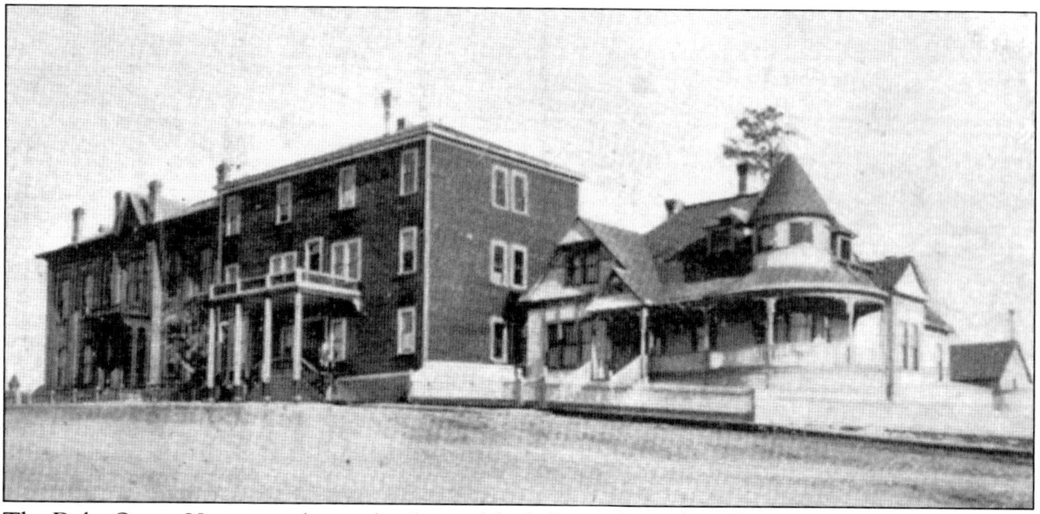

The Dake Opera House was located only one block from where the Elks Opera House now stands. Formerly known as the Patton Opera House, its demolition in 1903 helped persuade Prescott Lodge no. 330 to proceed with plans for its own theatrical edifice. (Sharlot Hall Museum Library and Archives.)

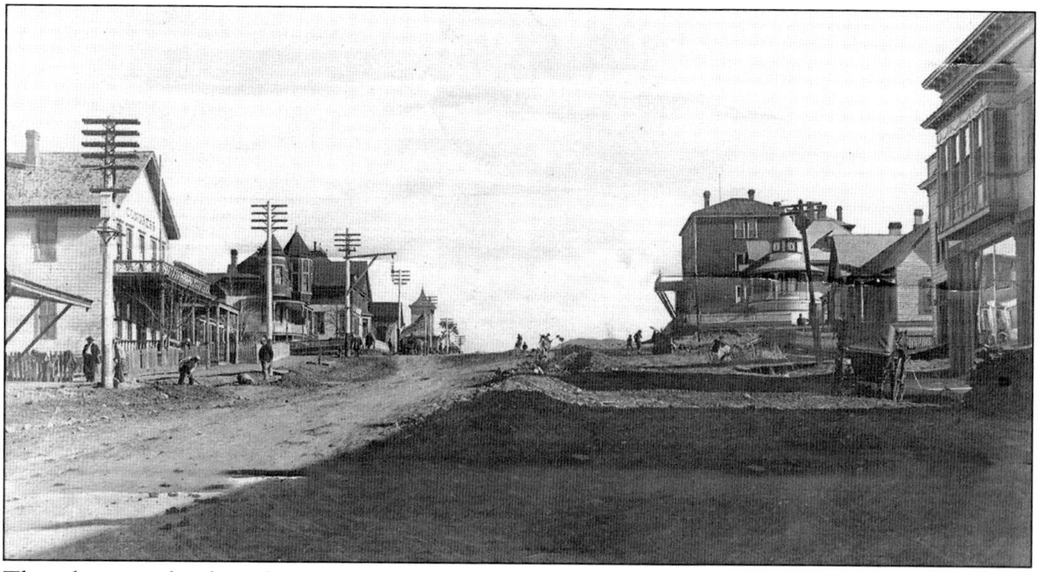

This photograph of Gurley Street facing east shows the area before the Elks Opera House was built. At the top of hill, on the right, is the Dake Opera House; the second building in from the right, shown here at its original location, is the former home of Territory of Arizona governor John C. Fremont. Gurley has been one of the main thoroughfares through downtown Prescott to the present day, and the decision to build the Elks Opera House here was a wise business move. (Sharlot Hall Museum Library and Archives.)

Members of Prescott Lodge no. 330 are standing on the steps of the Yavapai County Courthouse in 1902. It was around this time that plans for the Elks Building were well underway. Pictured here are many prominent Prescott townspeople, including Joseph P. Dillon, Al Brow, Henry D. Ross, Barney H. Smith, Reese M. Ling, chief of police S.A. Prince, former (and future) sheriff George C. Ruffner, attorney Joseph E. Morrison, Henry Brinkmeyer, and lodge treasurer Benjamin Belcher. (Sharlot Hall Museum Library and Archives.)

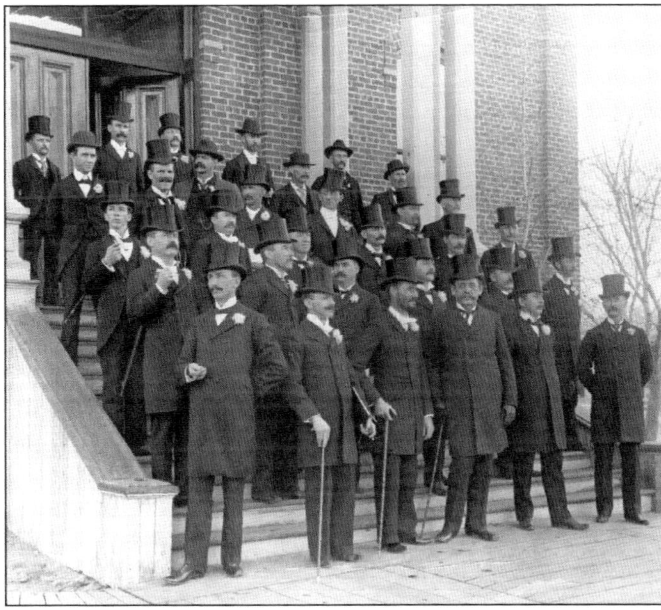

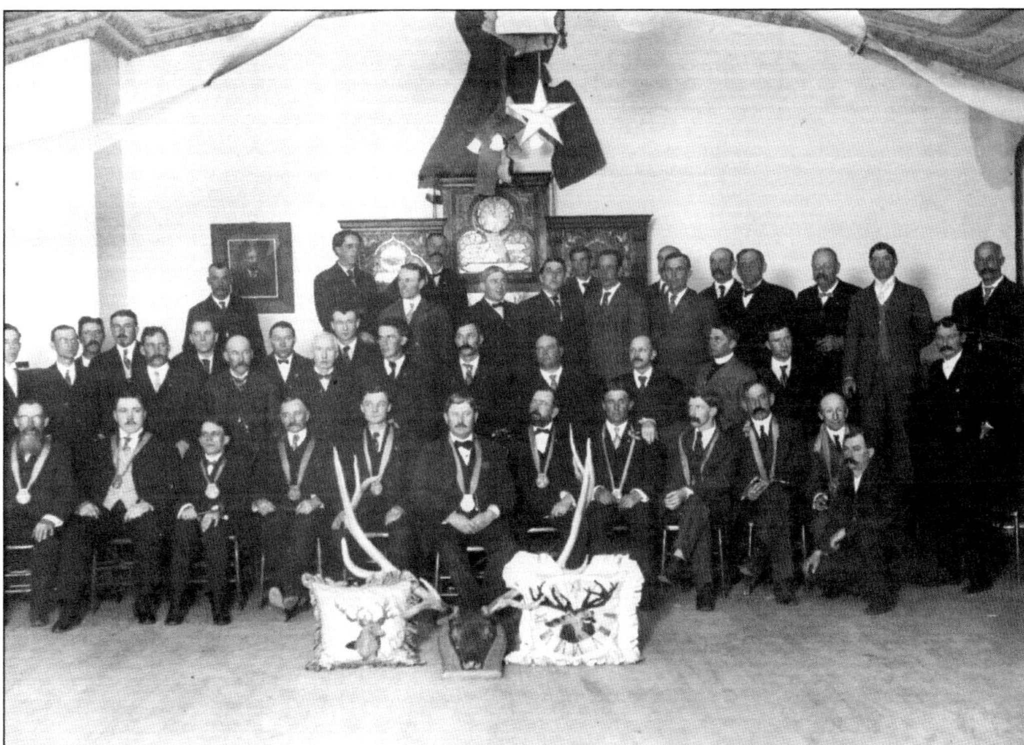

Members of Prescott Lodge no. 330 are shown in a 1908 group photograph. Many of the men pictured were responsible for the building of the Elks Opera House, including Joseph P. Dillon, Benjamin Belcher, R.M. Lamson, chief of police S.A. Prince, mortician H.M. Maus, Dr. Harry T. Southworth, Harry Harter, Barney H. Smith, Dennis A. Burke, and others. (Sharlot Hall Museum Library and Archives.)

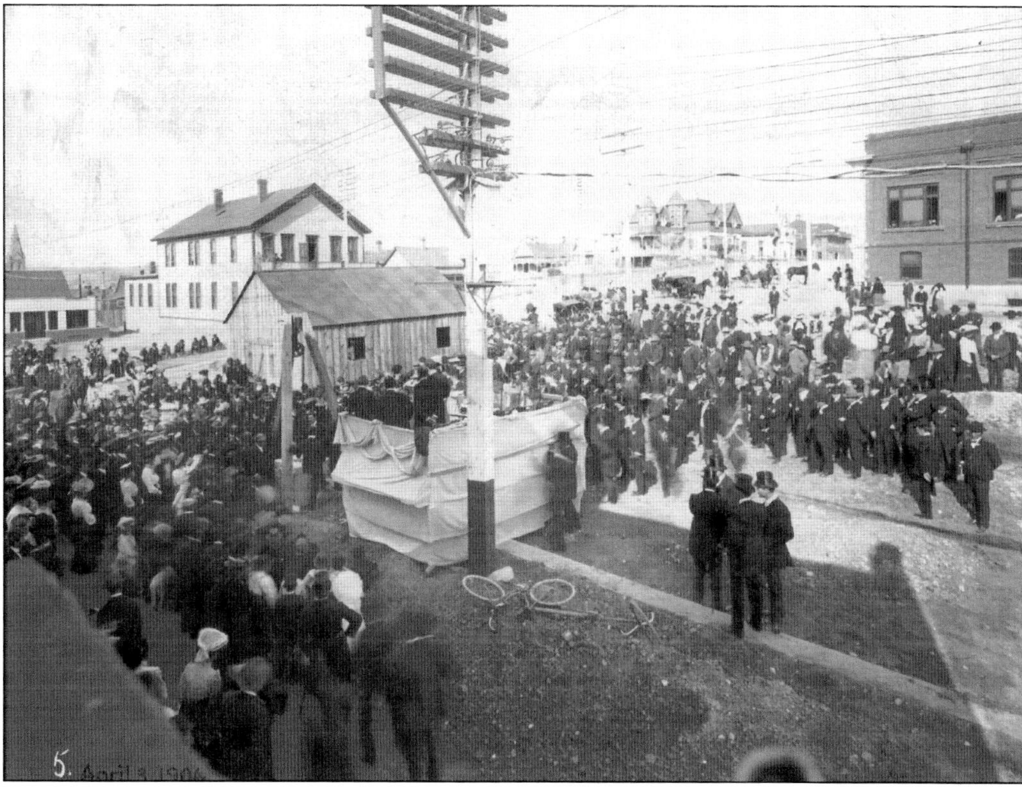

Laying the cornerstone for the building occurred on April 3, 1904, amid much fanfare, including street parades and speeches. The Elks Lodge and the residents of Prescott believed the construction of the new opera house would change the small mining community for generations to come. (Above, Sharlot Hall Museum Library and Archives; below, Elisabeth Ruffner collection.)

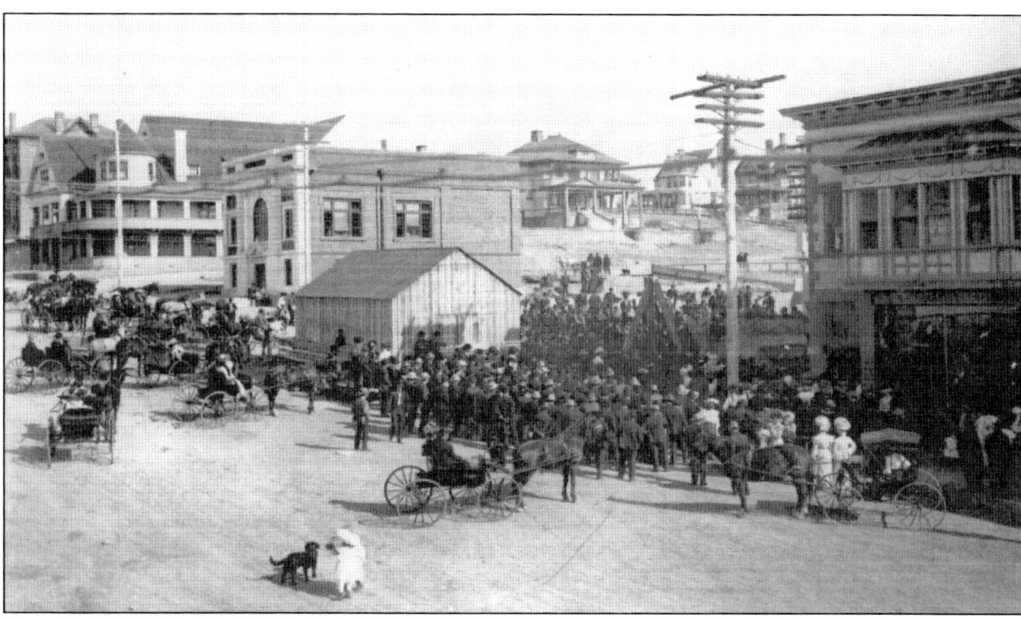

The cornerstone of the Elks Building, which had been laid with so much fanfare in 1904, is seen here in the present day and is starting to look a bit weatherworn after 107 years. (Photograph by Terry Berrett.)

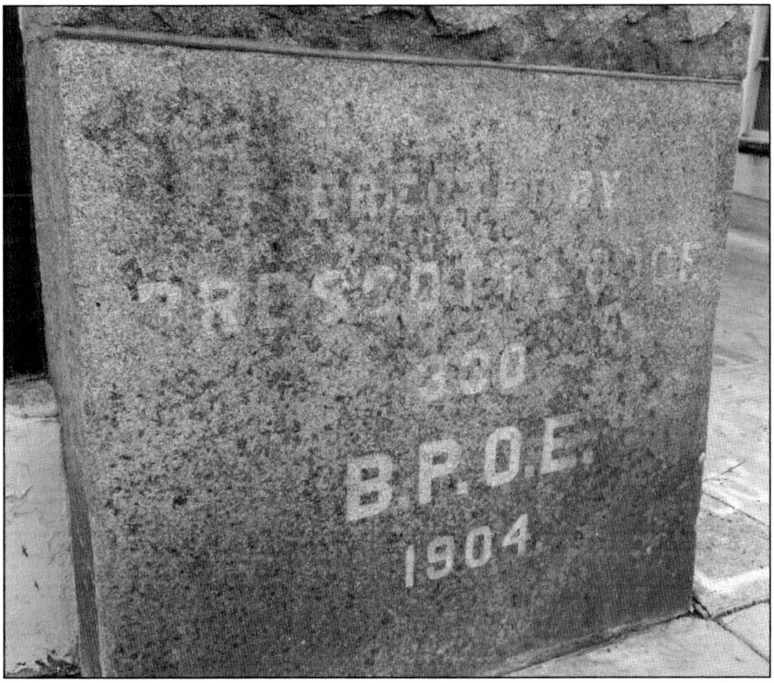

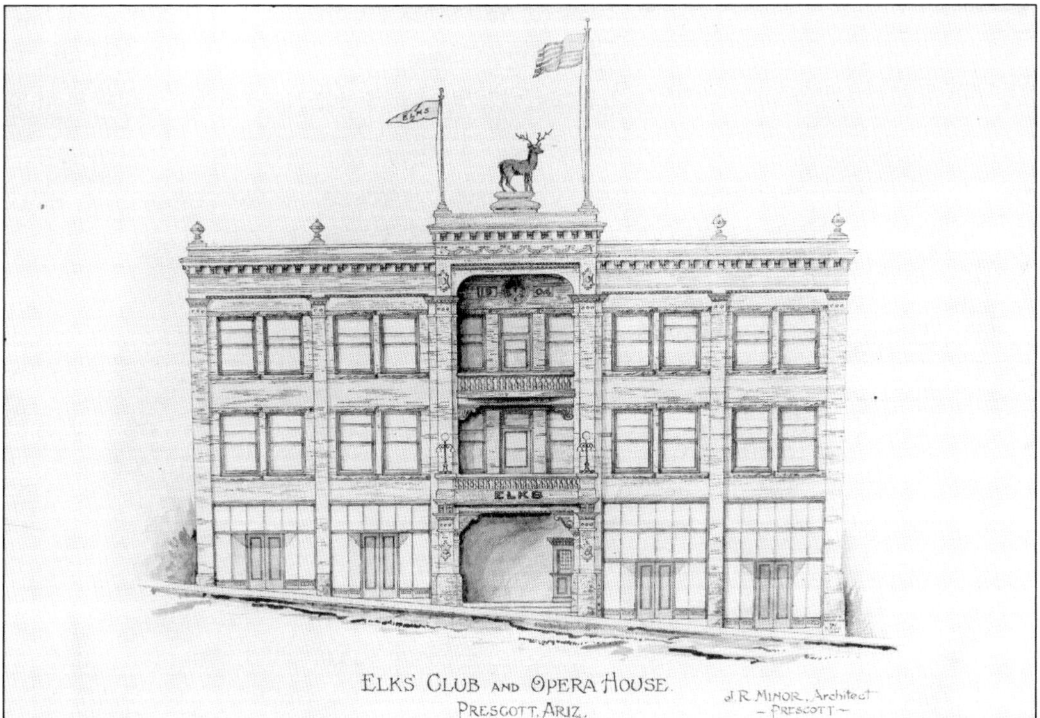

Architect John R. Minor was hired to design and construct the Elks Building. The initial blueprint of what he envisioned in 1903 was erected with only a couple of variations. Minor is today buried in Richmond, Virginia, in the same cemetery as Confederate leaders Jefferson Davis and Robert E. Lee. (Sharlot Hall Museum Library and Archives.)

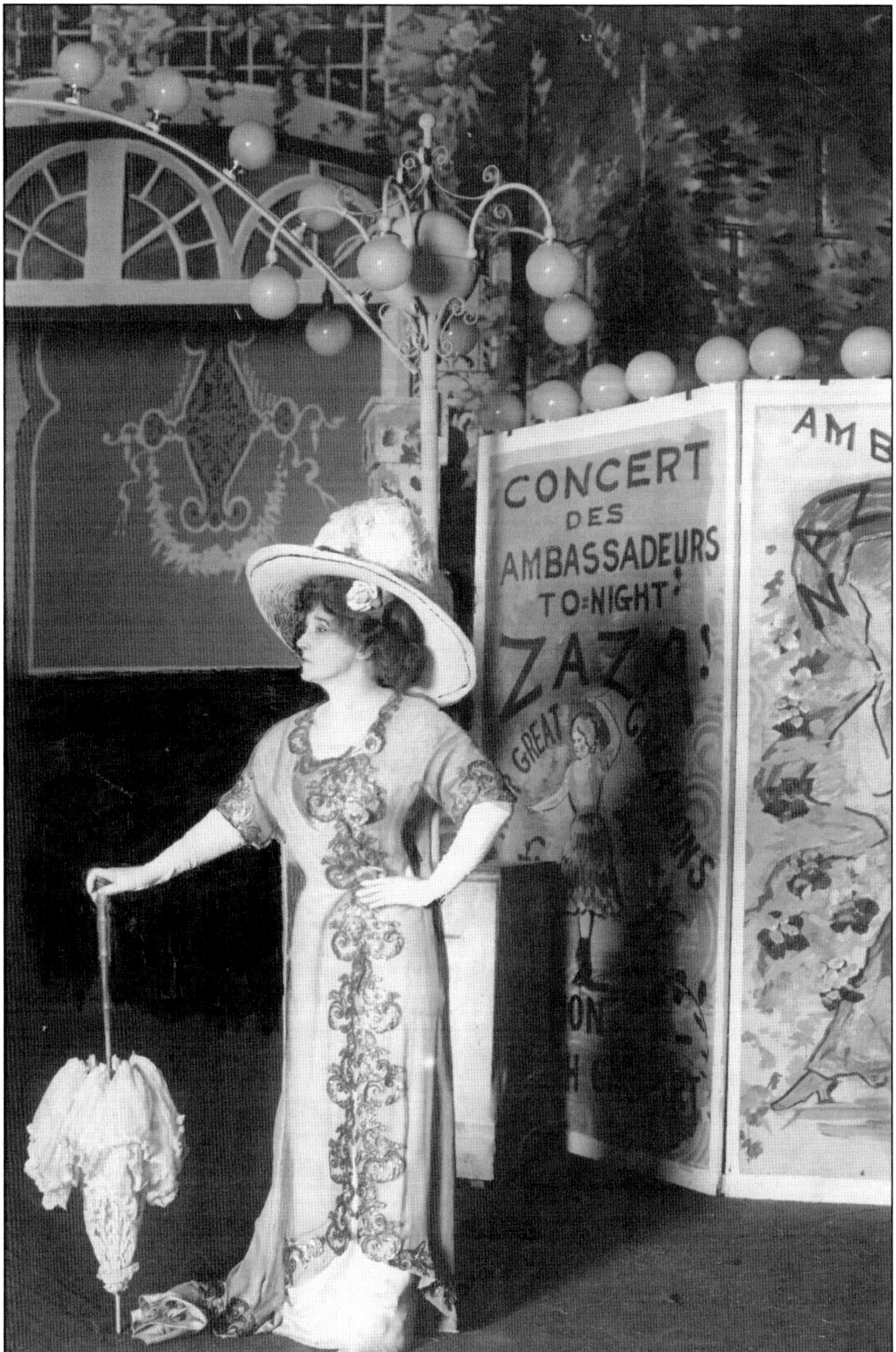

Florence Roberts was one of the most prominent touring actresses of her day. She and her troupe opened the Elks Opera House on February 20, 1905, with the acclaimed Spanish Catalan play *Marta of the Lowlands* by Angel Guimera. This undated photograph shows Roberts, probably in San Francisco where she lived, in her most famous role as Zaza in a play of the same name. (Parker Anderson collection.)

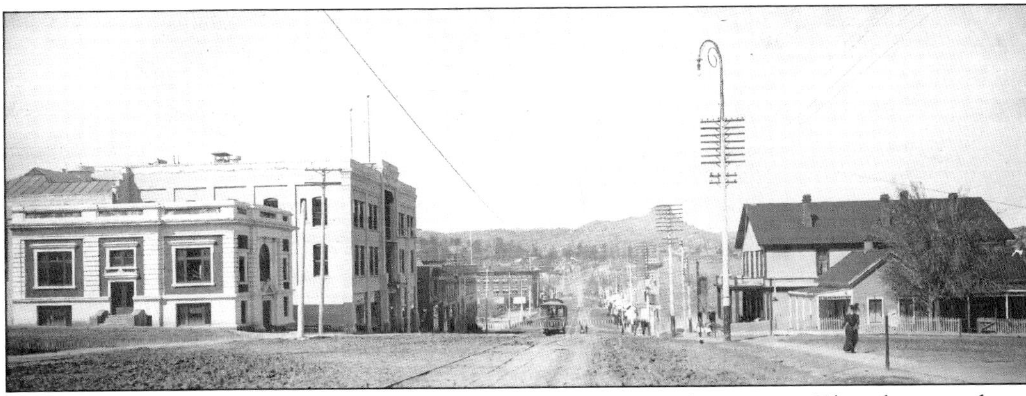

Pictured is the newly completed Elks Building on Gurley Street facing west. This photograph was clearly taken prior to June 1905, as the copper elk that graced the top of the building for many years does not appear here. To the far left is the Carnegie Library building, constructed in 1903. (Sharlot Hall Museum Library and Archives.)

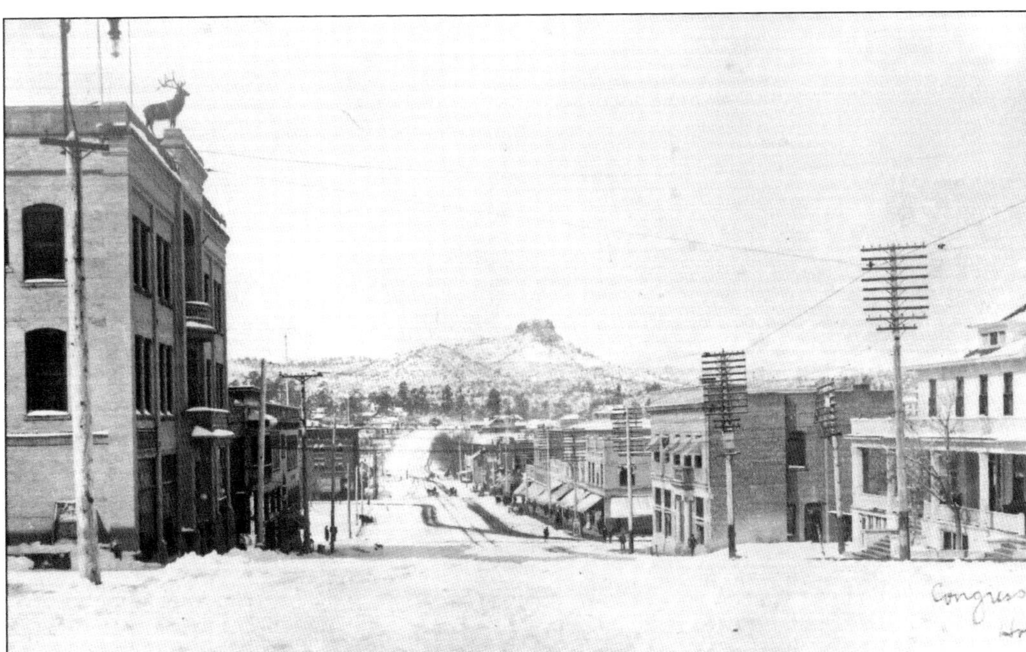

This image shows a winter scene on Gurley Street in front of the Elks Opera House with a snow-covered Thumb Butte clearly in the distance. Gurley Street was a primary east-west street in the early days of Prescott and became a prominent street once Highway 69 was developed as an alternative route to Phoenix. The photograph is undated but was probably taken prior to 1910, as the Elks sign has yet to be added above the opera house entrance. (Sharlot Hall Museum Library and Archives.)

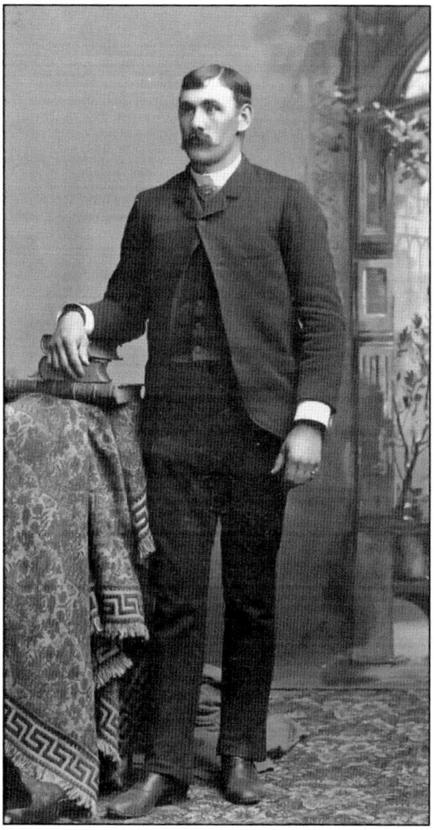

Joseph P. Dillon was the first manager of the Elks Opera House. Prominent in his lodge, he was also an important figure in the local Democratic Party and had served for a time as a Yavapai County deputy sheriff in the late 19th century. Dillon was the hoodman at the 1898 hanging of convicted murderer Fleming "James" Parker. (Sharlot Hall Museum Library and Archives.)

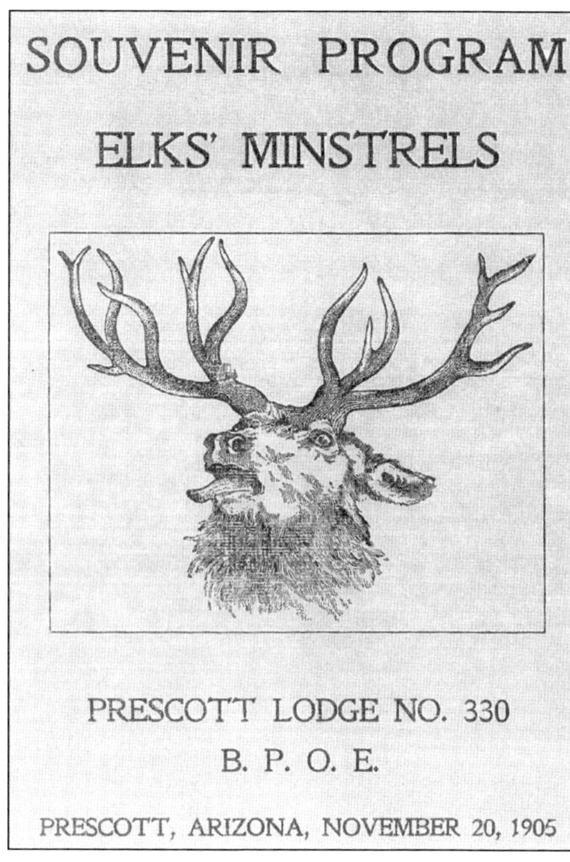

This is a program cover for an Elks Minstrel Show. Although blackface minstrel shows are considered offensive today, they were very popular in the early 20th century, and Elks Lodges nationwide staged them almost yearly as fundraisers for themselves and for local charity drives. (Elisabeth Ruffner collection.)

This is one of the best surviving photographs of the Elks Building exterior and dates from the early 1900s. The J.S. Acker storefront is on the left; the members of Prescott Lodge no. 330 reportedly met in this room while the finishing touches were being put on the upstairs lodge rooms. (Sharlot Hall Museum Library and Archives.)

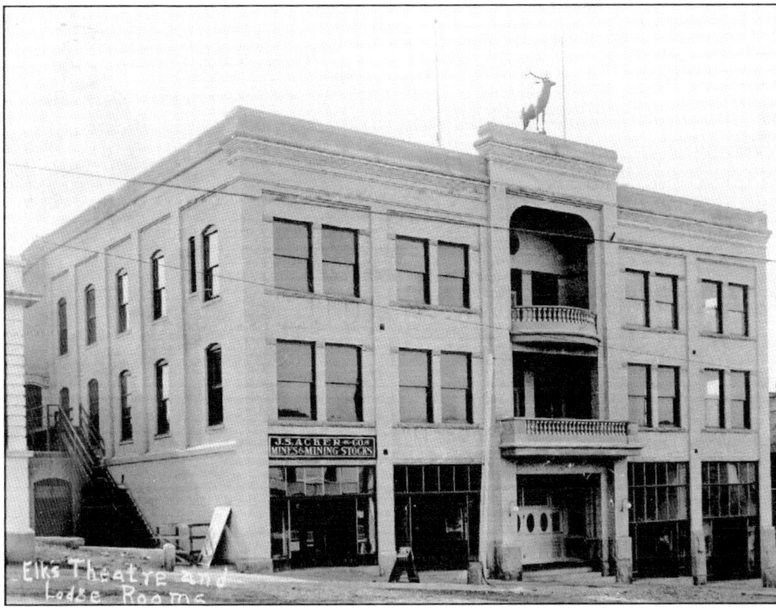

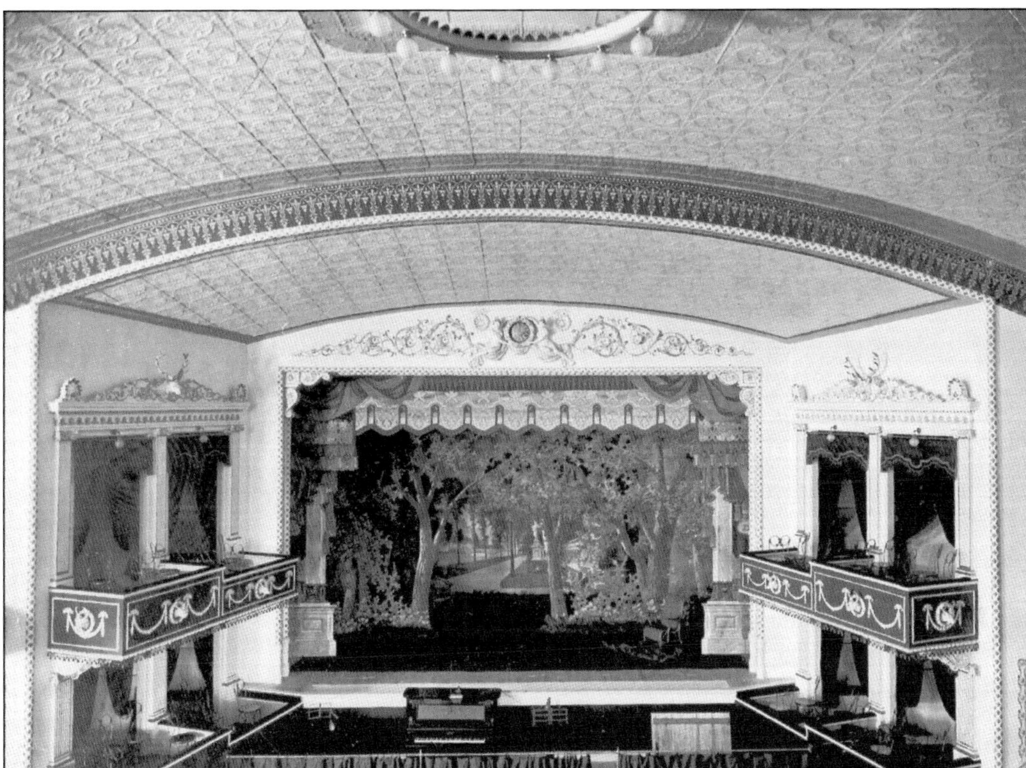

This undated image is the oldest known photograph of the Elks Opera House interior. The opera house was considered one of the finest theaters in the West at the time, as demonstrated by the exotic ornamentation around the box seats and the proscenium as well as the ceiling-light ring at the top of the image. The impressive forest set pieces on stage were replicated in 2010 as part of the restoration of the theater (see chapter five). (Sharlot Hall Museum Library and Archives.)

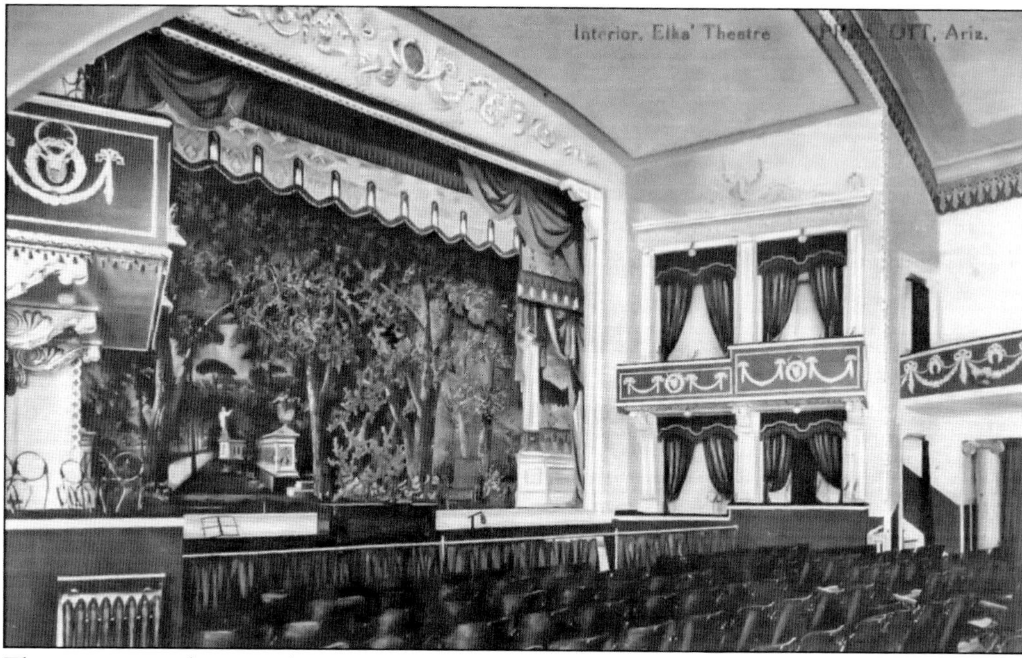

These interior side views show the original seats, which were designed to be removable so the auditorium could be converted into a dance ballroom for the annual Elks May Day ball and other dances. Important details include the steam radiator heater and the stenciled designs on the balcony and walls. (Both, Sharlot Hall Museum Library and Archives.)

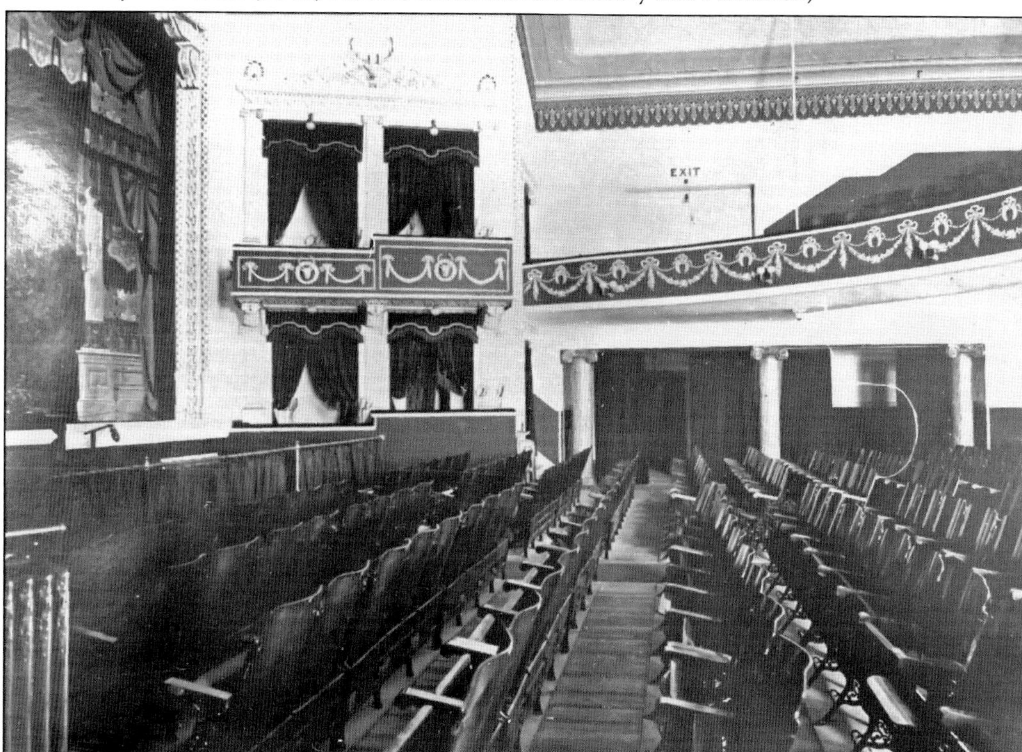

This is an advertisement for *The Twins of Bistritz*, a locally written 1905 operetta by Prescott's Nellie von Gerichten-Smith that attracted almost as much attention as the opening of Elks Opera House had. Smith wrote sheet music, many songs, and other compositions, but fame outside of the immediate area eluded her. (Parker Anderson collection.)

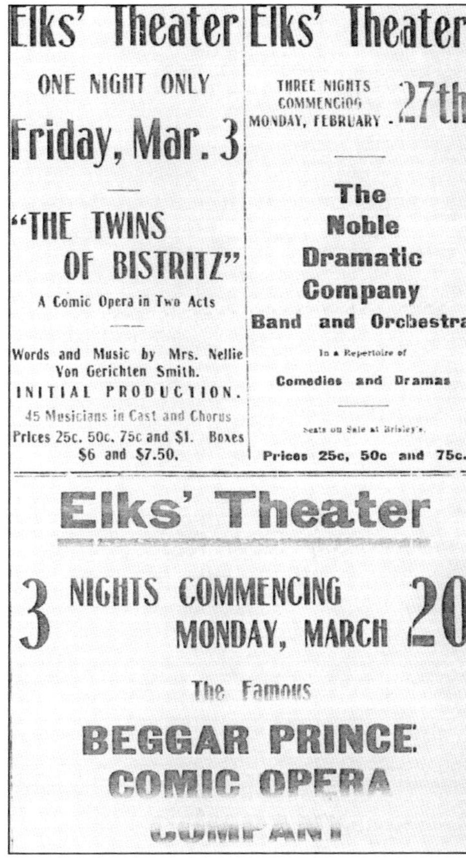

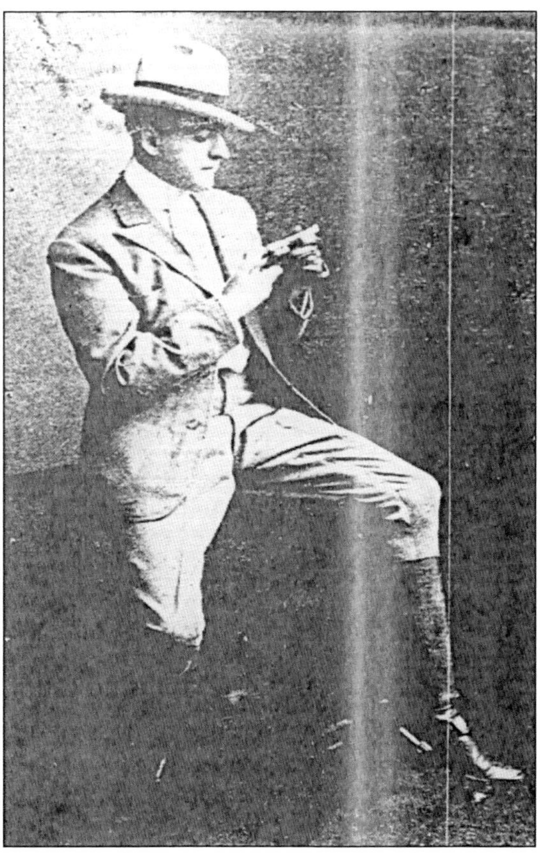

San Francisco actor White Whittlesey arrived at the Elks Opera House with his troupe in 1905 shortly after his Bay Area colleague Florence Roberts had been there. As San Francisco was prominent in theater circles, Prescott residents considered the appearance of these famous actors a great honor. (Parker Anderson collection.)

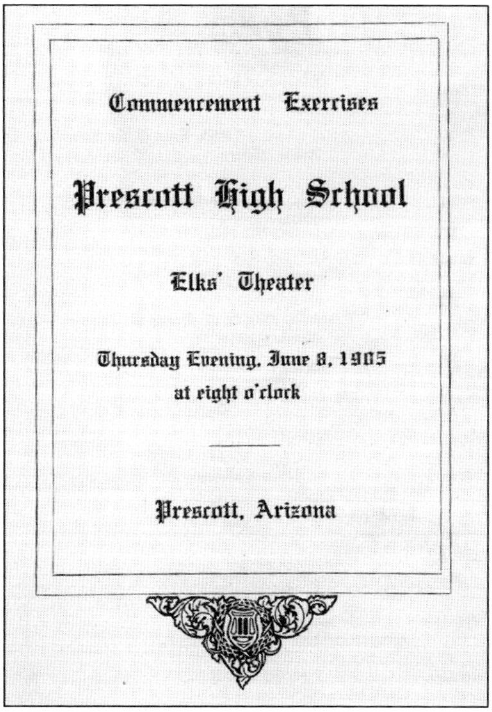
Commencement Exercises

Prescott High School

Elks' Theater

Thursday Evening, June 8, 1905
at eight o'clock

Prescott, Arizona

Prescott High School held its graduation ceremonies (then called "commencement exercises") in the Elks Opera House in 1905 and continued to do so for a number of years. There were only four graduates in 1905. (Both, Parker Anderson collection.)

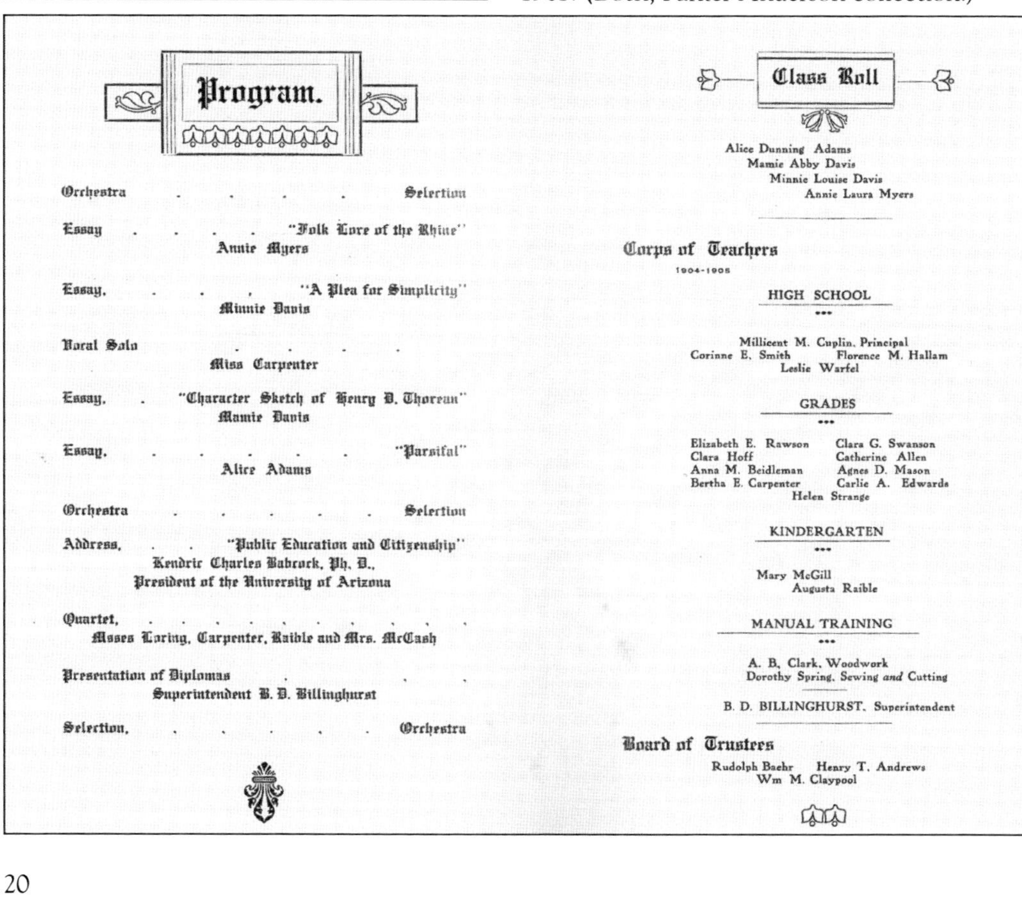
Program.

Orchestra . . . . . Selection

Essay . . . . . "Folk Lore of the Rhine"
Annie Myers

Essay. . . . . "A Plea for Simplicity"
Minnie Davis

Vocal Solo . . . .
Miss Carpenter

Essay. . "Character Sketch of Henry D. Thoreau"
Mamie Davis

Essay. . . . . . . "Parsifal"
Alice Adams

Orchestra . . . . . . Selection

Address. . . "Public Education and Citizenship"
Kendric Charles Babcock, Ph. D.,
President of the University of Arizona

Quartet. . . . .
Misses Loring, Carpenter, Raible and Mrs. McCash

Presentation of Diplomas . . . .
Superintendent B. D. Billinghurst

Selection. . . . . . . Orchestra

Class Roll

Alice Dunning Adams
Mamie Abby Davis
Minnie Louise Davis
Annie Laura Myers

Corps of Teachers
1904-1905

HIGH SCHOOL

Millicent M. Cuplin, Principal
Corinne E. Smith   Florence M. Hallam
Leslie Warfel

GRADES

Elizabeth E. Rawson   Clara G. Swanson
Clara Hoff   Catherine Allen
Anna M. Beidleman   Agnes D. Mason
Bertha E. Carpenter   Carlie A. Edwards
Helen Strange

KINDERGARTEN

Mary McGill
Augusta Raible

MANUAL TRAINING

A. B. Clark, Woodwork
Dorothy Spring, Sewing *and* Cutting

B. D. BILLINGHURST, Superintendent

Board of Trustees
Rudolph Baehr   Henry T. Andrews
Wm M. Claypool

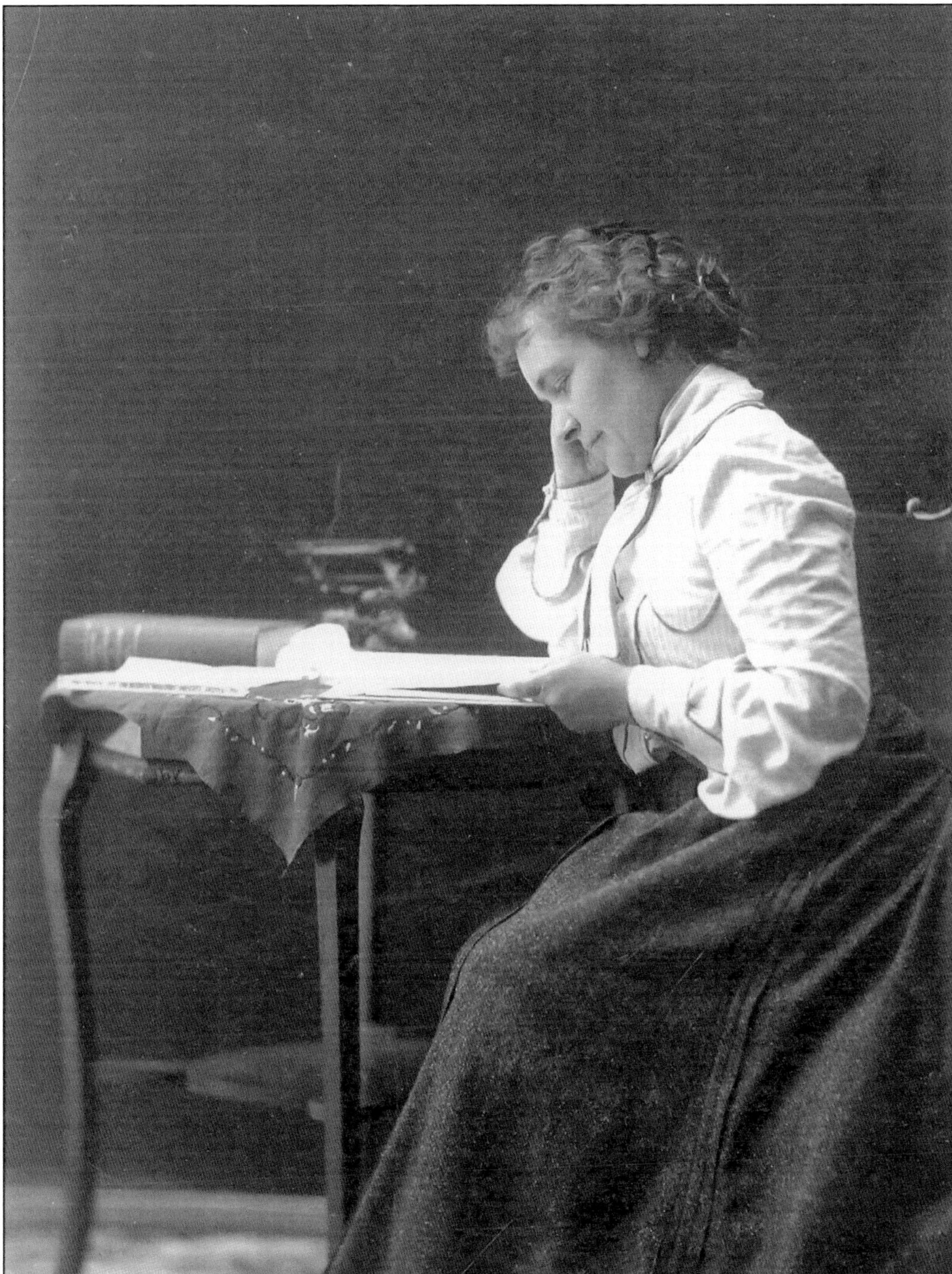

Sharlot Mabridth Hall is the legendary poetess, Arizona historian, and founder of Sharlot Hall Museum and Archives. In 1907, she began her 20-year campaign to save the Territorial Governor's Mansion on the stage of the Elks Opera House with a variety show she produced with the Monday Club. The only known time Hall appeared live at this venue is when she read a number of her own poems on stage. (Sharlot Hall Museum Library and Archives.)

The Elks' Theatre

MONDAY and TUESDAY, OCTOBER 2d and 3d

TALLY & LEWIS

Expert moving picture exhibitros of the world, will present the

PALACE OF THE Arabian Nights

The greatest spectacular production ever presented to the American people; also giving scenes of the great Naval Battle of the Sea of Japan, the greatest modern sea fight. There will also be sbown numerous funny scenes and mysterous objects, such as the Moon's Lover, the hit of the season; the Devil's Works, Rube and Mandy's Trip to Coney Island, and many others. Six shousand feet of film will be shown, making the entertainment two hours long. Something new every minute of the time.

ADMISSION, 25c and 50c. PERFORMANCE at 8:20 p.m.

ELKS' THEATER

J. P. DILLON, MANAGER

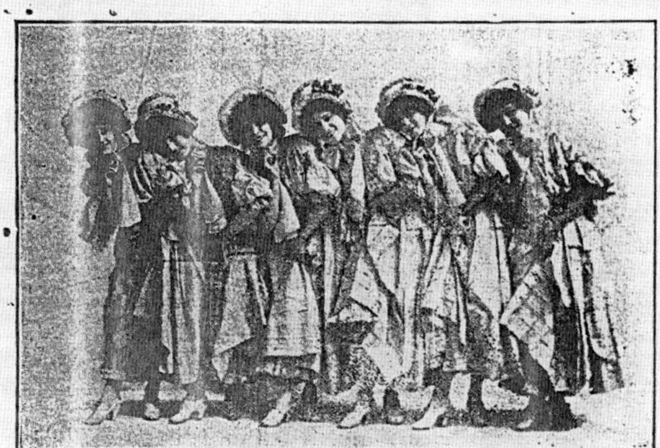

One Night Only, Monday, Nov. 4th

80 PEOPLE

Geo. M. Cohen's Great Musical Success

LITTLE JOHNNY JONES

The Largest and Best Attraction on the Road

ABSOLUTE CAPACITY IN EVERY CITY WE HAVE PLAYED THOUSANDS TURNED AWAY NIGHTLY THE RECORD BUSINESS EVERYWHERE	All-Star Cast—This is No. 1 Company Entirely New Scenery and Costumes. Reserved Seats on Sale, Brisley Drug Company, Saturday Morning, November 2nd. PRICES—$2.50, $2.00, $1.50 and $1.00. FREE LIST SUSPENDED	ONE BIG SCREAM THE MOST FASCINATING MUSIC EVER WRITTEN THE LARGEST AND PRETTIEST CHORUS ON THE ROAD

The first motion picture shown at the Elks Opera House was *Palace of the Arabian Nights* (1905), the Georges Melies import from France. Movies were in their infancy, but an entertainment revolution was brewing that would affect all theaters nationwide, including the Elks Opera House. (Parker Anderson collection.)

George M. Cohan's *Little Johnny Jones* was a Broadway smash, and a professional tour of the show drew sellout crowds across the country. According to Prescott newspapers, the city council cancelled its regular meeting so members could attend this performance at the Elks Opera House. (Parker Anderson collection.)

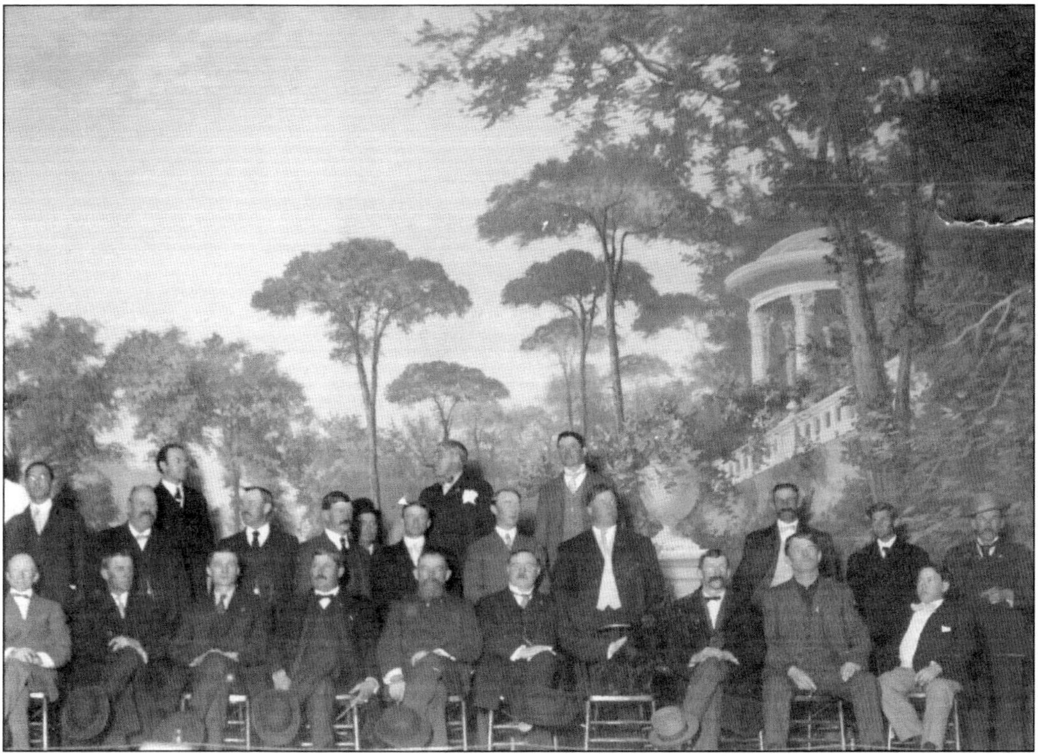

This group of men is at an unidentified 1908 event at the Elks Opera House. As denoted by the beautiful theater scrim behind the men, the Elks Lodge spared no expense for its events, providing the finest in theater scenery. (Sharlot Hall Museum Library and Archives.)

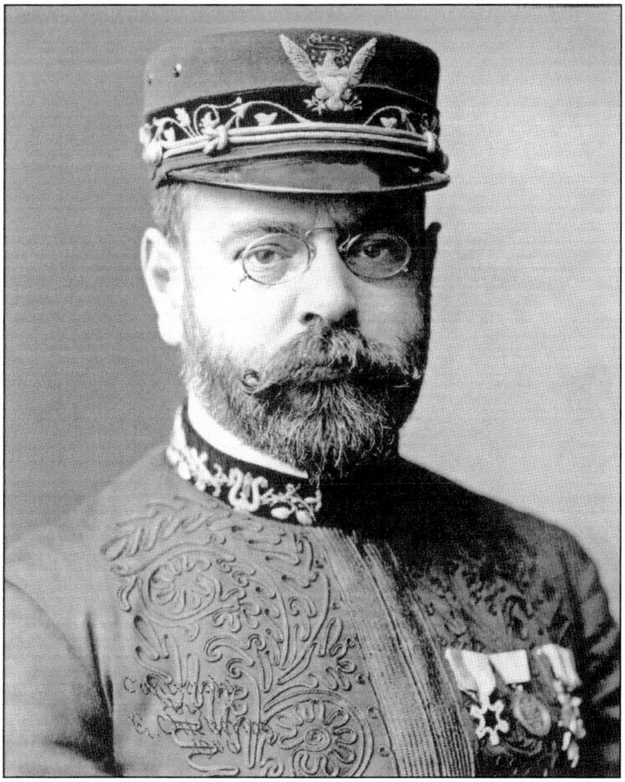

John Philip Sousa and his orchestra appeared live at the Elks Opera House in 1909, again demonstrating the quality of entertainers the famed opera house was able to draw at this time. Sousa is now one of the legendary figures in American music history. (Library of Congress Prints and Photographs Collection, LC-USZ62-110617.)

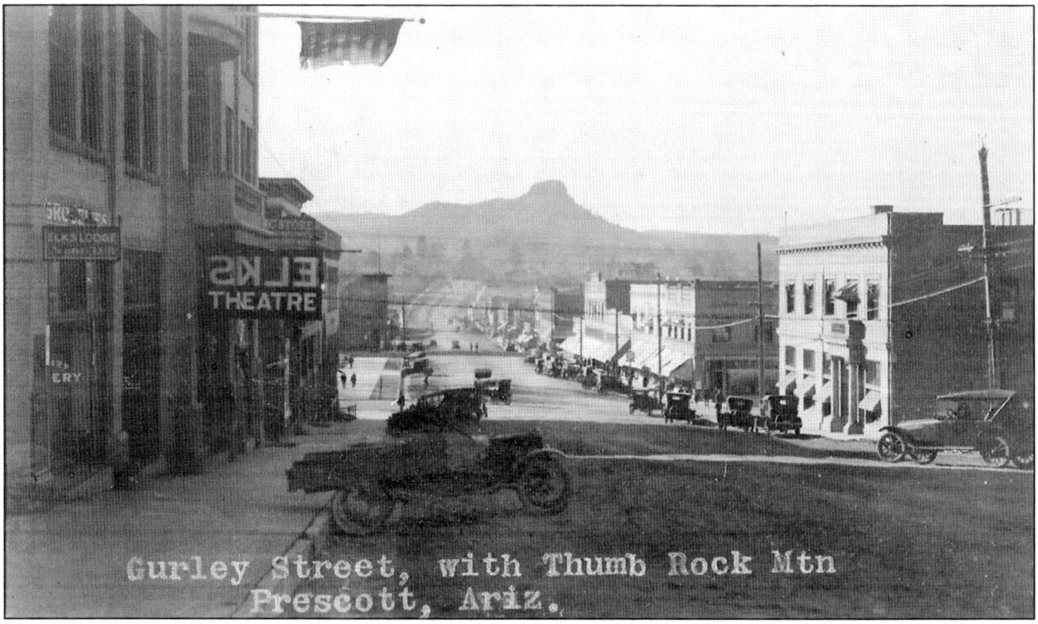

The Elks Opera House, then known as the Elks Theatre because of the advent of films, is shown in both views looking west on Gurley Street around 1910. Notable details include the oddity of the sign spelling and a small sign designating the entrance to the upstairs lodge room and Elks Club for members. (Both, Sharlot Hall Museum Library and Archives.)

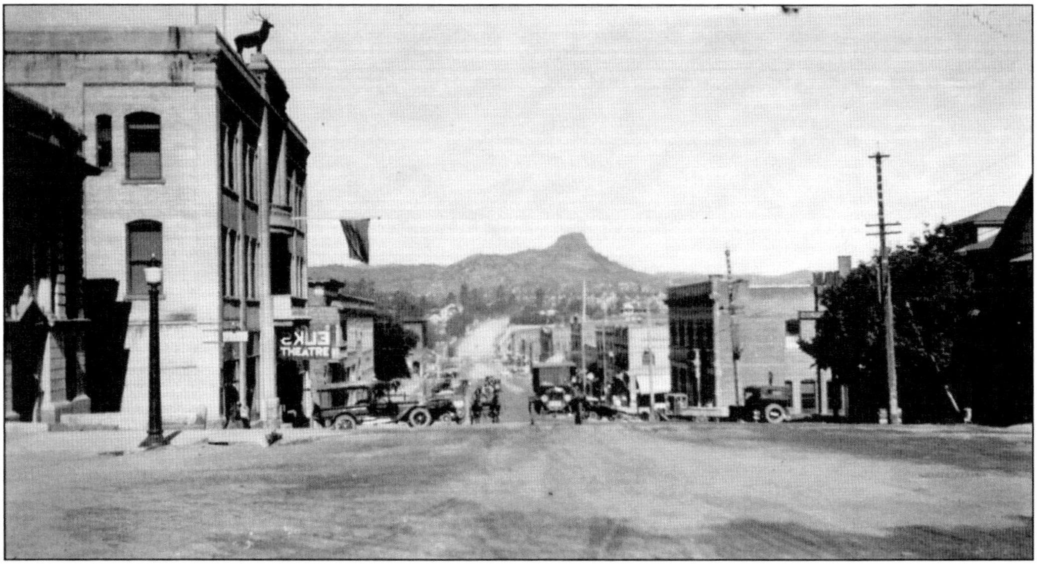

Two

Vaudeville and the Roaring Twenties

By 1910, the entertainment scene had changed drastically throughout the world. Motion pictures had revolutionized evenings out, and every town demanded a moving-picture house. Elks Lodge no. 330 was also feeling some financial growing pains from the first five years of operating the Elks Opera House, so members made a decision to start leasing the theater to an independent manager. The first man to pick up the gauntlet was Charles Howard, who had owned a competing vaudeville house on Cortez Street called the Electric Theatre.

After taking the reins of management, Howard turned the Elks Opera House (often referred to as the Elks Theatre) into a vaudeville house with motion pictures every night. The movies would stay at the Elks Opera House for more than 70 years. By the mid-teens when vaudeville was dying, William Mays, Ray Vyne, and Charles Born guided the Elks Opera House into becoming a full-fledged movie theater as well as one of the most successful businesses in Prescott. Born would eventually become the full manager.

During the 1920s, there were some live performances, including some by notable people, as well as continuing events by local playwrights, performers, actors, and musicians. But motion pictures changed virtually every night in those days, and the Elks Theatre gave Prescott residents a wide variety of entertainment from which to choose.

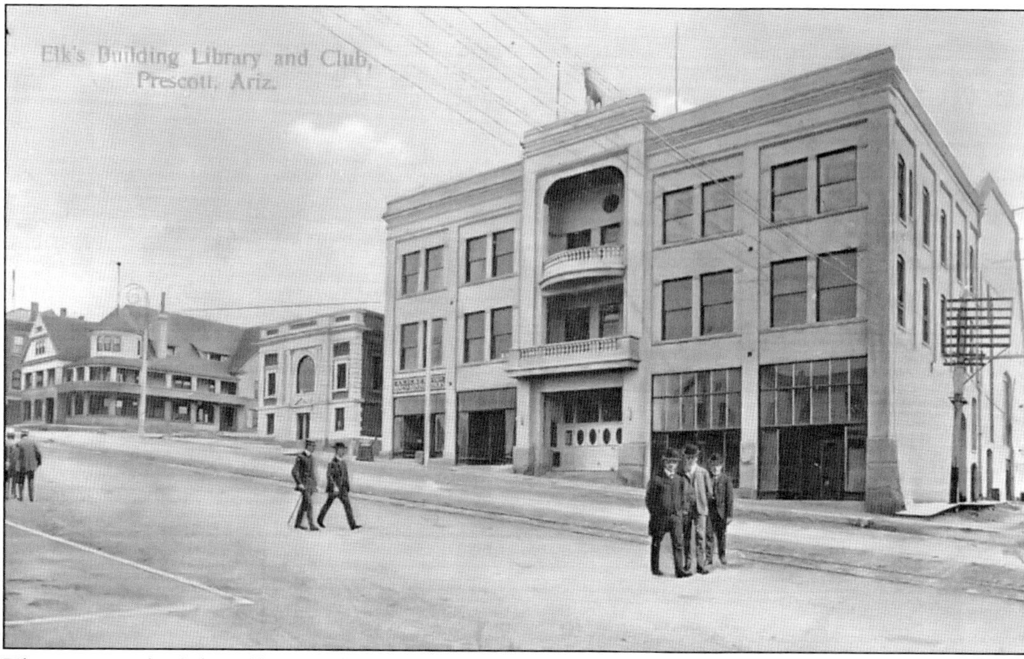

This postcard of the Elks Building shows the exterior in considerable detail. Notable features include the open balconies (now enclosed), the streetcar tracks, and the low electric wires. (Sharlot Hall Museum Library and Archives.)

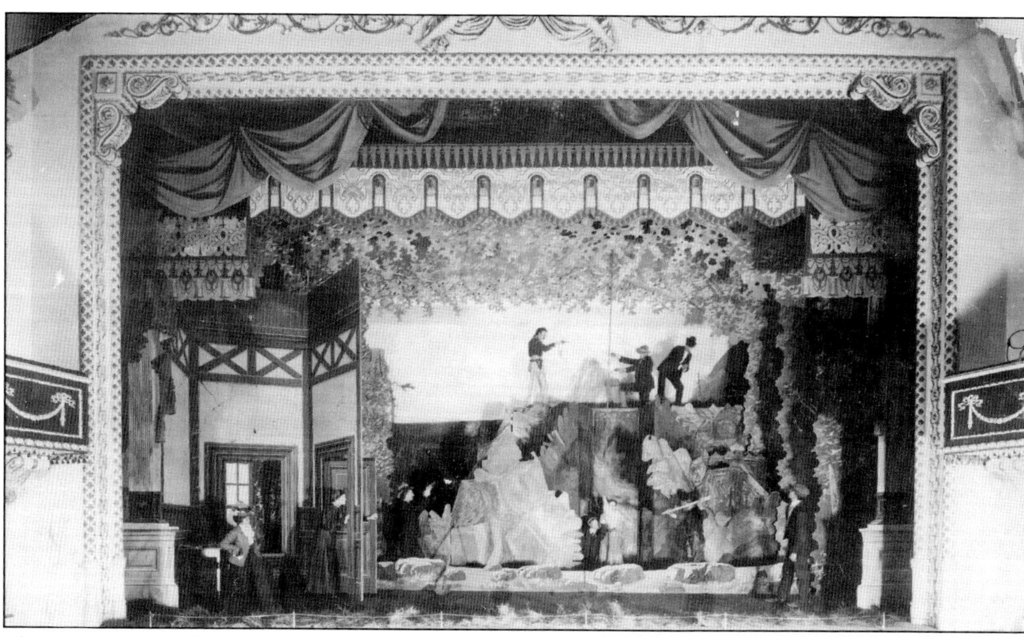

Shown is an unidentified stage play at the Elks Theatre with an elaborate two-story set and numerous actors on stage. The photograph is undated, but it gives an idea of the extravagance of early productions at the Elks Theatre. (Sharlot Hall Museum Library and Archives.)

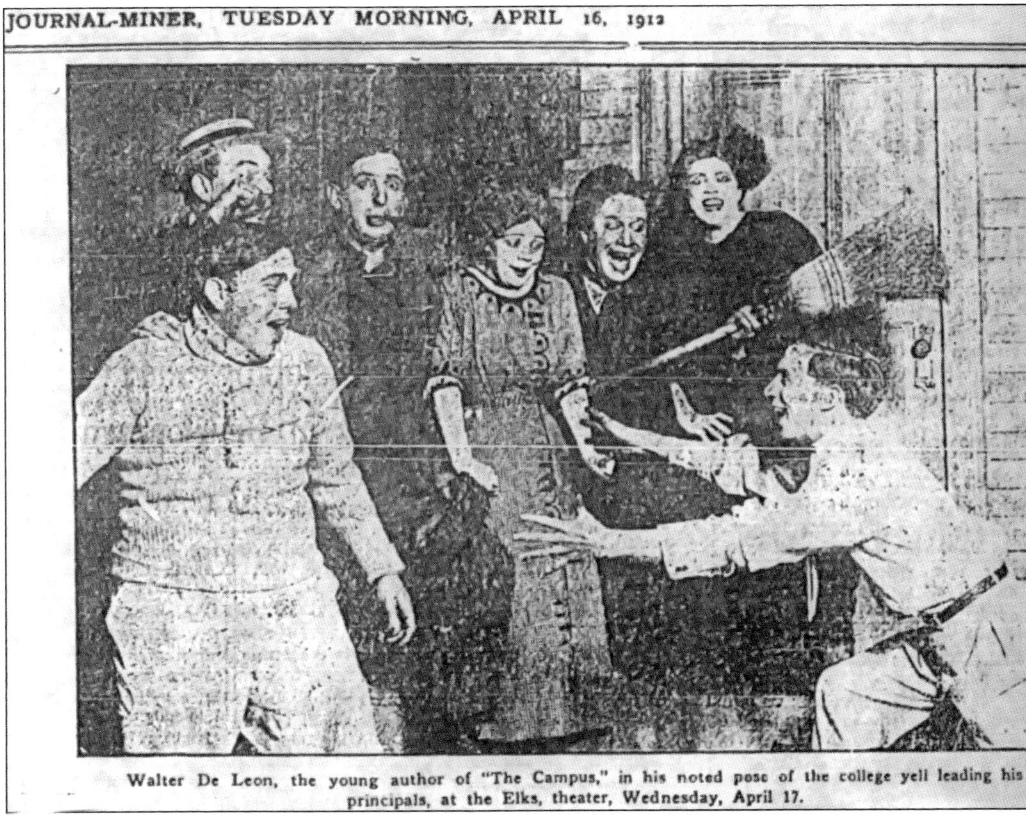

JOURNAL-MINER, TUESDAY MORNING, APRIL 16, 1912

Walter De Leon, the young author of "The Campus," in his noted pose of the college yell leading his principals, at the Elks, theater, Wednesday, April 17.

The Campus was a professional touring stage play in 1912. This poor-quality newspaper photograph is the only known relic of the show, notable for the presence of Roscoe Arbuckle in the cast only a year from hitting the big time as "Fatty" Arbuckle. (Parker Anderson collection.)

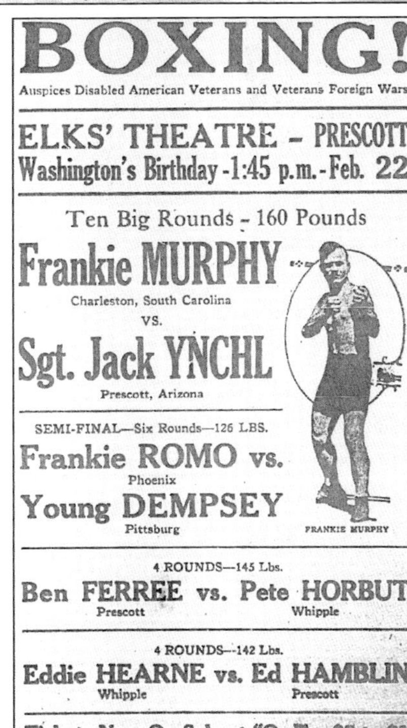

Boxing matches were held in the Elks Theatre periodically during these early days as well. Participating fighters tended to be local celebrities instead of nationally known fighters. There is an obvious typographical error in Jack Lynch's name. (Parker Anderson collection.)

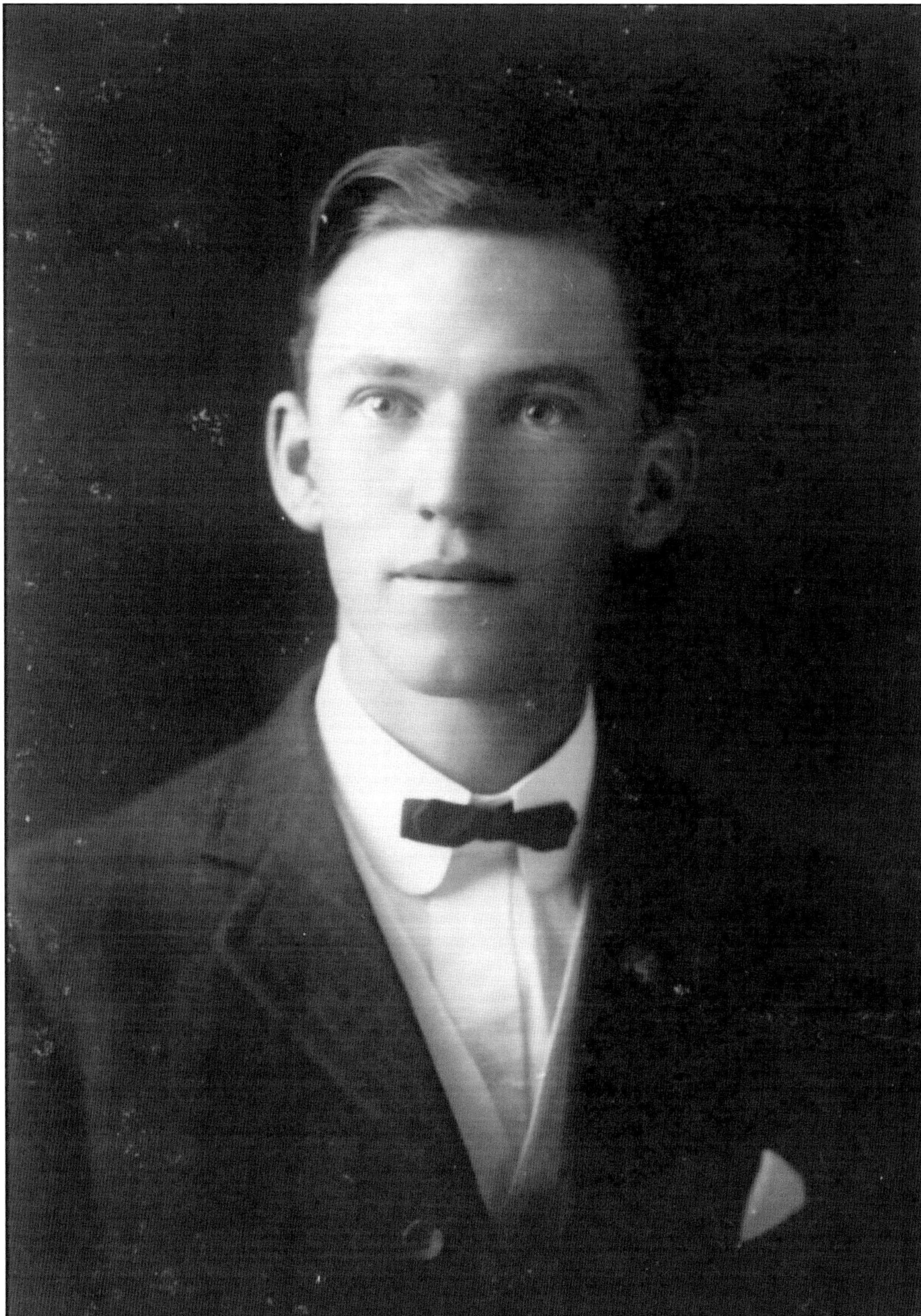

Lester and Mary Ruffner were two of Prescott's most prominent residents. They performed in many locally written and produced variety shows at the Elks Theatre. (Elisabeth Ruffner collection.)

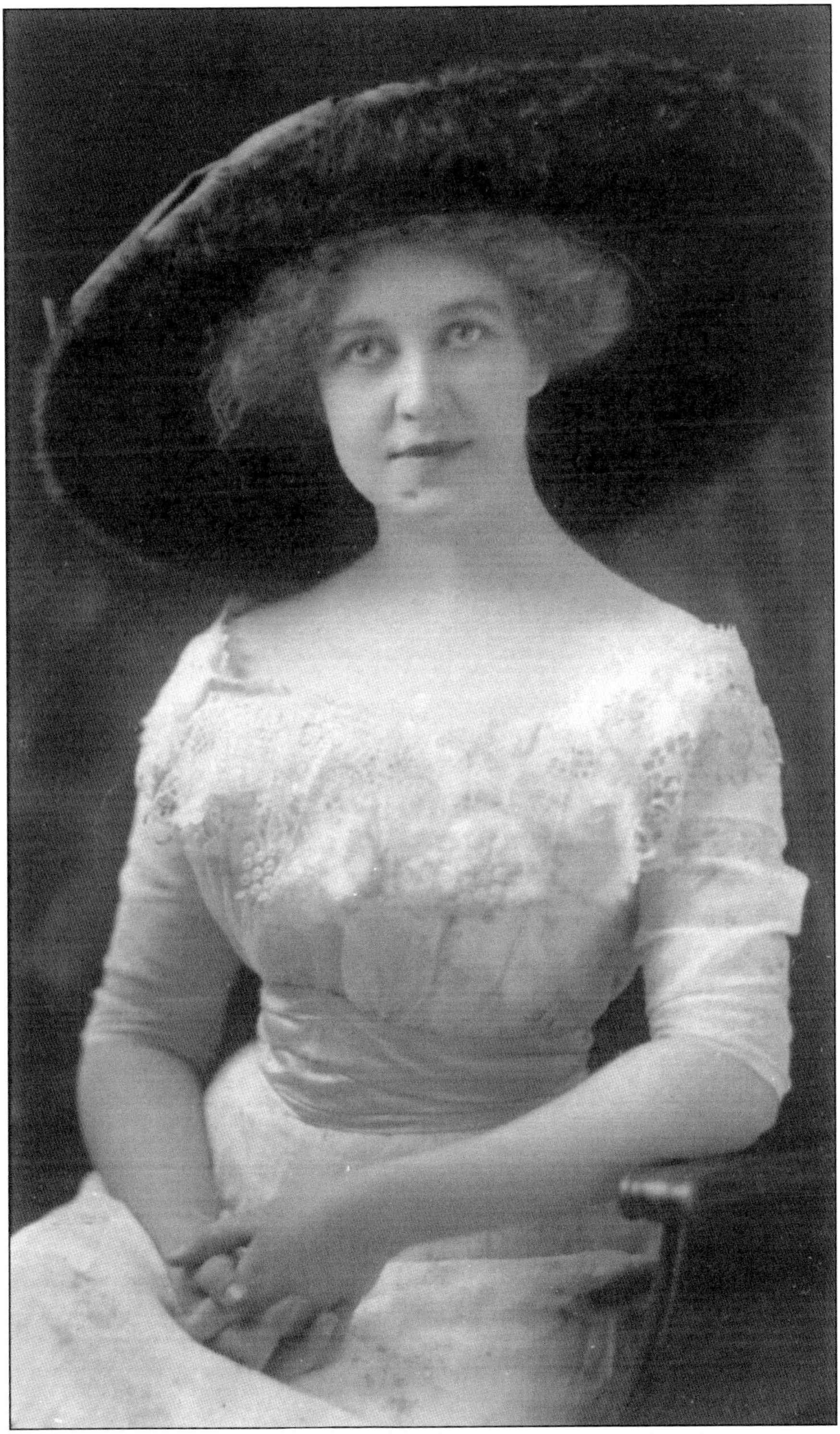

Mary is believed to have appeared on the Elks Theatre stage more often than anyone else who has been documented. (Elisabeth Ruffner collection.)

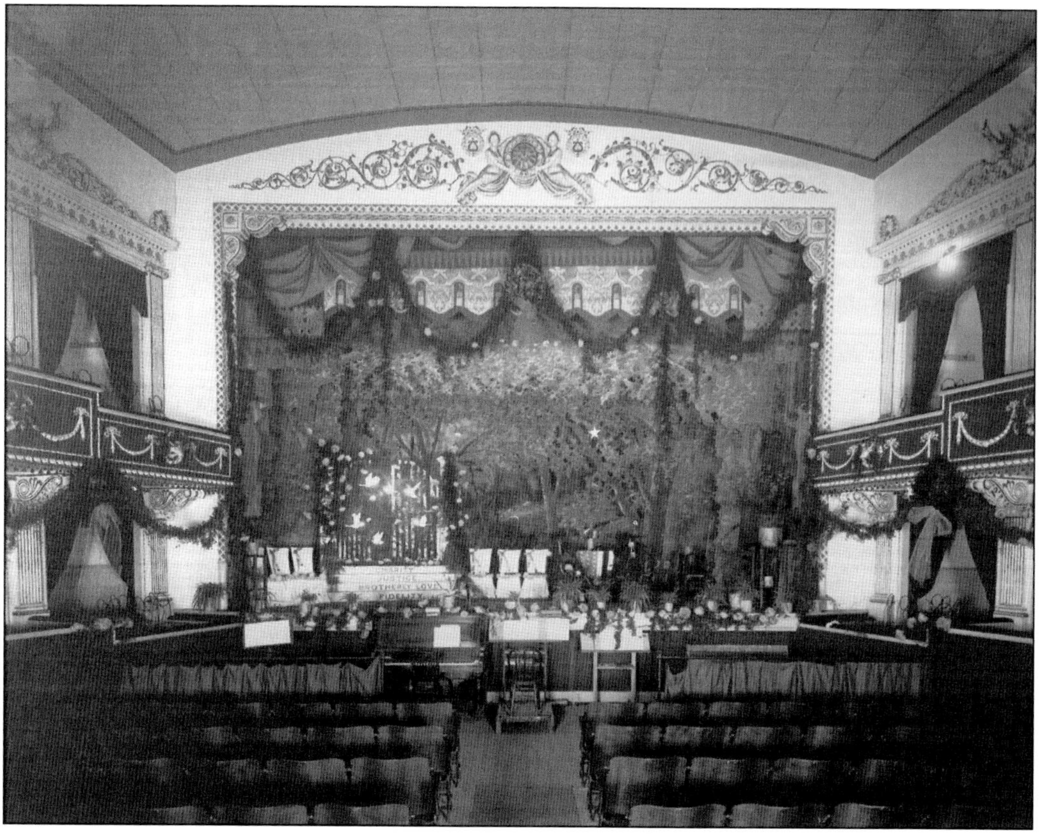

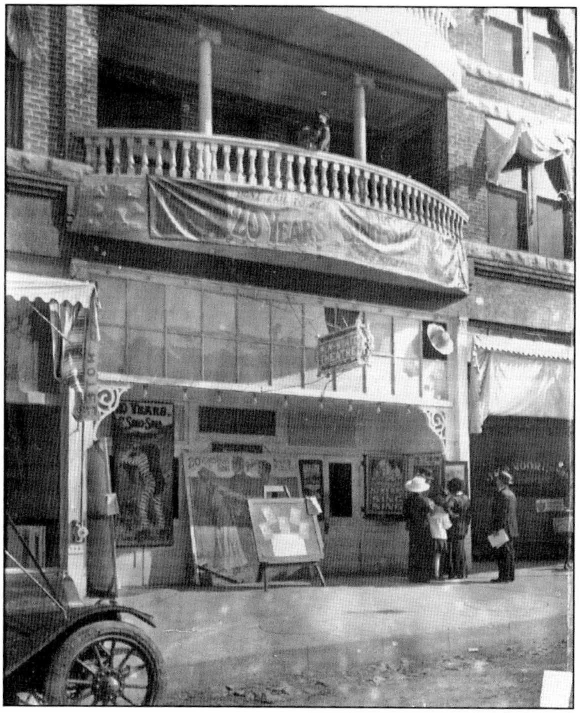

In this undated image, the interior of the Elks Theatre is decorated, perhaps for Christmas or some other festive gathering. (Sharlot Hall Museum Library and Archives.)

The New State Theatre on Cortez Street is shown around 1910. Previously known as the Electric Theatre, it opened as a vaudeville house with motion pictures and gave stiff competition to the Elks Theatre initially. Eventually, New State manager Charles Howard took over the reins of the Elks Theatre for a time. (Sharlot Hall Museum Library and Archives.)

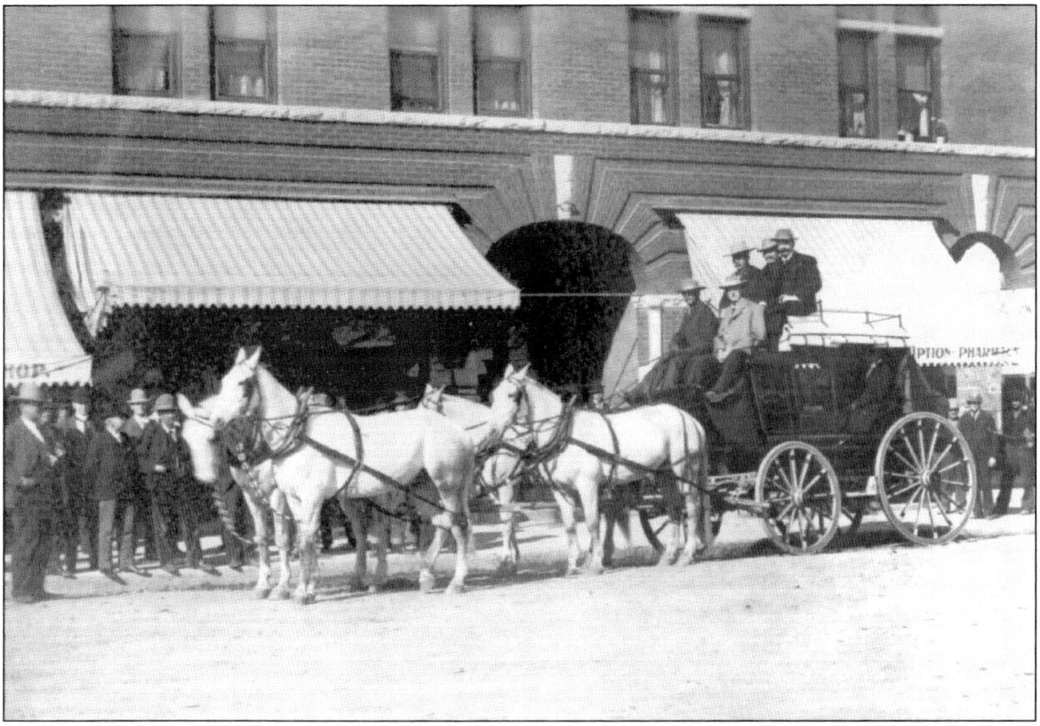

Famed presidential-candidate-turned-evangelist William Jennings Bryan made two appearances at the Elks Theatre while touring the nation giving oratorical speeches. In this photograph, Bryan is seen in the front seat of a Ruffner Livery Stable coach in the light suit. He is seated next to Yavapai County sheriff George C. Ruffner in front of the St. Michael Hotel in downtown Prescott. (Elisabeth Ruffner collection.)

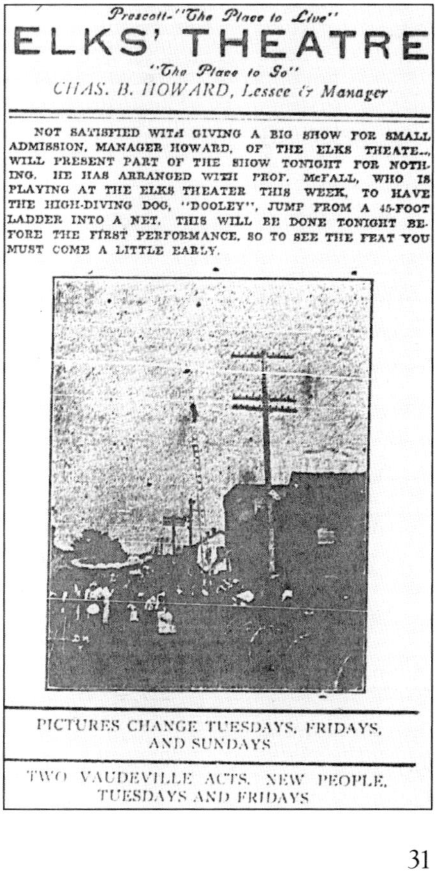

Prescott-"The Place to Live"

ELKS' THEATRE

"The Place to Go"

CHAS. B. HOWARD, Lessee & Manager

NOT SATISFIED WITH GIVING A BIG SHOW FOR SMALL ADMISSION, MANAGER HOWARD, OF THE ELKS THEATER, WILL PRESENT PART OF THE SHOW TONIGHT FOR NOTHING. HE HAS ARRANGED WITH PROF. McFALL, WHO IS PLAYING AT THE ELKS THEATER THIS WEEK, TO HAVE THE HIGH-DIVING DOG, "DOOLEY", JUMP FROM A 45-FOOT LADDER INTO A NET. THIS WILL BE DONE TONIGHT BEFORE THE FIRST PERFORMANCE, SO TO SEE THE FEAT YOU MUST COME A LITTLE EARLY.

PICTURES CHANGE TUESDAYS, FRIDAYS, AND SUNDAYS

TWO VAUDEVILLE ACTS, NEW PEOPLE, TUESDAYS AND FRIDAYS

Did Dooley the dog really jump off a 45-foot-tall tower in front of the Elks Building as advertised? Animal acts were a part of most vaudeville circuits in the days when the Humane Society was not around to monitor their treatment. (Parker Anderson collection.)

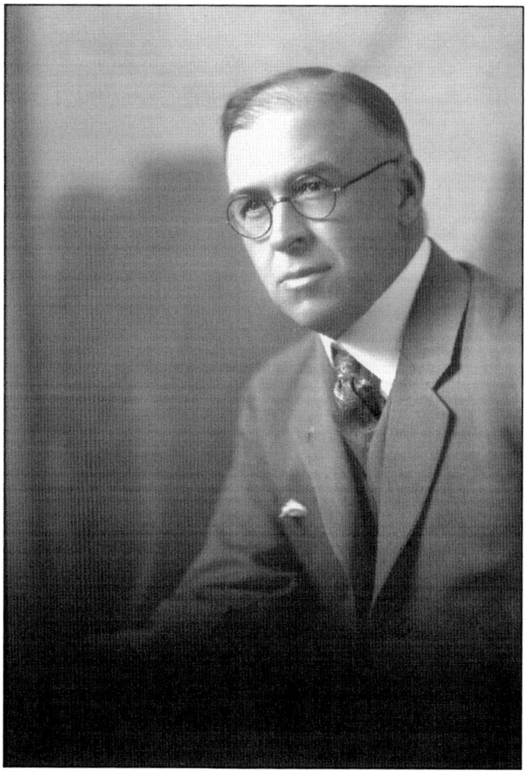

Dr. Harry T. Southworth and Harriet Fay Southworth, two of Prescott's most respected residents, appeared on the Elks stage many times in local variety productions. Their daughter Dorothy Fay Southworth married famed country-western singer Tex Ritter and was the mother of television actor John Ritter. (Both, Sharlot Hall Museum Library and Archives.)

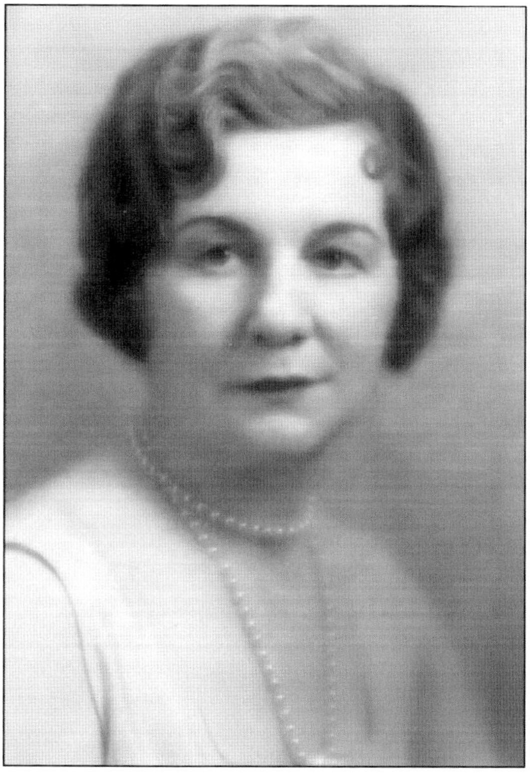

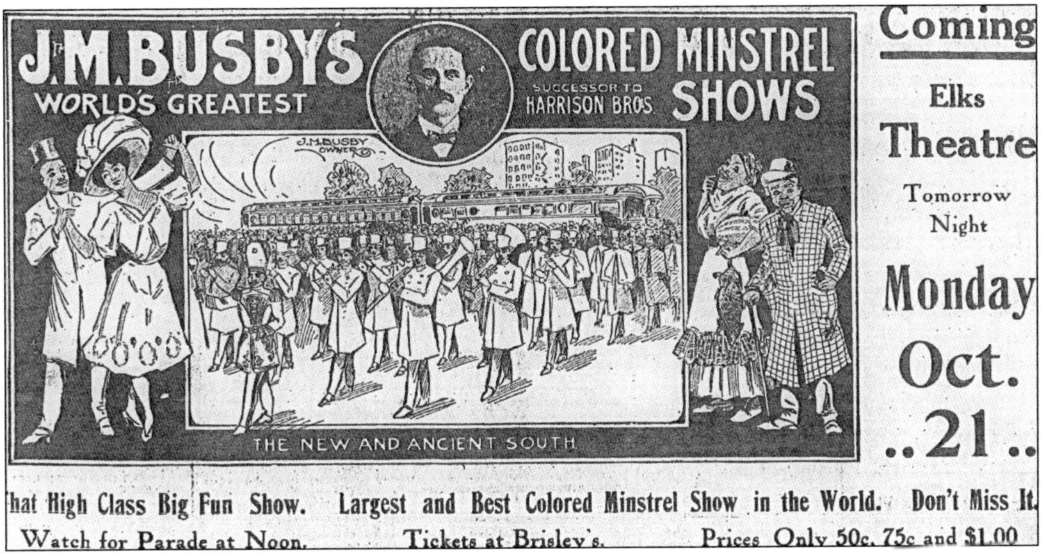

Many traveling shows performed daytime street parades in small towns to advertise later appearances. This was especially common with blackface minstrel shows. The photograph below shows an unidentified minstrel parade at the corner of Gurley and Cortez Streets. The Elks Theatre is near the top left of the photograph. (Above, Parker Anderson collection; below, Sharlot Hall Museum Library and Archives.)

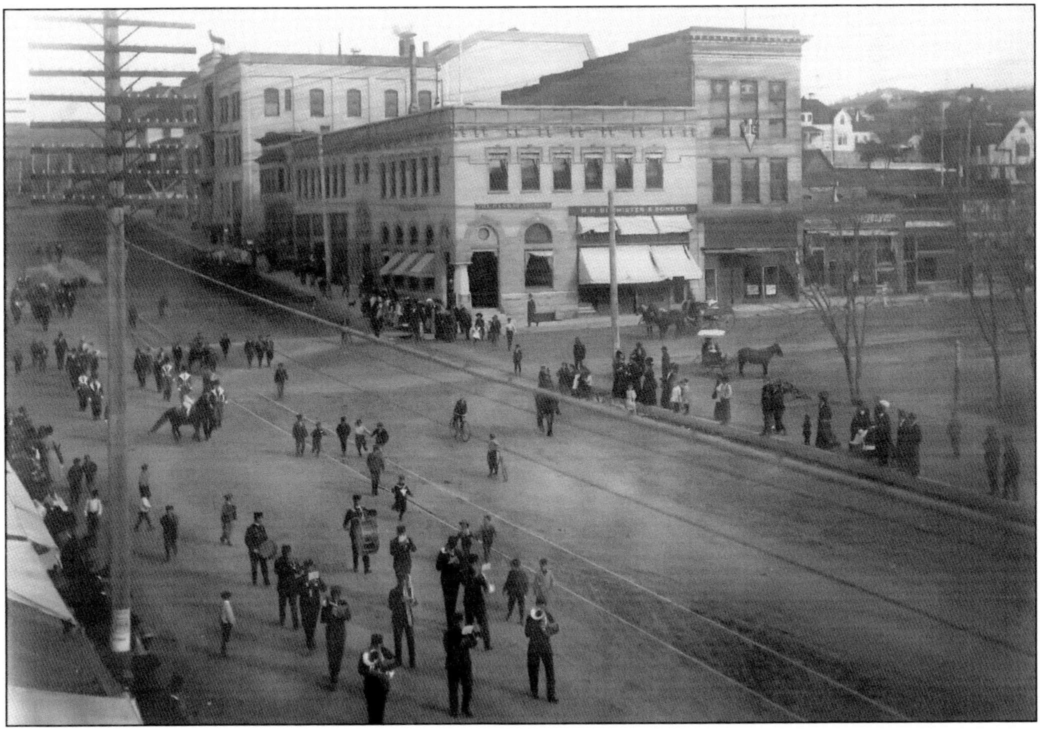

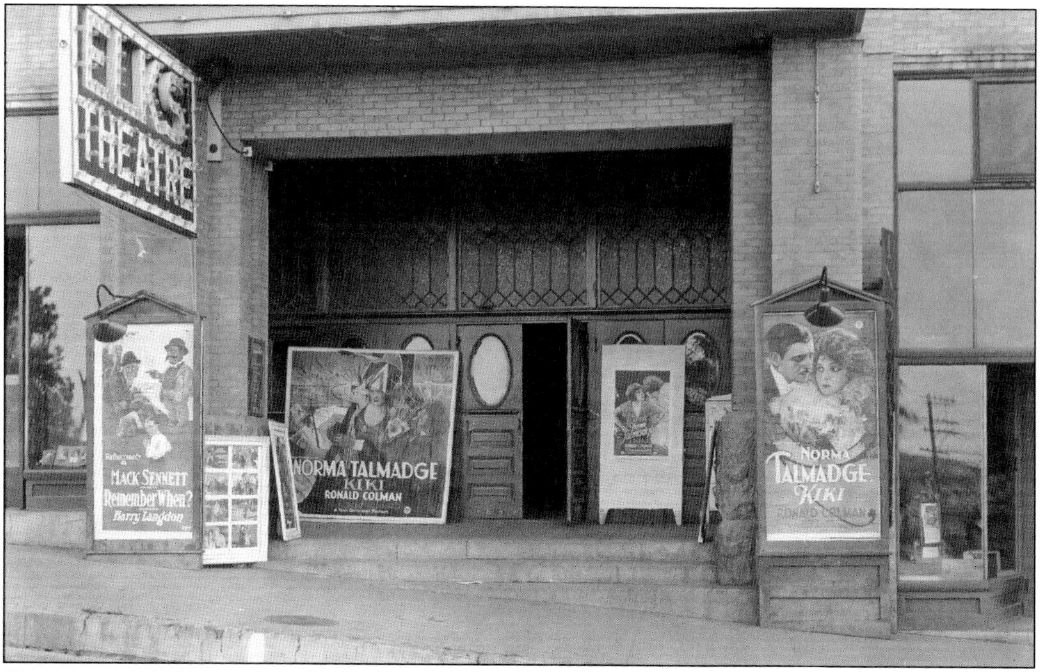

Shown around the 1920s is the entrance to the Elks Theatre with beautiful oval windows in the doors and decorative glass. Virtually the entire center of the entrance would be replaced by a box office in later years. (Sharlot Hall Museum Library and Archives.)

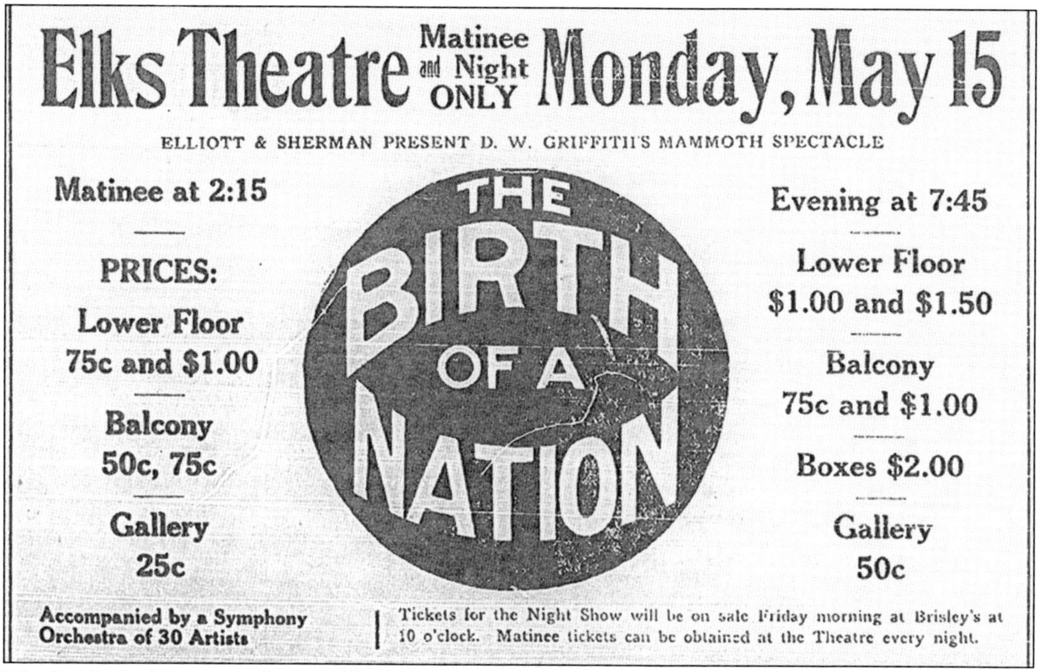

The Birth of a Nation, still arguably the most controversial motion picture ever made, first played at the Elks Theatre in 1916. Local African American residents unsuccessfully petitioned the city council to ban the showing at the theater, a situation that had also happened in other cities at the time. (Parker Anderson collection.)

Elks Theatre manager Charles Born poses for a photograph with silent film actress May McAvoy, who was a major star in the 1920s. Along with partners William Mays and Ray Vyne, Born turned the Elks Theatre into a movie theater of the first magnitude, which included lavish promotions, press conferences, and major remodeling of the theater interior. (Sharlot Hall Museum Library and Archives.)

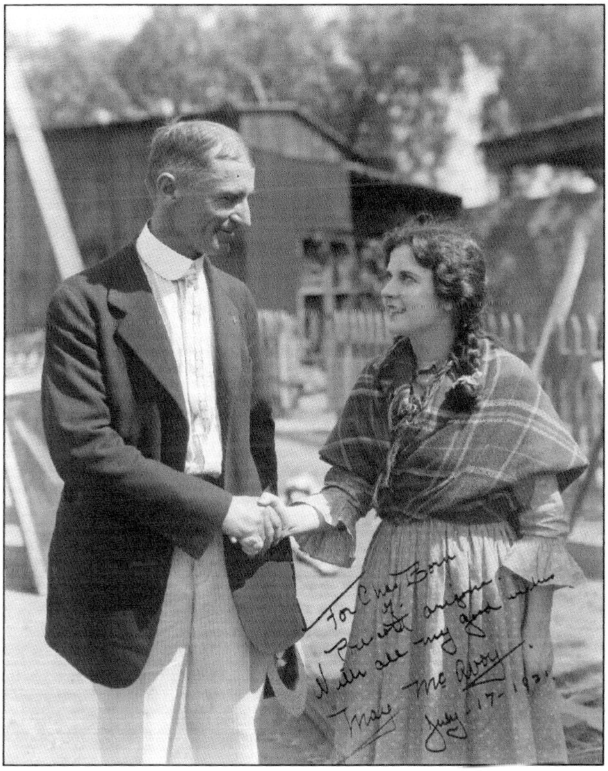

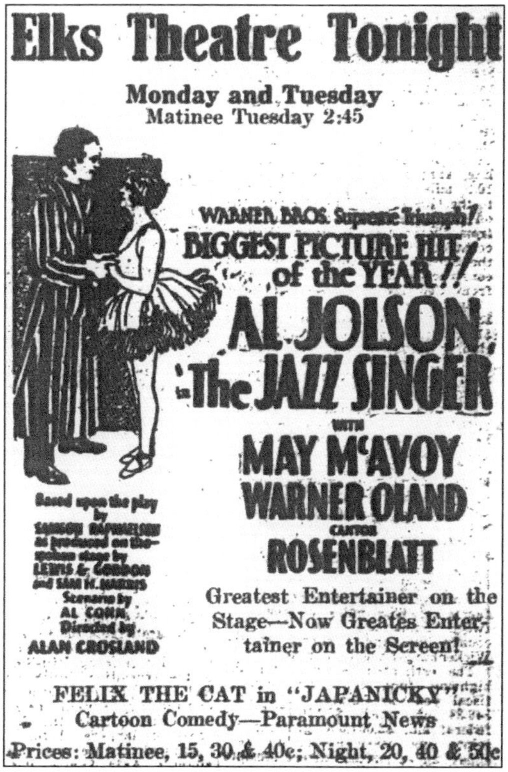

The Jazz Singer is remembered as the first genuine sound film, although this was undoubtedly a special silent print that played the Elks Theatre. This was common in the early days of talkies, as most theaters throughout the country, including the Elks Theatre, had not yet acquired the audio and projection equipment necessary to show sound motion pictures. Note that May McAvoy, shown in the photograph at the top of the page, is in the cast. (Parker Anderson collection.)

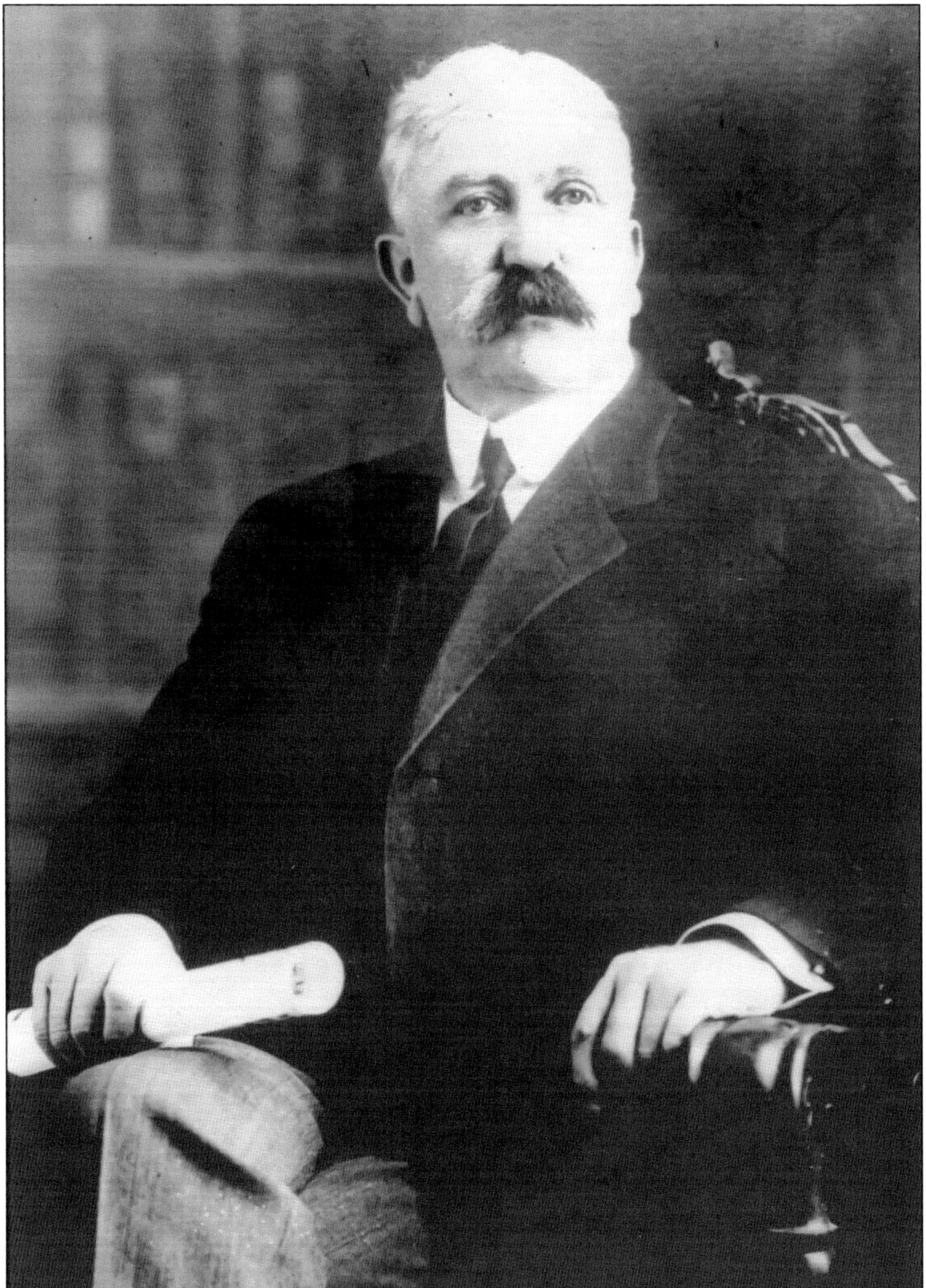

Marcus Aurelius Smith served as Arizona's territorial delegate to the US House of Representatives sporadically in the late 19th and early 20th centuries and later became one of Arizona's first two US senators following statehood in 1912. Smith also appeared in political rallies at the Elks Opera House. Even though Smith was not in office at the time Arizona was accepted into the Union as a state, statehood historians remember him far more fondly than his successor Ralph Cameron. (Library of Congress Prints and Photographs Division, George Grantham Bain Collection, LC-DIG-ggbain-06708.)

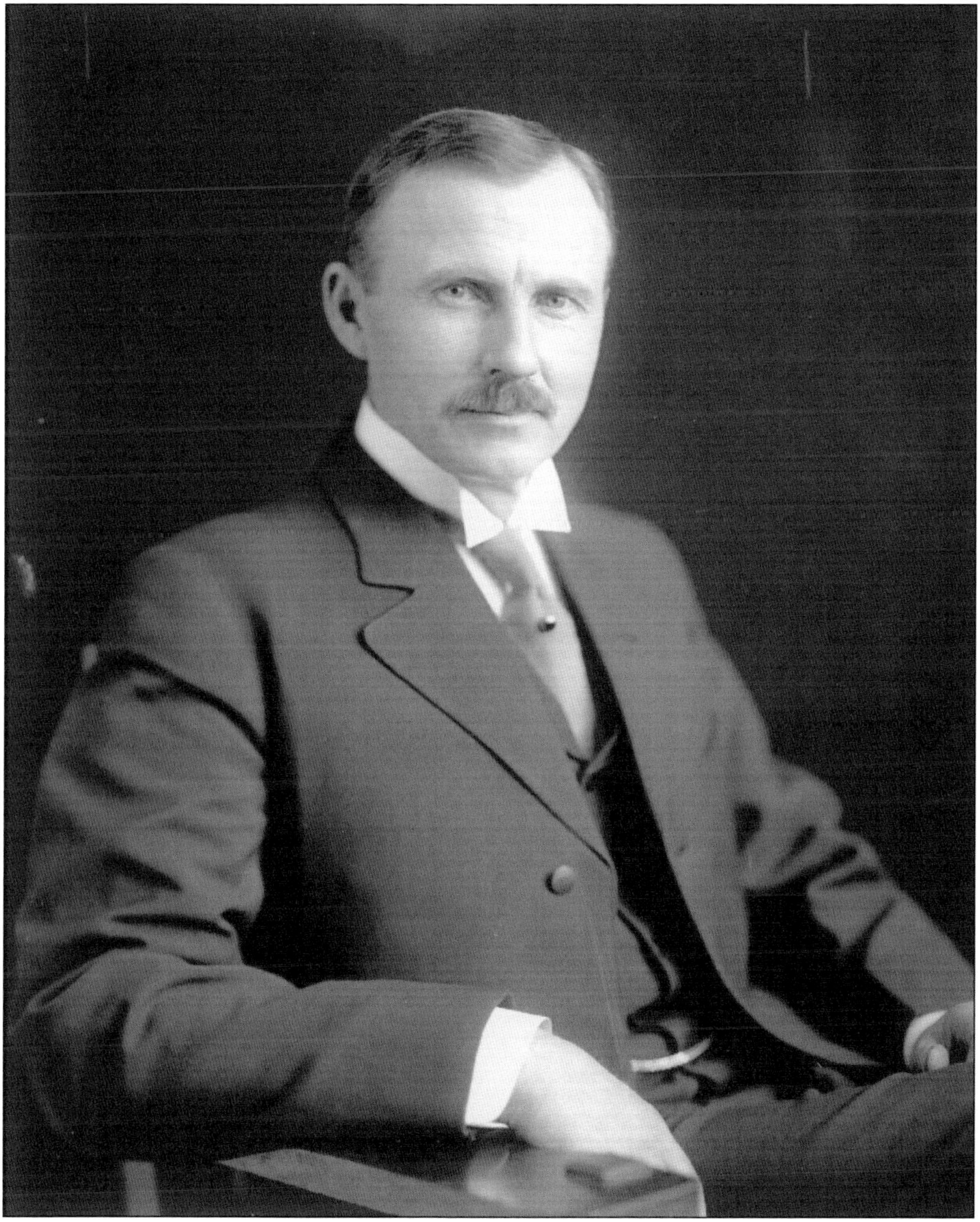

Ralph Henry Cameron was the last Arizona territorial delegate to the U.S. House of Representatives in the years before Arizona statehood, and he appeared several times at the Elks Theatre in political rallies. Although a household name in Arizona politics in his era, he is seldom remembered today, and the few times he is mentioned, it is usually with disdain due to his attempts to keep the Grand Canyon from becoming a National Park. (Library of Congress Prints and Photographs Division, Harris & Ewing Collection, LC-DIG-hec-16125.)

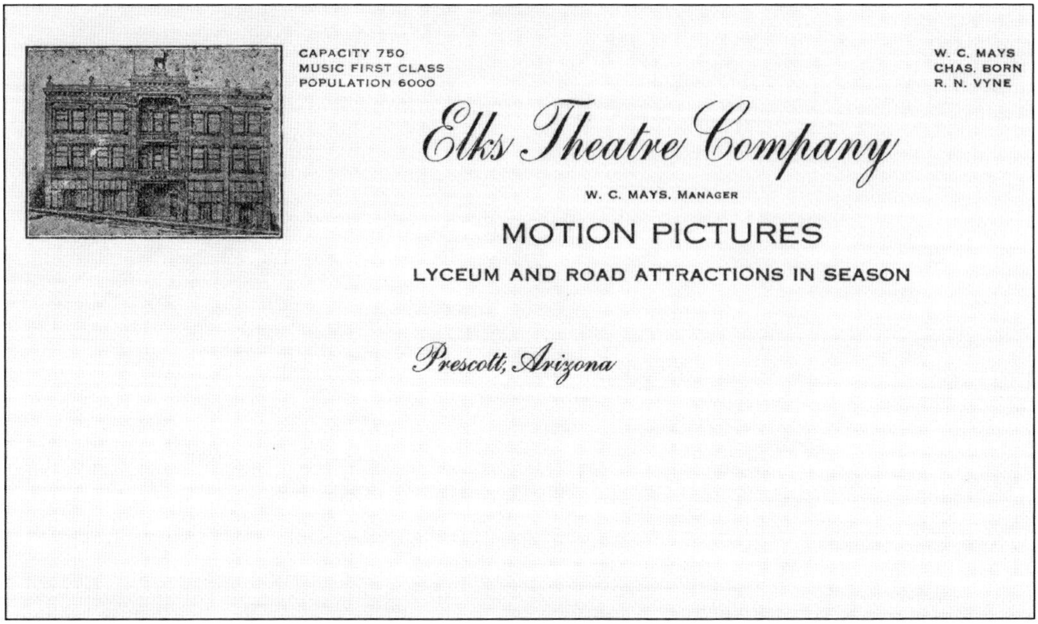

CAPACITY 750
MUSIC FIRST CLASS
POPULATION 6000

W. C. MAYS
CHAS. BORN
R. N. VYNE

Elks Theatre Company

W. C. MAYS, MANAGER

MOTION PICTURES

LYCEUM AND ROAD ATTRACTIONS IN SEASON

Prescott, Arizona

This is a rare surviving sheet of Elks Theatre letterhead stationery from the 1910s. Included are the names of the three managers, with the printing of W.C. Mays's name twice. (Sharlot Hall Museum Library and Archives.)

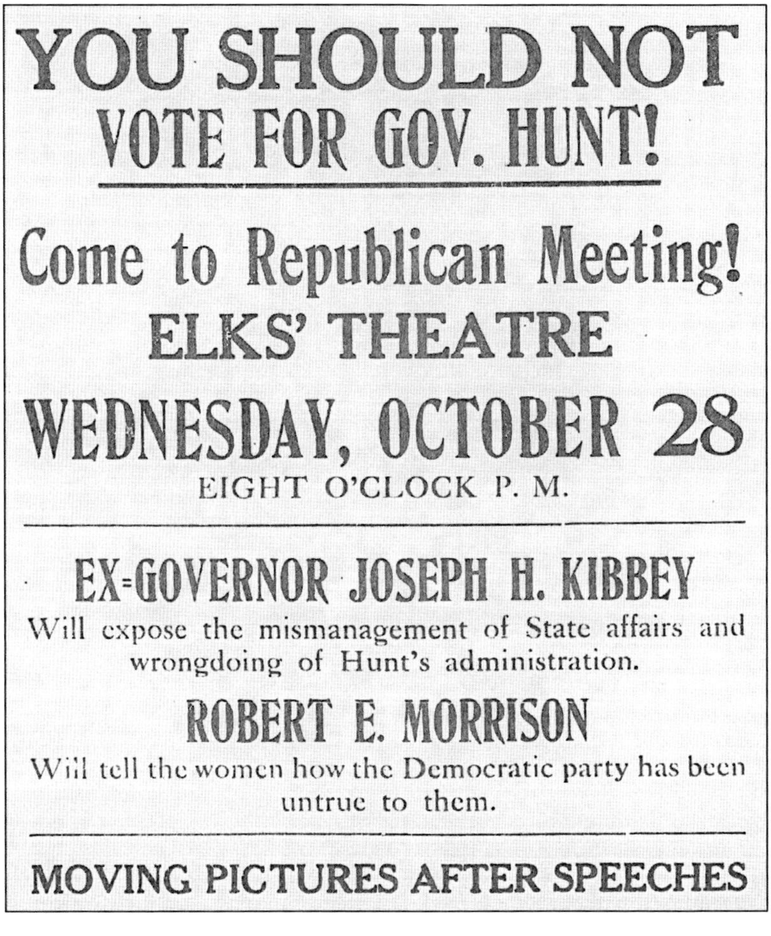

Many political rallies took place at the Elks Theatre in the 1910s and 1920s. This advertisement for a Republican rally shows that politically things have not changed all that much. (Parker Anderson collection.)

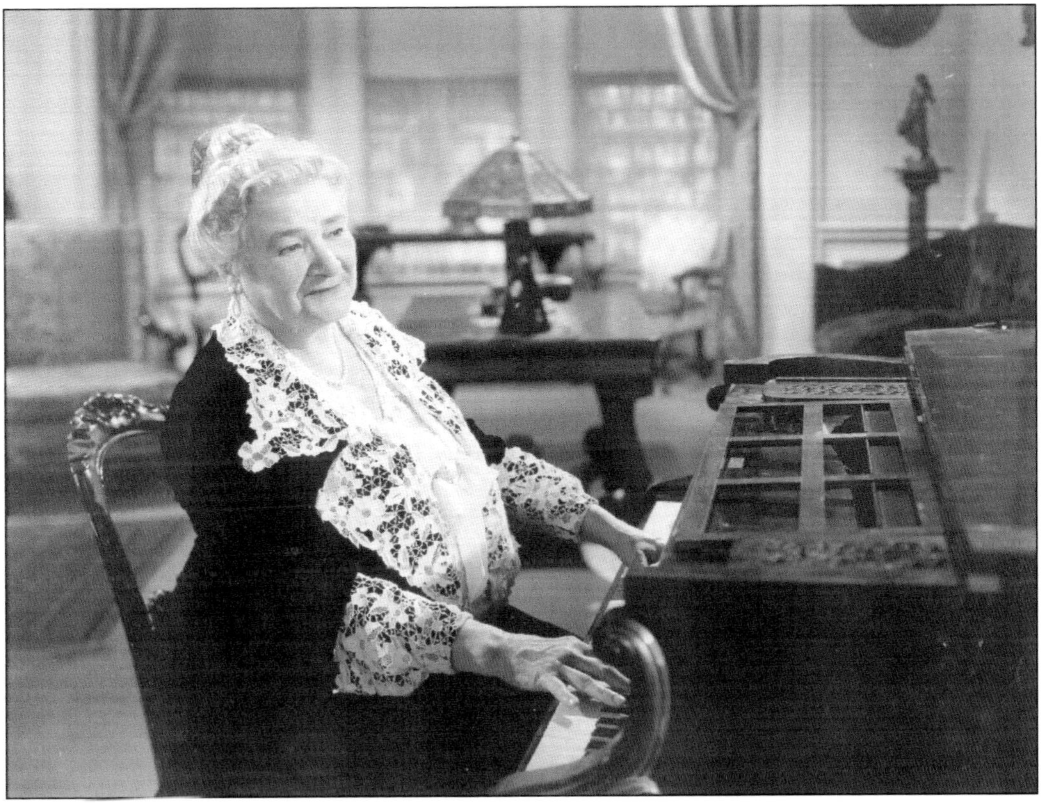

World-famous opera contralto Mme. Ernestine Schumann-Heink made a much-heralded appearance at the Elks Theatre in 1921. At the time, she was one of the best-known performers to appear on stage there, and Prescott residents talked about it for decades after. She promised the audience she would return to Prescott to perform again, but she never did. This photograph is from the 1935 film *Here's to Romance* in which she starred. That film also played at the Elks Theatre. (Parker Anderson collection.)

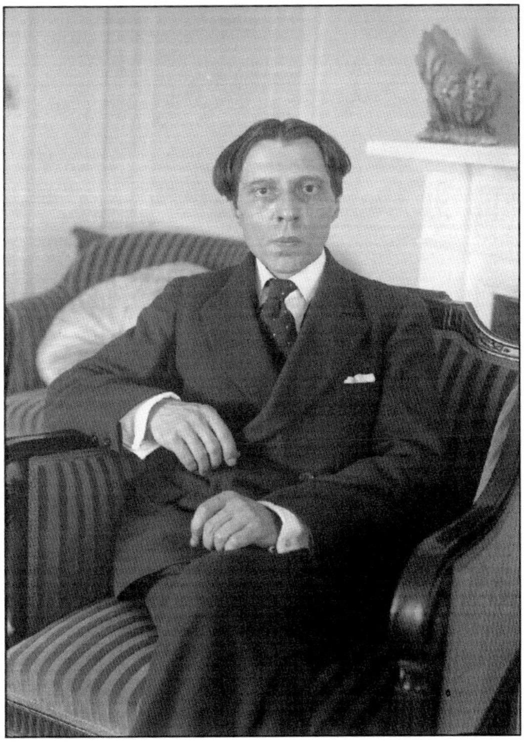

Alfred Cortot was regarded as one of the finest classical pianists in the world at the time he appeared at the Elks Theatre in the 1920s. An effort was made by Charles Born and the Prescott Chamber of Commerce to bring a number of well-known classical performers to the Elks Theatre in the early part of that decade. (Library of Congress Prints and Photographs Division, George Grantham Bain Collection, LC-DIG-ggbain-27618.)

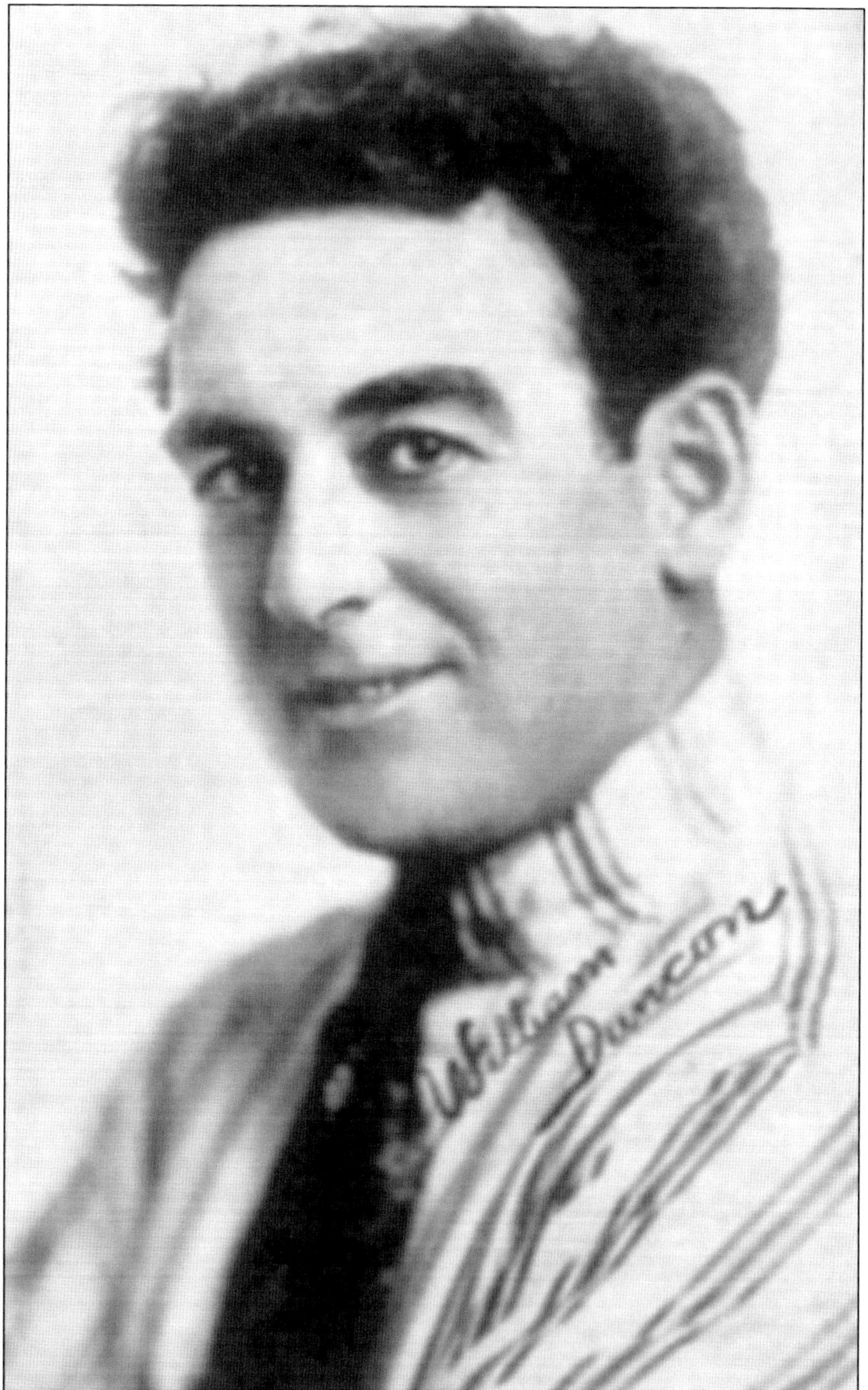

Silent film actor William Duncan, of the Selig Polyscope Company, arrived in Prescott to shoot a number of films, most of which have regrettably not survived. He and other members of the Selig Polyscope Company also appeared live at the Elks Theatre while in town. Duncan passed away in 1961.

Myrtle Stedman also came to Prescott as part of the Selig Polyscope film company. She was one of the first major female stars. It was a different time then; the actors greeted Prescott residents as their friends and neighbors, they made live appearances at the Elks Theatre and other venues during their stay, and Myrtle Stedman even agreed to sing at a local resident's funeral. Although she played leading roles for Selig, she was reduced to bit parts by the 1920s. (Library of Congress Prints and Photographs Division, George Grantham Bain Collection, LC-DIG-ggbain-32953.)

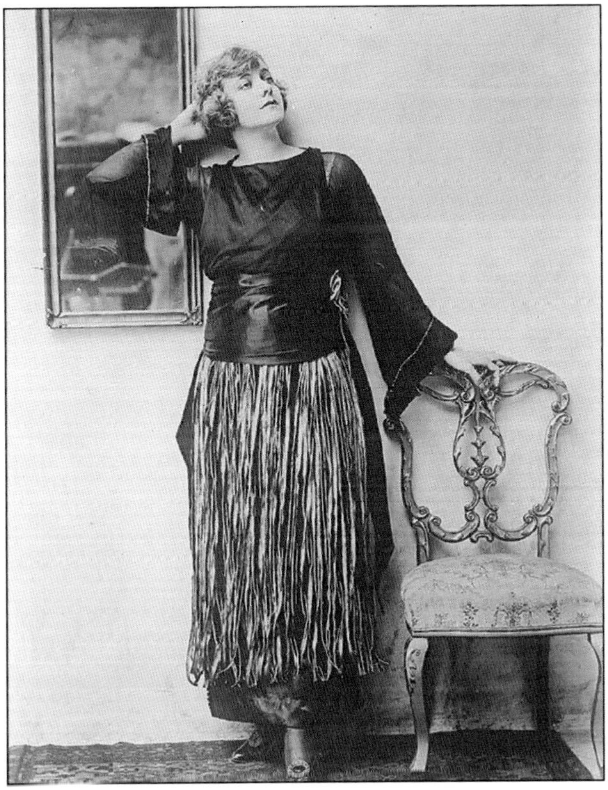

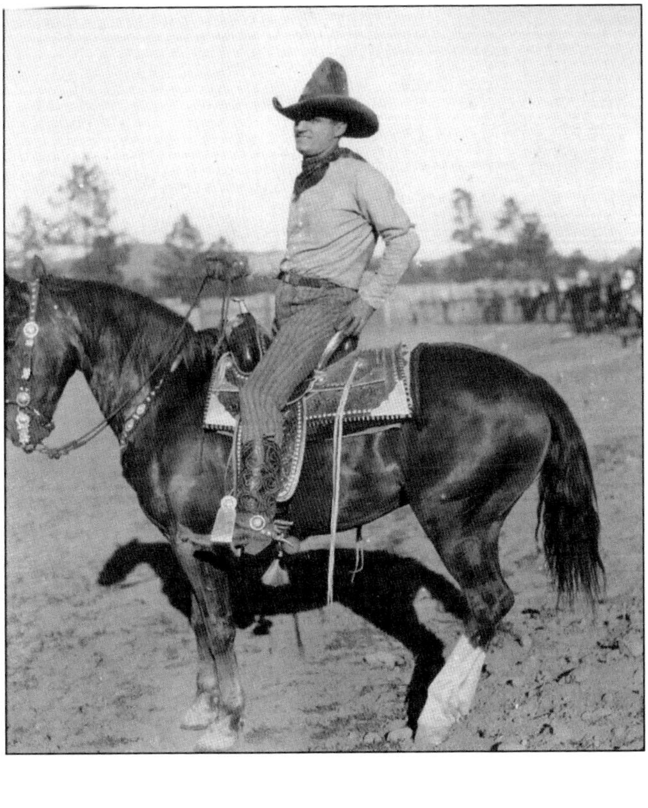

Famed cowboy star Tom Mix first came to Prescott as part of the Selig Polyscope Company and filmed many of his movies in the Prescott area between 1912 and 1927. He was fond of the community and made numerous live appearances at the Elks Theatre, often at fundraisers for local causes. This July 4, 1920, photograph shows Mix in Prescott astride his horse Tony. (Sharlot Hall Museum Library and Archives.)

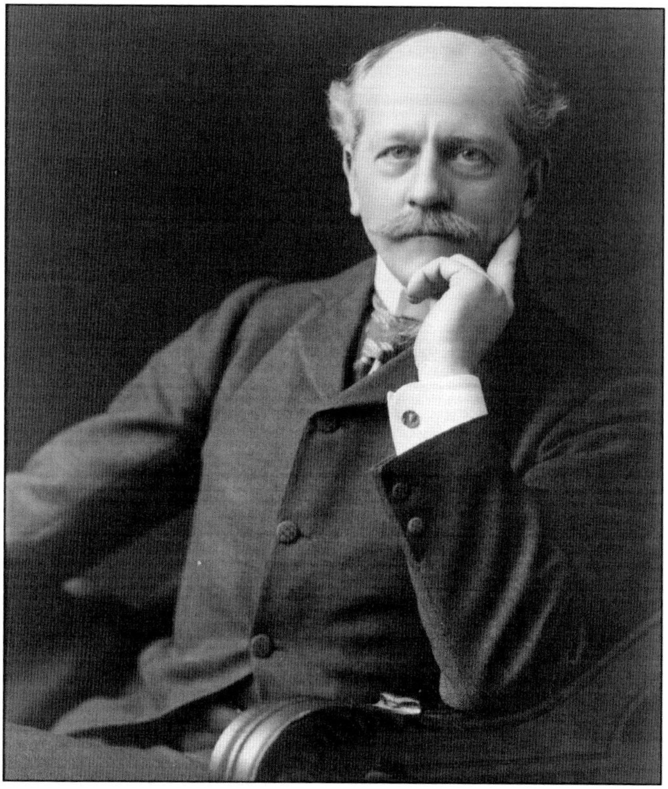

World-famous astronomer Percival Lowell (founder of Lowell Observatory in Flagstaff, Arizona) came to the Elks Theatre for a lecture in 1911. Although his place in astronomy is indisputable, his memory has been derided a bit in recent years for his belief that there is life on Mars. With the increase in Mars space missions to find signs of life at the molecular level, he may someday be proven correct. (Library of Congress Prints and Photographs Division, LC-USZ62-128068.)

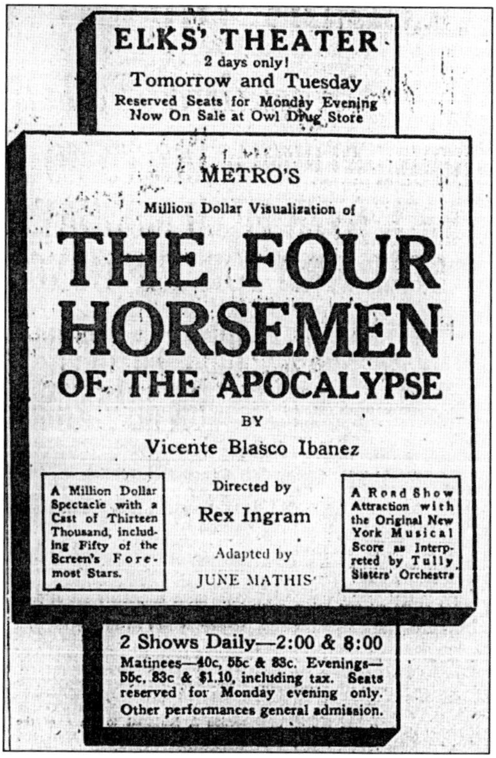

Although his name does not appear in the advertisement, *The Four Horseman of the Apocalypse* solidified Rudolph Valentino as a major star in motion pictures. The advertisement references the Tully Sisters, a Prescott musical group that performed regularly at the Elks Theatre and often contributed to the live music scores for silent films. (Parker Anderson collection.)

New York Metropolitan Opera star Anna Case was another famous 1920s contralto performer to appear at the Elks Theatre. In addition to her stage performances, she also recorded extensively for Edison records. (Sharlot Hall Museum Library and Archives.)

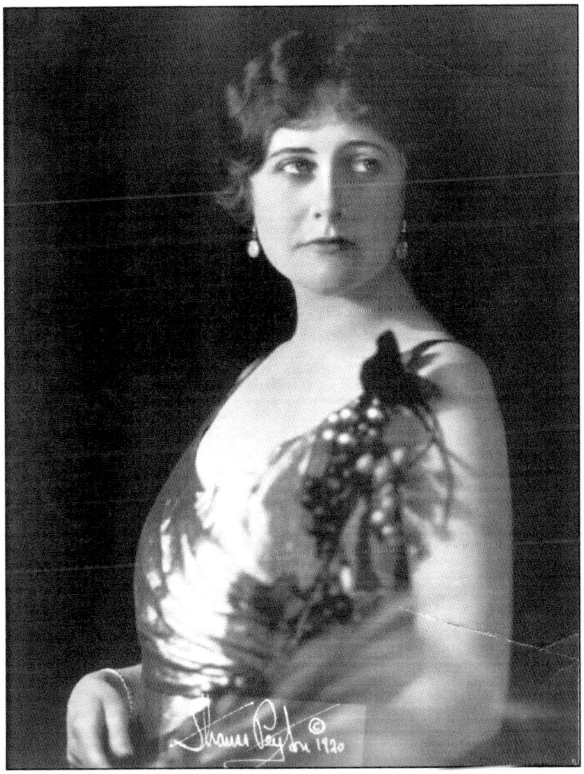

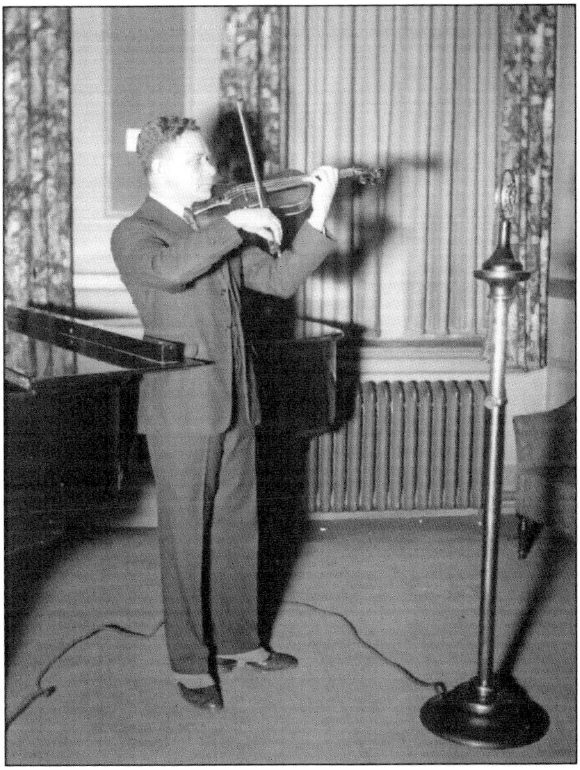

Violinist Efrem Zimbalist Sr. came to Prescott to play the Elks Theatre during the 1920s. Although a famous classical musician in his day, he is overshadowed in the public's memory by his son, television actor Efrem Zimbalist Jr., and his granddaughter, television actress Stephanie Zimbalist. (Library of Congress Prints and Photographs Division, LC-DIG-ggbain-39119.)

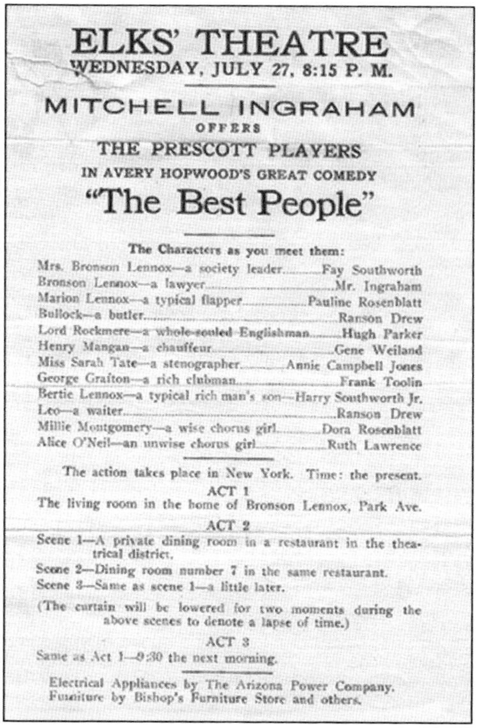

ELKS' THEATRE
WEDNESDAY, JULY 27, 8:15 P. M.

MITCHELL INGRAHAM
OFFERS
THE PRESCOTT PLAYERS
IN AVERY HOPWOOD'S GREAT COMEDY
"The Best People"

The Characters as you meet them:

Mrs. Bronson Lennox—a society leader..........Fay Southworth
Bronson Lennox—a lawyer..........Mr. Ingraham
Marion Lennox—a typical flapper..........Pauline Rosenblatt
Bullock—a butler..........Ranson Drew
Lord Rockmere—a whole-souled Englishman..........Hugh Parker
Henry Mangan—a chauffeur..........Gene Weiland
Miss Sarah Tate—a stenographer..........Annie Campbell Jones
George Grafton—a rich clubman..........Frank Toolin
Bertie Lennox—a typical rich man's son—Harry Southworth Jr.
Leo—a waiter..........Ranson Drew
Millie Montgomery—a wise chorus girl..........Dora Rosenblatt
Alice O'Neil—an unwise chorus girl..........Ruth Lawrence

The action takes place in New York. Time: the present.

ACT 1
The living room in the home of Bronson Lennox, Park Ave.

ACT 2
Scene 1—A private dining room in a restaurant in the theatrical district.
Scene 2—Dining room number 7 in the same restaurant.
Scene 3—Same as scene 1—a little later.
(The curtain will be lowered for two moments during the above scenes to denote a lapse of time.)

ACT 3
Same as Act 1—9:30 the next morning.

Electrical Appliances by The Arizona Power Company.
Furniture by Bishop's Furniture Store and others.

This is a program for the live stage production of *The Best People*, which was produced by local Prescott resident Mitchell Ingraham, who also directed and cast himself in the show. Ingraham produced a number of such events at the Elks Theatre in the 1920s before moving to Hollywood, where he tried to break into the movies. He only succeeded in playing a number of unbilled bit parts in film before passing away in 1944. (Parker Anderson collection.)

A rare surviving photograph of Mitchell Ingraham shows him on stage in an unidentified play in San Francisco in the 1920s. He occasionally left Prescott for stage opportunities elsewhere, but he always returned until 1932, when he left Prescott for good. (Parker Anderson collection.)

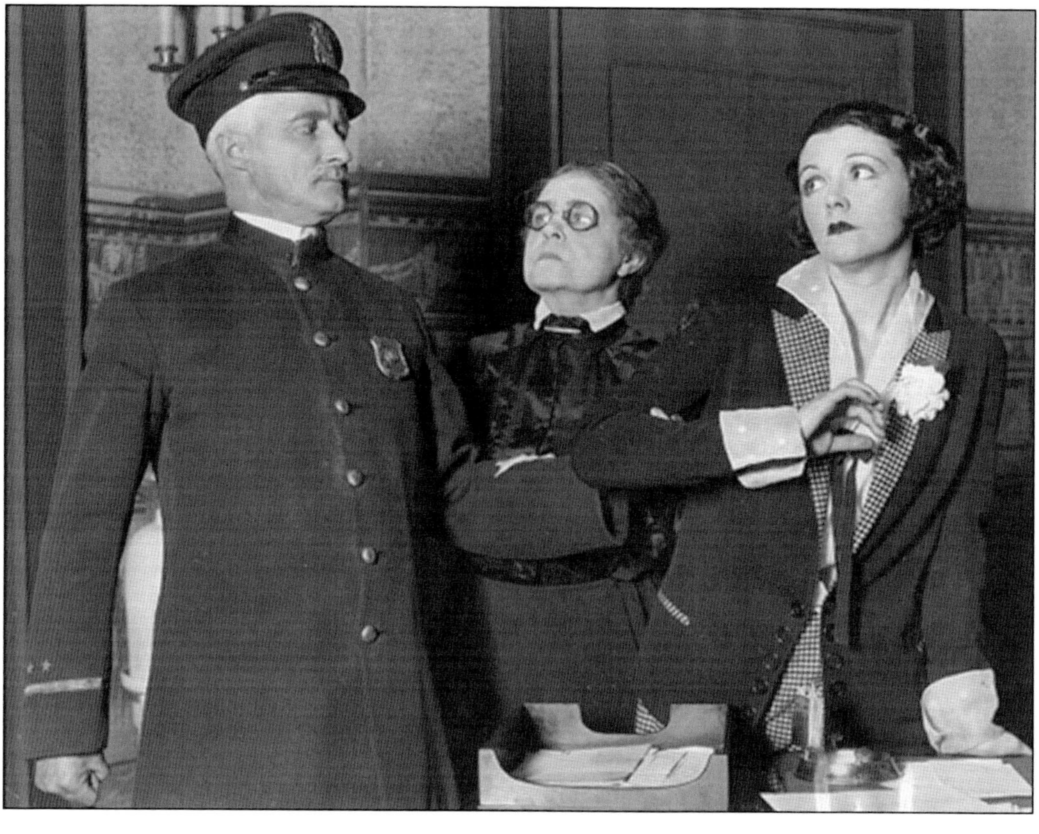

Shown is an Elks Theatre program for Mitchell Ingraham's 1929 play *Fifty Years from Now* in which he and his cast depicted (probably for comic effect) what Prescott would be like 50 years later in 1979. It is unfortunate that no script is known to have survived. (Parker Anderson collection.)

ELKS' THEATRE PROGRAM

Saturday Evening, Oct. 26

1—"Movie Night," an M. G. M. Comedy

2—Mitchell Ingraham Presents:—

"Fifty Years From Now"

A problem playlet of the future

THE CHARACTERS

Jean, the wife .... Miss Clara Steiner

Edward, the husband .... Mr. Ingraham

Florence, the home wrecker .... Miss Vera Voge

THE DANCING DOLLS

The Misses—Katharine Durham, Maxine Boville, Marie Netherby, Louis Rosenblatt, Betty Brooks and Lillian Napier

Michael Ganey .... Stage Manager

Time, 1979; Place—The 59th floor of an apartment house in Prescott, Arizona.

We do not presume to be an authority on the dress of this period

3—John Gilbert in "Desert Nights."

YAVAPAI COUNTY SAVINGS BANK

"A SAFE PLACE FOR YOUR SAVINGS"

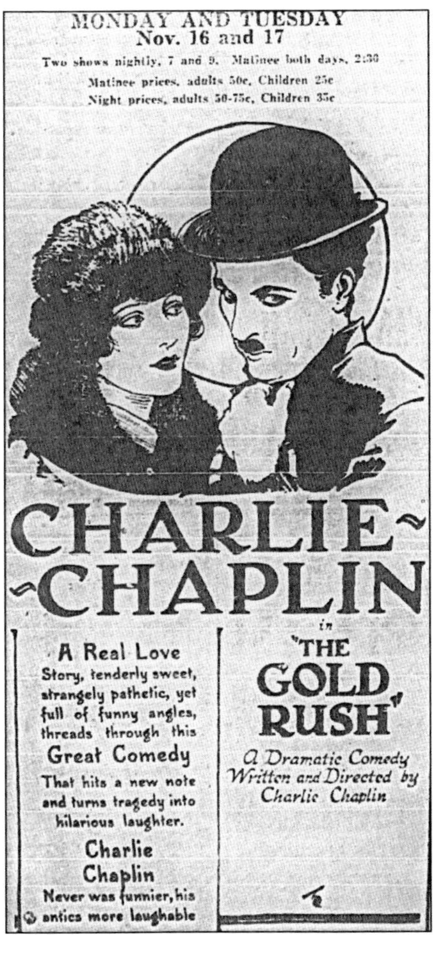

Who could ever forget Charlie Chaplin's immortal *The Gold Rush* in 1925? The "Little Tramp" was never more poignant. (Parker Anderson collection.)

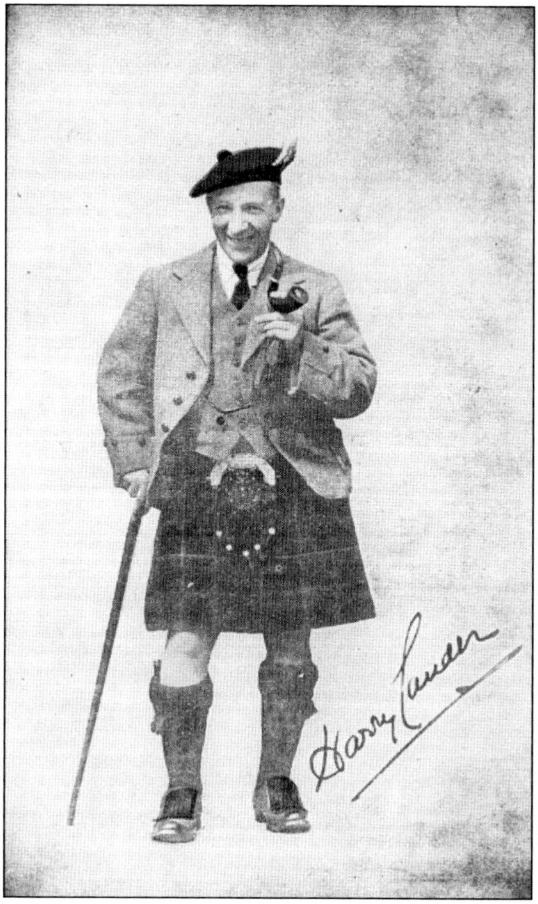

Sir Harry Lauder, the Scottish singer, comedian, and entertainer, was a legendary figure in his own lifetime. He made two memorable appearances at the Elks Theatre: first in 1923 and again in 1932. As of this writing, Prescott resident Hazel Deming, shown in a photograph on page 110, is undoubtedly the last living eyewitness to Sir Harry's appearance at the Elks Theatre. (Parker Anderson collection.)

Elks Theatre

PRESENTS

ANNE NICHOLS' COMEDY DRAMA

"ABIE'S IRISH ROSE"

"Shall I ask the brave soldier who fights by my side
In the cause of mankind, if our creeds agree?
Shall I give up the friend I have valued and tried,
If he kneel not before the same altar with me?"
From the heretic giry of my soul shall I fly,
To seek somewhere else a more orthodox kiss?
No, perish the hearts and the laws that try
Truth, valor and love, by a standard like this!"
—Tom Moore.

CAST OF CHARACTERS

(In the Order of Their First Appearance)

Isaac Cohen .... Edward Pascal
Mrs. Isaac Cohen .... Mildred Beverly
Rabbi Jacob Samuels .... Alfred Clarke
Solomon Levy .... Leo Hoyt
Abraham Levy (his son) .... Teddy Gibson
Rosemary Murphy .... Jenny Wren
Patrick Murphy .... John McCabe
Father Whalen .... Leo Brown

SYNOPSIS OF SCENES

ACT I

Solomon Levy's Apartment, New York City

Act II

Same as Act I. (One week later)

ACT III

Abie's and Rosemary's Apartments, New York

Christmas Eve, one year later

FOR ANNE NICHOLS

General Manager .... Wm. de Lignemare
Manager .... J. B. Moore
Stage Manager .... Leon Brown
Press Representative .... Harry Lambert

This is a program from the Elks Theatre in the 1920s, which was most likely for a traveling road-show production. Such shows were common in those days and still exist (albeit on a smaller level) even today. (Parker Anderson collection.)

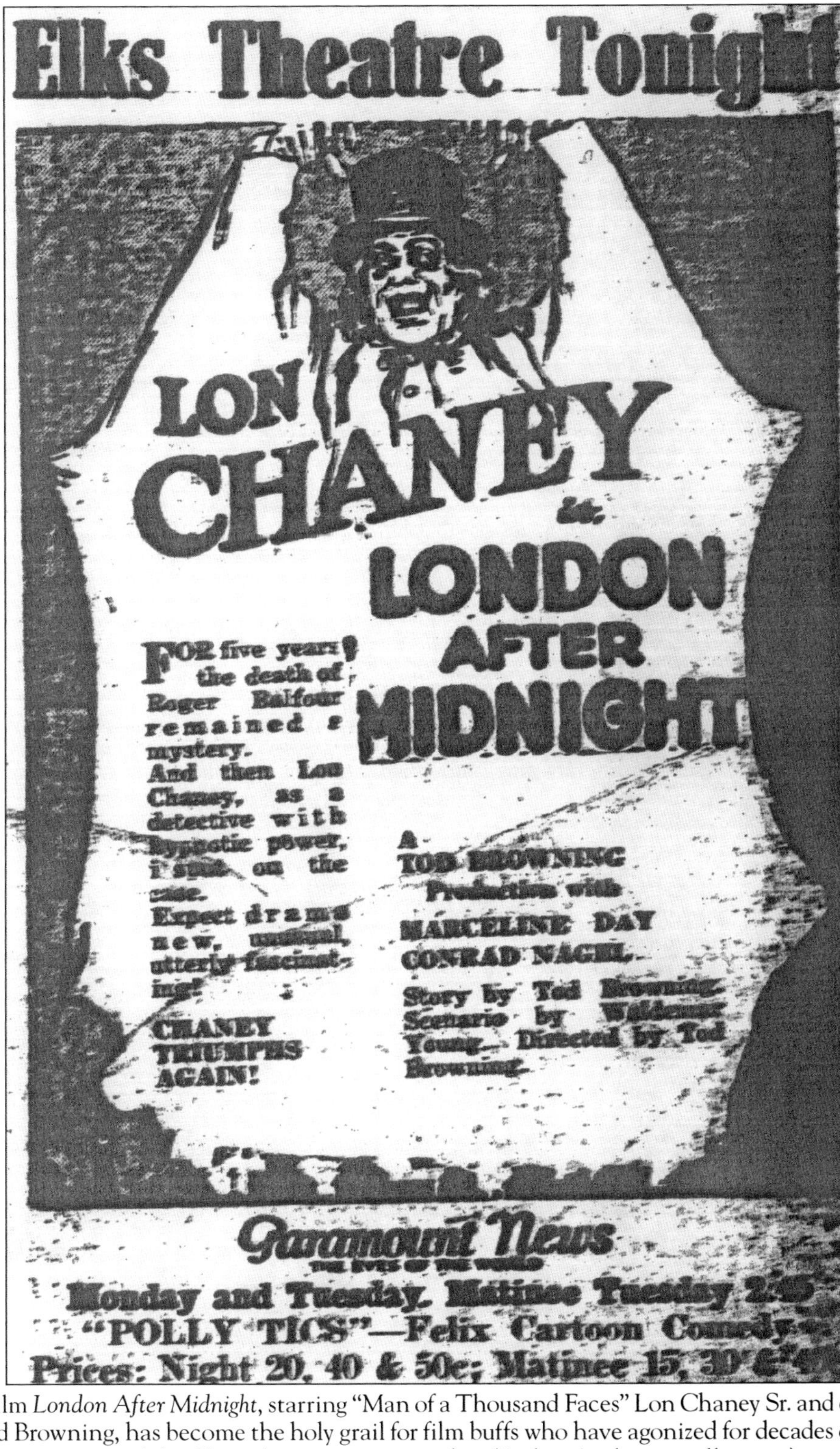

The film *London After Midnight*, starring "Man of a Thousand Faces" Lon Chaney Sr. and directed by Tod Browning, has become the holy grail for film buffs who have agonized for decades over the fact that no print of the film is known to exist today. (Parker Anderson collection.)

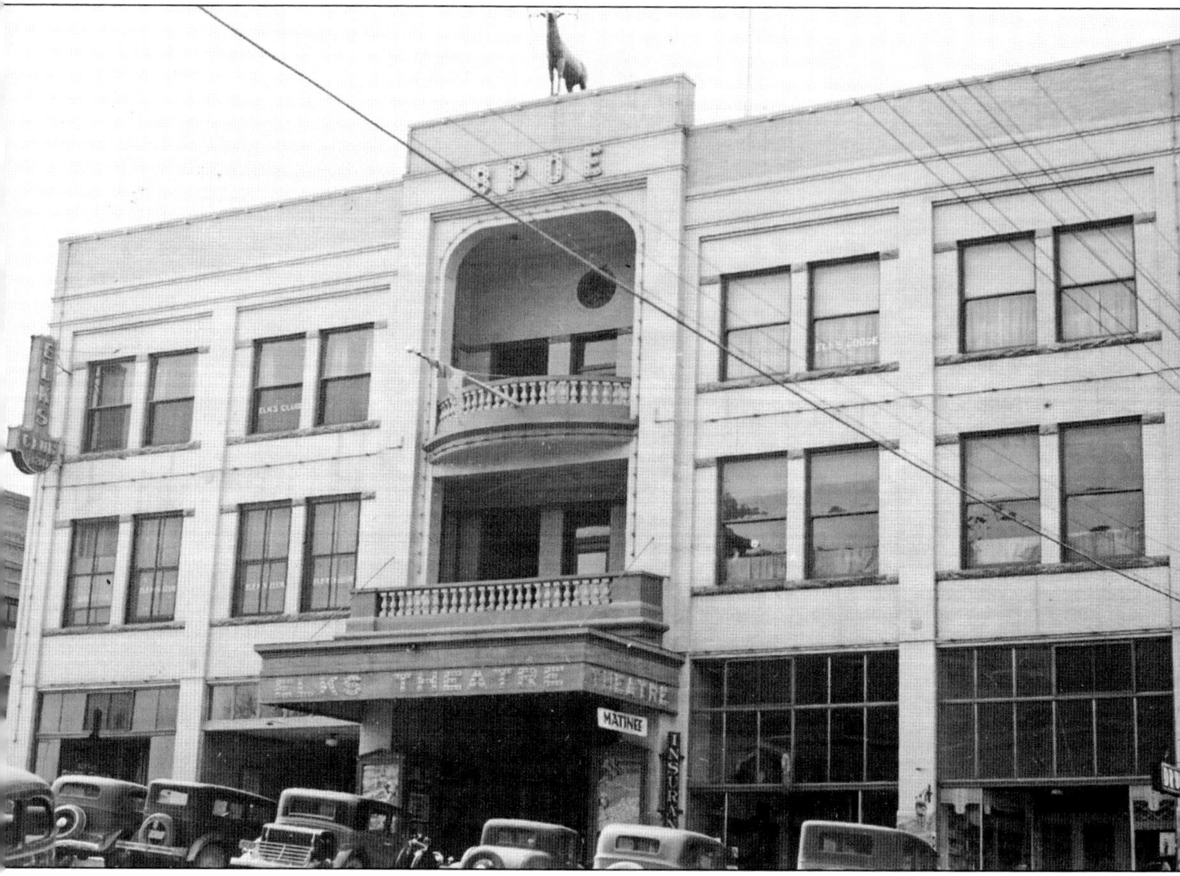

Shown is the exterior of the Elks Building from the late 1920s or early 1930s. Various changes to the facade include large *BPOE* letters on the front of the building, the Elks Club sign in the upper left, and the Elks Theatre marquee. (Sharlot Hall Museum Library and Archives.)

Three

Magical Movie Memories

Charles Born operated the Elks Theatre as a movie theater until his retirement in 1942. At that time, Claude Cline took over management and continued to operate it as a film venue. Charles Born's son Dewey Born continued to work at the Elks Theatre as a projectionist through the 1960s. Reportedly, Phoenix-area businessman and theater operator Harry Nace, who had some holdings in Prescott, became a silent partner and investor with Claude Cline in the management of the theater.

Although the Elks Theatre had undergone some major remodeling in previous years, Claude Cline removed the opera boxes and all of the ornamentation in 1945. This was done largely because a full-time movie theater was not deemed to need such extravagance, and the wood paneling walls that were put up where the box seats had been were somehow deemed to improve the picture and sound quality of the motion pictures.

Some historians have dismissed the movie-theater years as lacking in significance, but to this day, there remain Prescott residents who have many happy memories of seeing movies in the Elks Theatre. First dates and first kisses occurred there, and in 2011, *Arizona Highways* magazine quoted Sharlot Hall Museum and Archives education director Jody Drake as saying that her husband, Ron, proposed to her there. The grand old Elks Theatre continued to serve Prescott very well as a movie theater.

Claude Cline retired in 1980, and he is the longest-serving manager of the Elks Opera House to date. After building the Marina Theatres on Marina Street in Prescott in 1973 to show first-run movies, Cline converted the Elks Theatre to a more family-oriented venue, showing first-run children's films and second-run PG-rated movies.

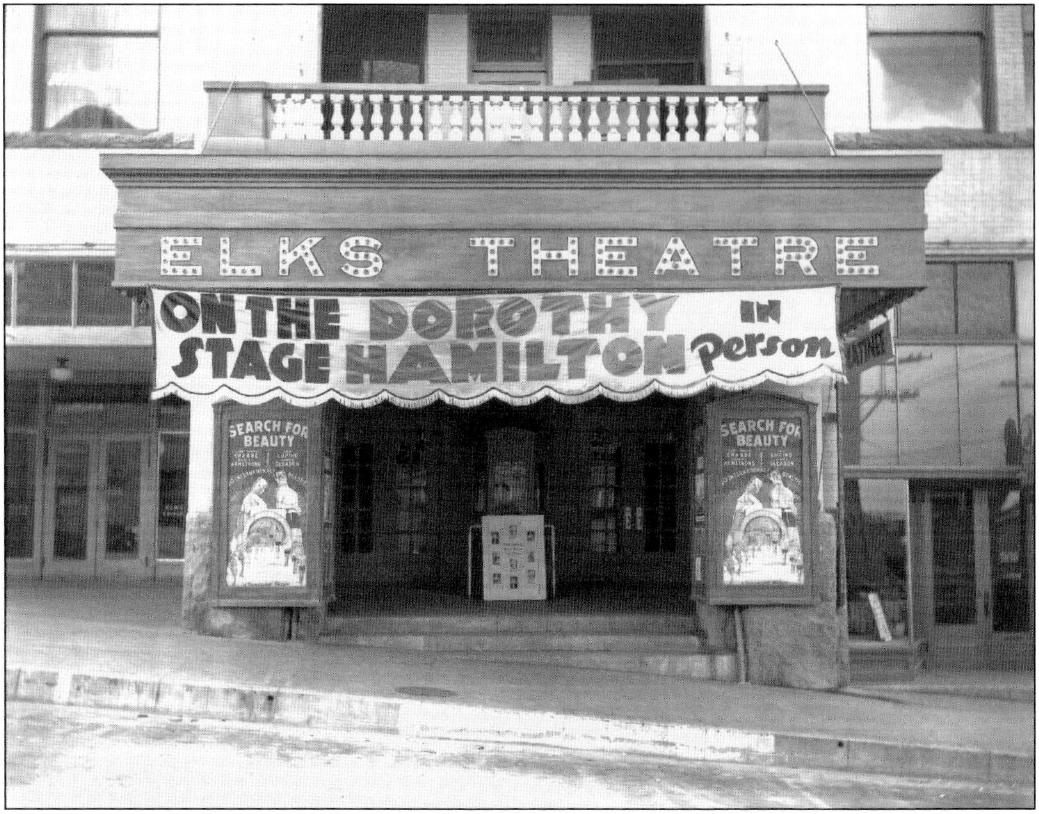

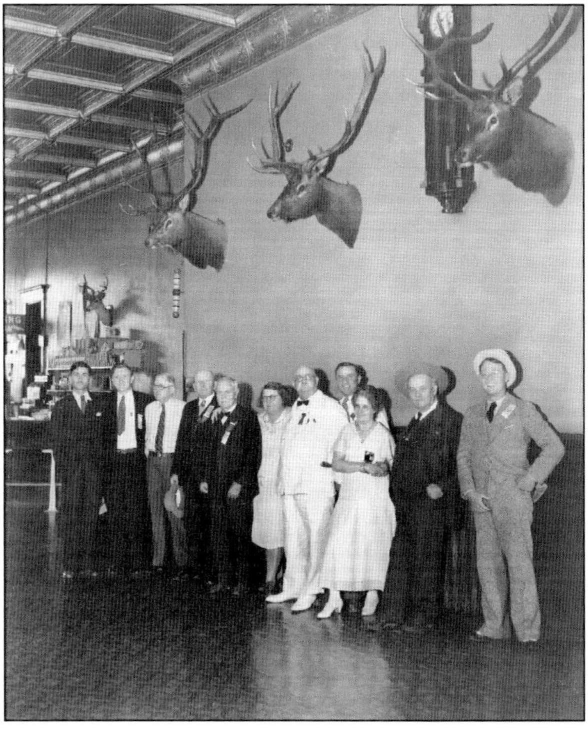

Around 1928, a large, marquee-style electric sign was installed outside of the Elks Theatre. It remained in use until 1942 when Claude Cline covered it over with a more traditional movie theater marquee. The original sign in this photograph was brought back in 2010 as part of the restoration of the opera house and is once again in use today. (Sharlot Hall Museum Library and Archives.)

This is a rare surviving interior shot of the Elks Club upstairs, taken at a United Indian War Veterans gathering on September 26, 1931. Arizona governor George W.P. Hunt (in the white suit and bow tie) is standing underneath the center Elk head with Yavapai County Chamber of Commerce secretary Grace Sparkes standing to the left of him; the others in the photograph are not identified. (Sharlot Hall Museum Library and Archives.)

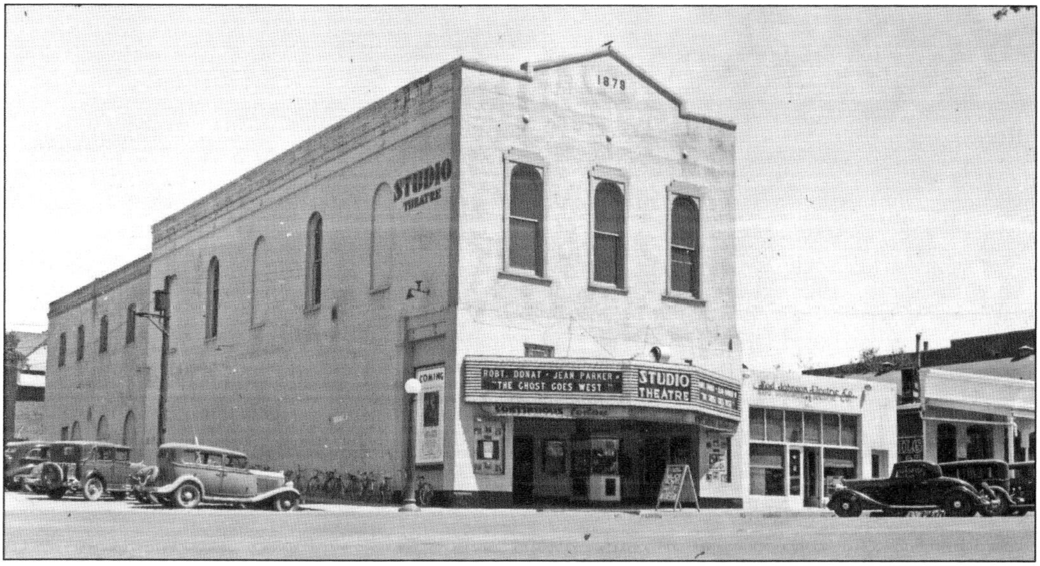

In 1933, Phoenix businessman Albert Stetson purchased the Goldwater Mercantile store on South Cortez Street (only a few blocks from the Elks Theatre) and turned it into a major movie theater that would compete with the Elks Theatre. Called the Studio Theater, the new establishment proved formidable for a while, but Elks Theatre manager Claude Cline assumed control of the Studio by the mid-1940s, and competition was no longer an issue. The Studio Theatre closed permanently in the early 1970s, and the building was demolished in 1978. The loss of this significant building led to a heightened interest in Prescott historic buildings. (Both, Sharlot Hall Museum Library and Archives.)

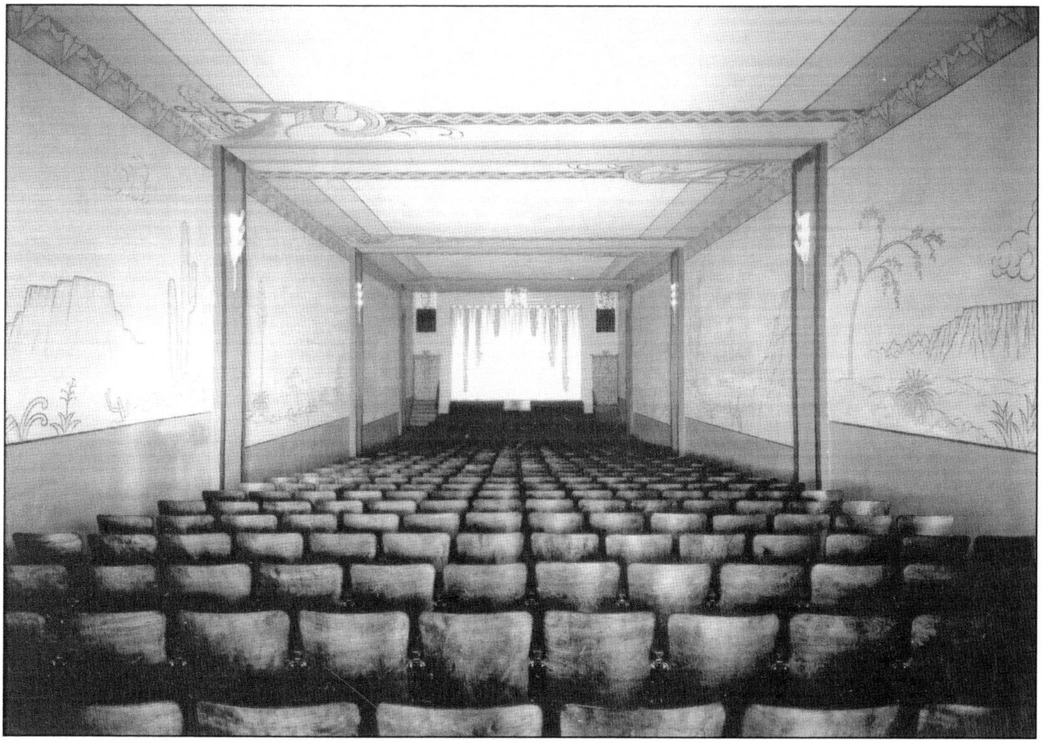

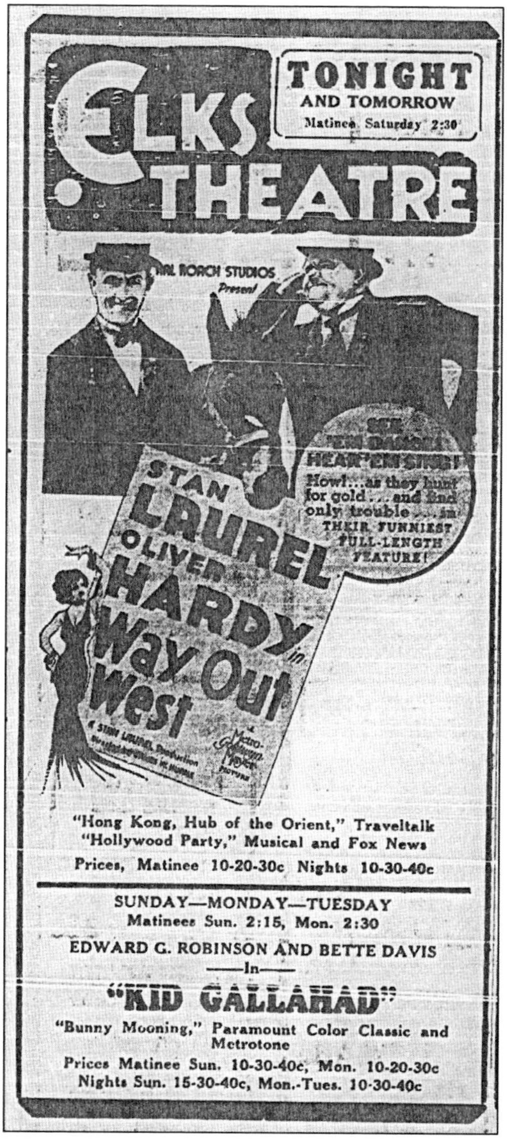

Laurel and Hardy remain one of the best-loved comedy teams of all time. *Way Out West* is regarded as perhaps the peak of their careers. (Parker Anderson collection.)

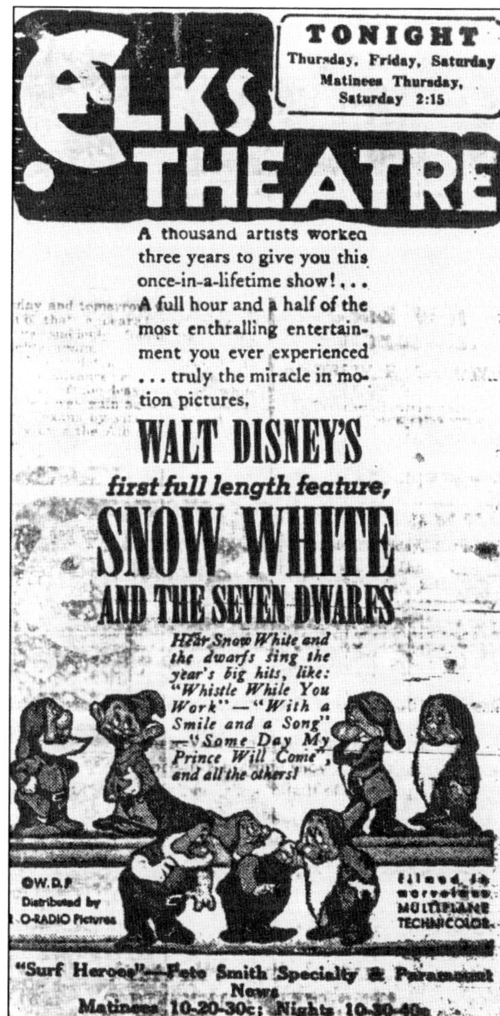

Walt Disney was initially derided for producing the first feature-length animated film in 1937, but he had the last laugh when *Snow White* became a huge success for his studio. This advertisement is from the film's first run that same year. (Parker Anderson collection.)

The publicity campaign accompanying *Gone with the Wind* was unprecedented in the United States. The studio demanded that movie theaters offer reserved seats for inflated prices. The $1.12 ticket price at the Elks Theatre was surely a shock to Prescott filmgoers. (Parker Anderson collection.)

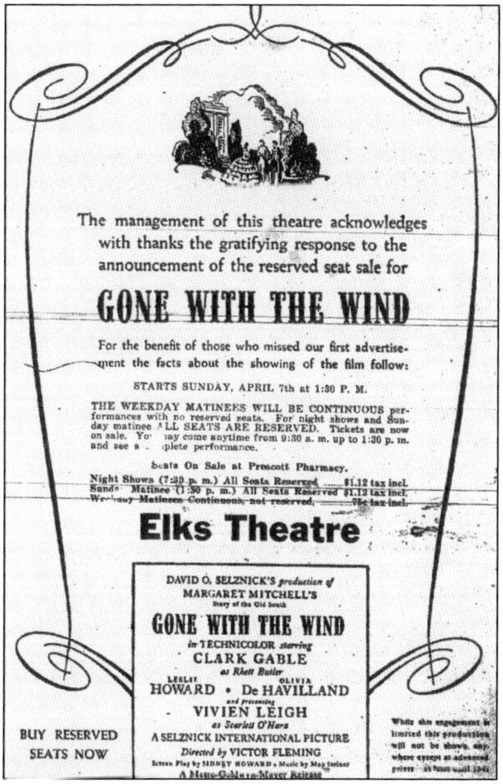

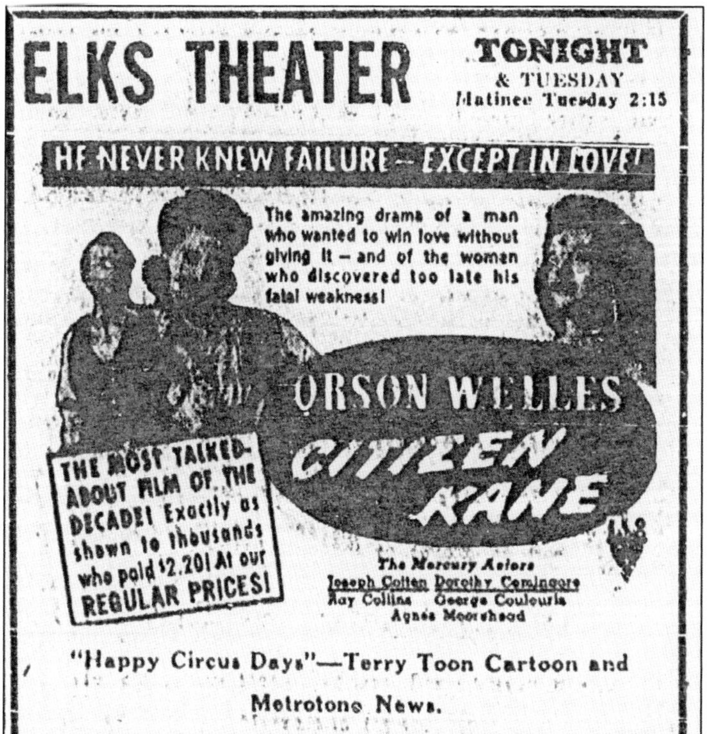

Orson Welles's *Citizen Kane* (1941) has long been cited by historians as one of the finest films ever made. Ironically, former Prescott resident and Elks Theatre persona Mitchell Ingraham had an unbilled bit part in the classic film. It is to be wondered if any of his old Prescott friends recognized him. (Parker Anderson collection.)

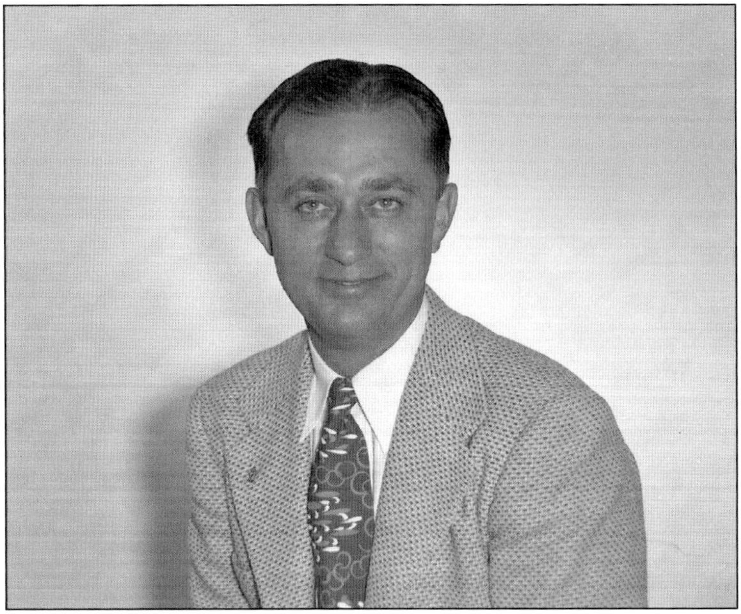

Claude Cline took over management of the Elks Theatre in 1942 and remained in the position until 1980. He was a major influence on the Elks Theatre, and perhaps the opera house would no longer be in existence if it had not been for his long stewardship. (Sharlot Hall Museum Library and Archives.)

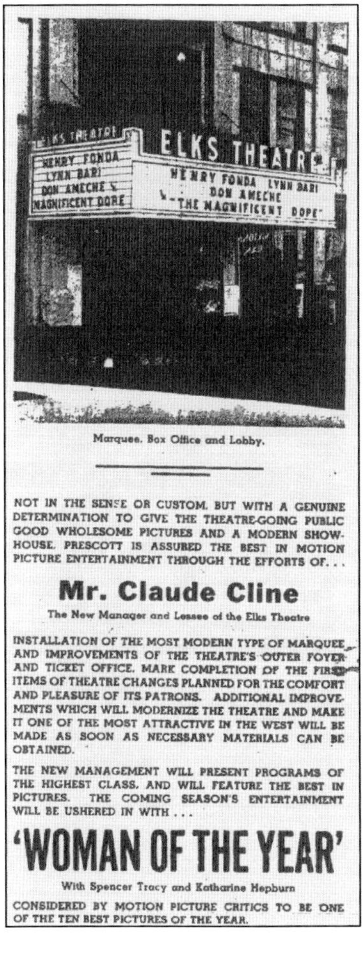

Marquee, Box Office and Lobby.

NOT IN THE SENSE OR CUSTOM, BUT WITH A GENUINE DETERMINATION TO GIVE THE THEATRE-GOING PUBLIC GOOD WHOLESOME PICTURES AND A MODERN SHOW-HOUSE, PRESCOTT IS ASSURED THE BEST IN MOTION PICTURE ENTERTAINMENT THROUGH THE EFFORTS OF . . .

Mr. Claude Cline

The New Manager and Lessee of the Elks Theatre

INSTALLATION OF THE MOST MODERN TYPE OF MARQUEE AND IMPROVEMENTS OF THE THEATRE'S OUTER FOYER AND TICKET OFFICE, MARK COMPLETION OF THE FIRST ITEMS OF THEATRE CHANGES PLANNED FOR THE COMFORT AND PLEASURE OF ITS PATRONS. ADDITIONAL IMPROVEMENTS WHICH WILL MODERNIZE THE THEATRE AND MAKE IT ONE OF THE MOST ATTRACTIVE IN THE WEST WILL BE MADE AS SOON AS NECESSARY MATERIALS CAN BE OBTAINED.

THE NEW MANAGEMENT WILL PRESENT PROGRAMS OF THE HIGHEST CLASS, AND WILL FEATURE THE BEST IN PICTURES. THE COMING SEASON'S ENTERTAINMENT WILL BE USHERED IN WITH . . .

'WOMAN OF THE YEAR'

With Spencer Tracy and Katharine Hepburn

CONSIDERED BY MOTION PICTURE CRITICS TO BE ONE OF THE TEN BEST PICTURES OF THE YEAR.

The first of Claude Cline's many renovations was to install a huge "traditional" movie theater marquee over the simple Elks Theatre sign that the building had sported for years. Not long after, he completely overhauled the interior, making it virtually unrecognizable from the earliest photographs. (Parker Anderson collection.)

Bambi remains one of the most beloved Disney films of all time despite the fact that generations of parents have never forgiven Walt Disney for the fate of Bambi's mother. This advertisement is from the very first release. (Parker Anderson collection.)

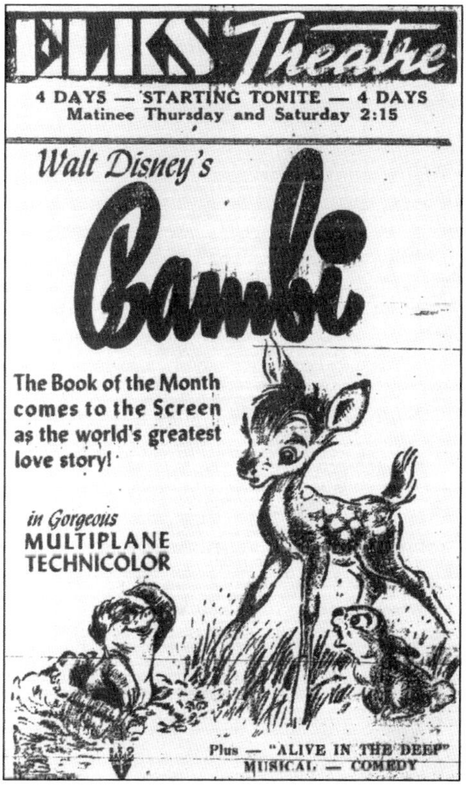

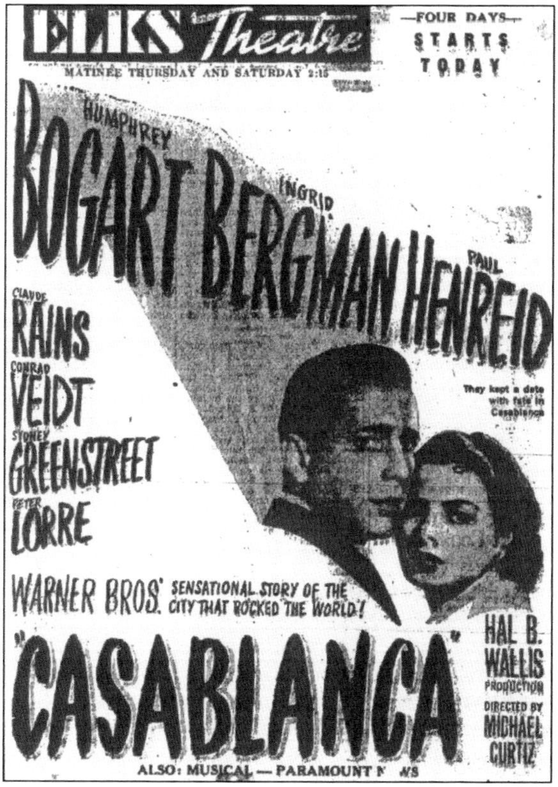

There is nothing to say about the legendary film *Casablanca* that has not already been mentioned. Despite the presence of the Studio Theater in Prescott at this time, the Elks Theatre was still exhibiting the best in motion pictures. (Parker Anderson collection.)

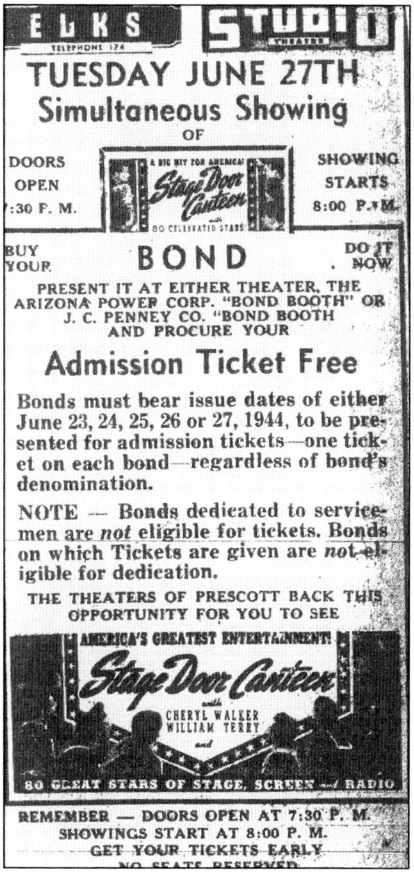

During World War II, theaters nationwide sold war bonds to help finance the war effort, and Prescott's two movie theaters were no exception. Residents who purchased bonds were rewarded with free admission. *Stage Door Canteen* was specifically produced by Hollywood for the war-bond effort and was considered important enough that the US government reportedly filed a print away in a time capsule for preservation. Ironically, the film is now in the public domain and is easily obtained on home video and DVD. (Parker Anderson collection.)

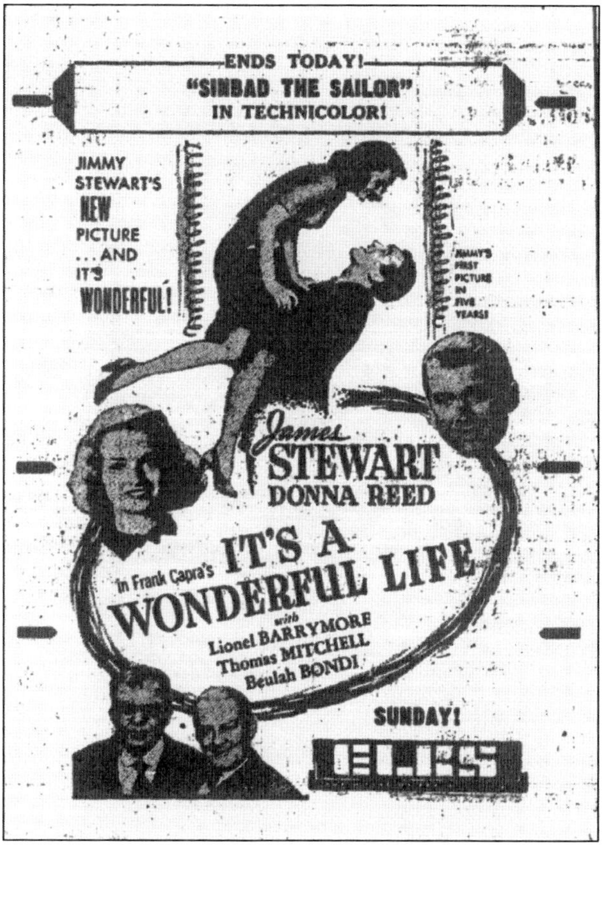

Frank Capra's *It's a Wonderful Life* (1946) was not regarded as a great film upon its first release and did not come to be regarded as a Christmas classic until it was shown on network television in the 1970s and became readily available for personal use with the home-video revolution of the 1980s. (Parker Anderson collection.)

Disney's *Song of the South* (1946), shown at the Elks Theatre on its first run, was beloved by Americans for many years until changing times rendered the film too offensive in the eyes of many. The present-day controversy has kept Disney from releasing the film in any home-video format in America to date. (Parker Anderson collection.)

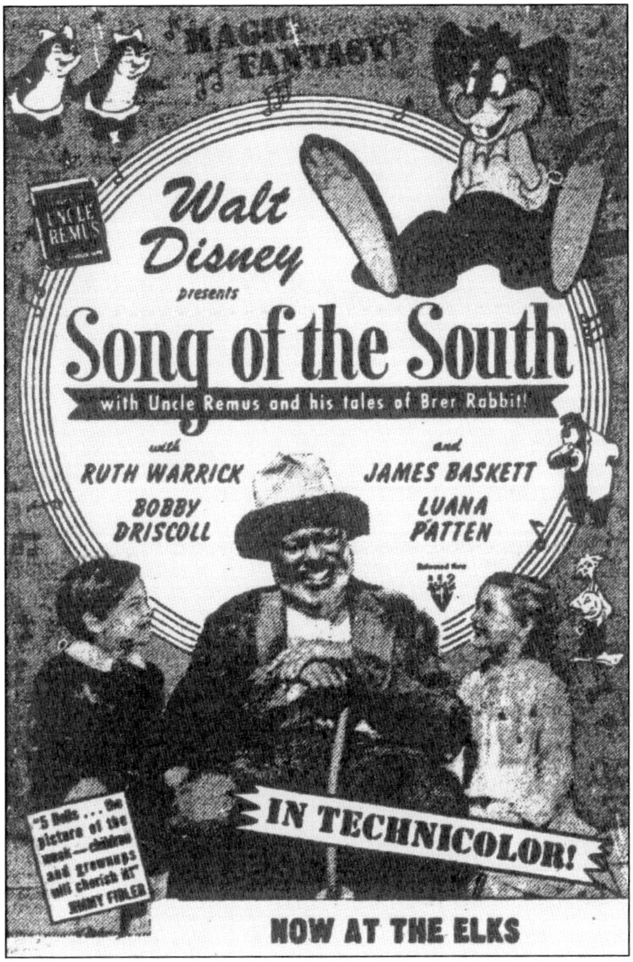

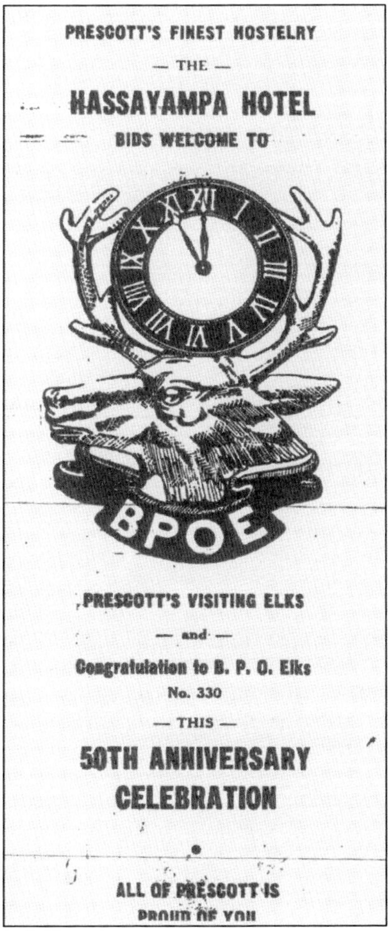

In 1946, Prescott Elks Lodge no. 330 celebrated the 50th anniversary of its installation with much fanfare and celebration. This congratulatory advertisement was purchased by the Hassayampa Hotel, which was built in 1927 directly across the street from the Elks Building. The Hassayampa remains open to this day and has always had a close relationship with the Elks Theatre. (Parker Anderson collection.)

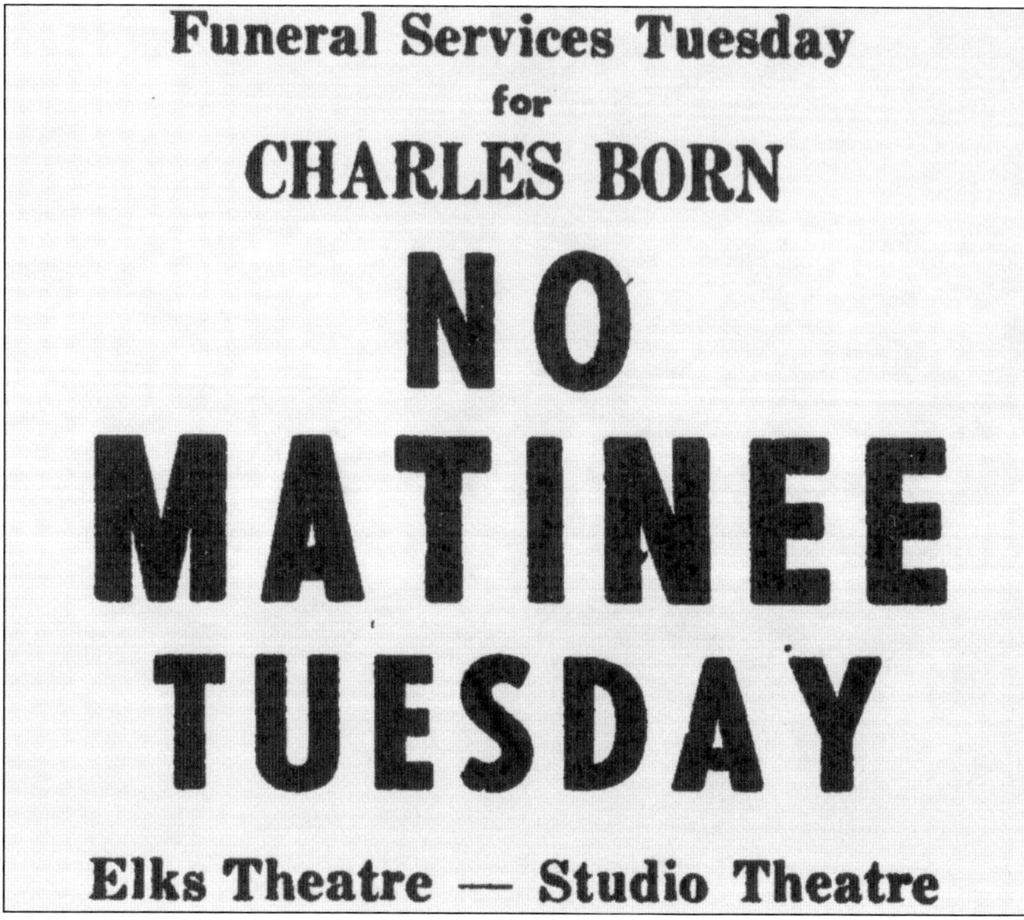

In the 1950s, in small towns such as Prescott, businesses would often close to honor the deaths of prominent individuals. There were two such cases in Prescott: movie theaters closed out of respect for former Elks Theatre manager Charles Born in 1951 and for the death of Phoenix entrepreneur Harry Nace in 1953, who had been a "silent partner" in Prescott's theaters. (Both, Parker Anderson Collection.)

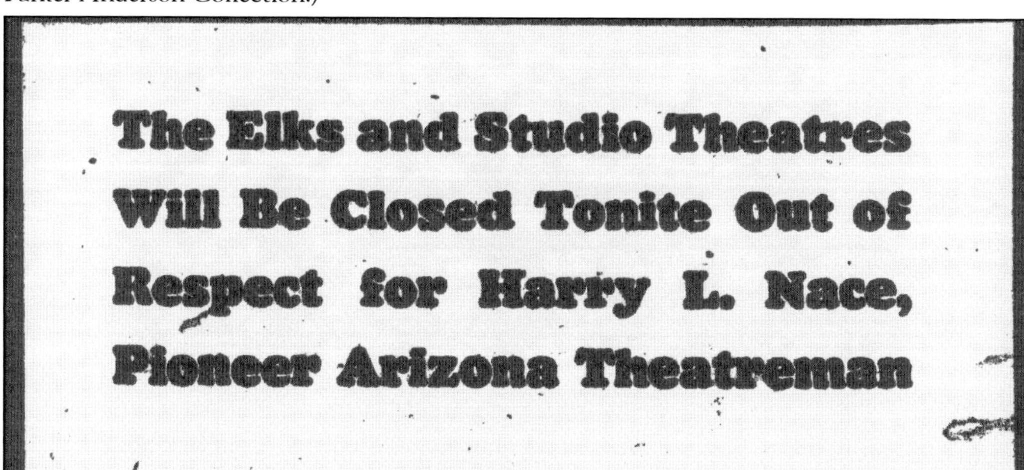

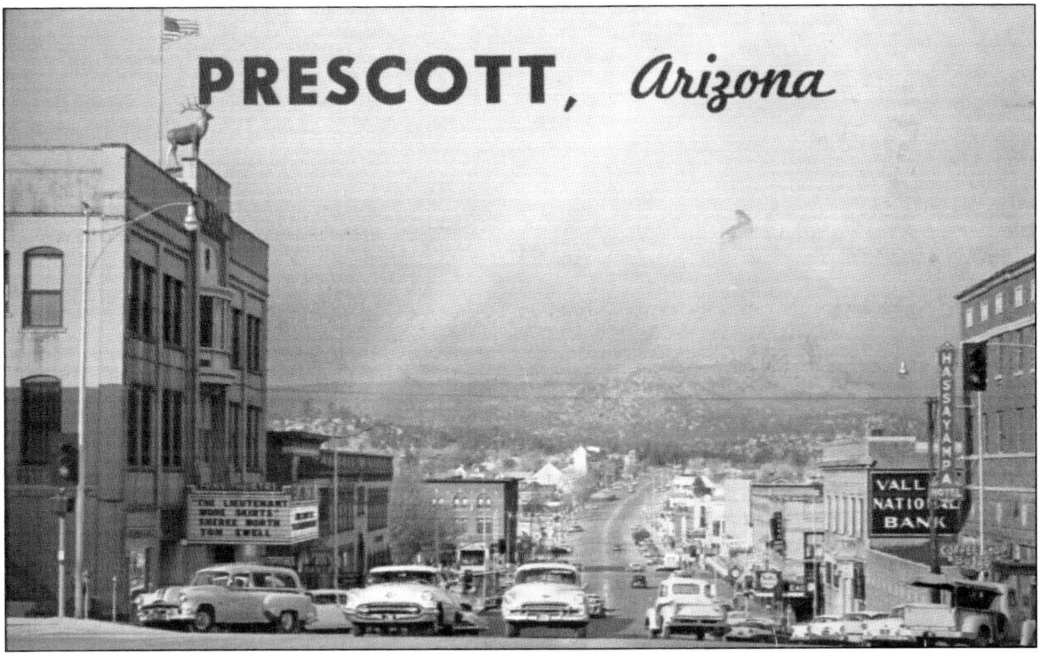

A 1950s postcard of Gurley Street shows a rainbow and storm clouds overhead. The theater was showing the film *The Lieutenant Wore Skirts* with Tom Ewell and Sheree North when this postcard was produced. (Debra Matthews collection.)

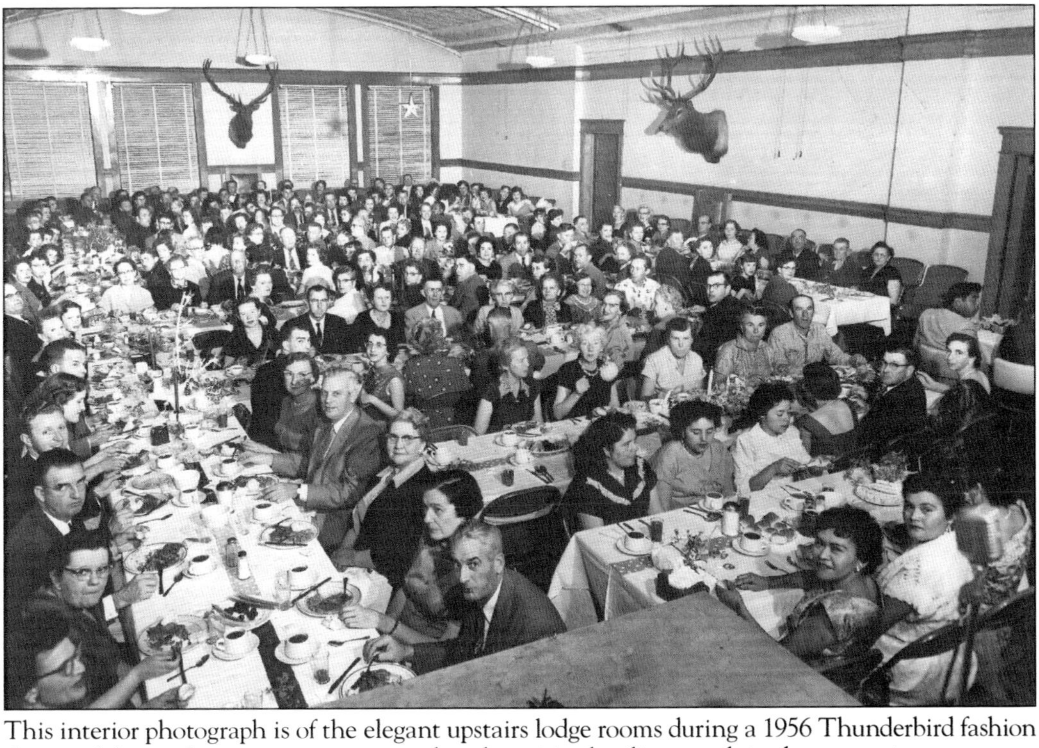

This interior photograph is of the elegant upstairs lodge rooms during a 1956 Thunderbird fashion show and dinner. It is interesting to note that the original ceiling panels in these upstairs rooms were identical to those installed in the opera house. (Sharlot Hall Museum Library and Archives.)

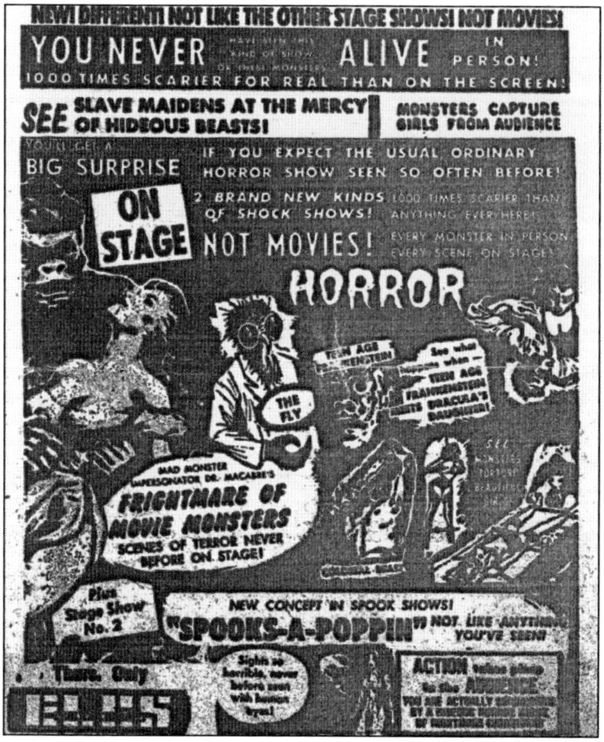

Live traveling road shows still existed as late as the 1960s, and some had taken on a horror theme to try to compete with the growing popularity of horror movies at this time. Although there were many "costumed monsters" on the road, this is the only known such road show to play the Elks Theatre. (Parker Anderson collection.)

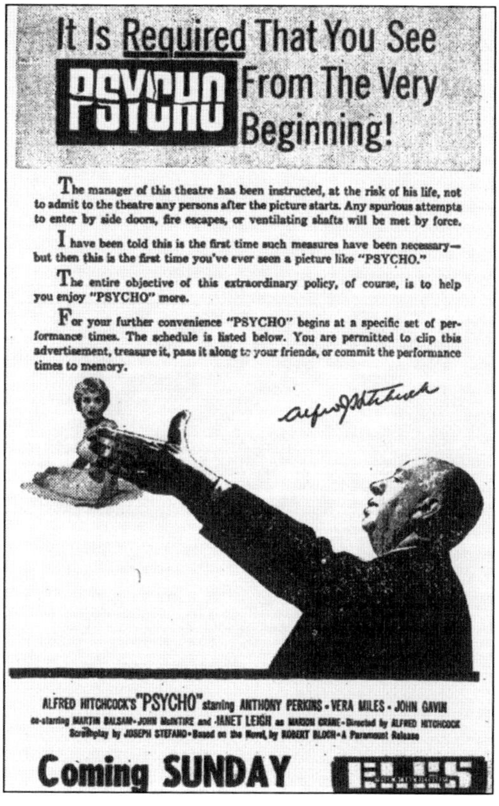

Everything that could be said about Alfred Hitchcock's classic film *Psycho* has already been mentioned, but its audacious advertising campaign for its first run remains very entertaining. (Parker Anderson collection.)

In a small town, the endorsement of the theater manager for a film meant something to residents, and occasionally Claude Cline did just that. The ongoing popularity of the film *The Magnificent Seven* shows that Claude Cline was right on the mark with his endorsement. (Parker Anderson collection.)

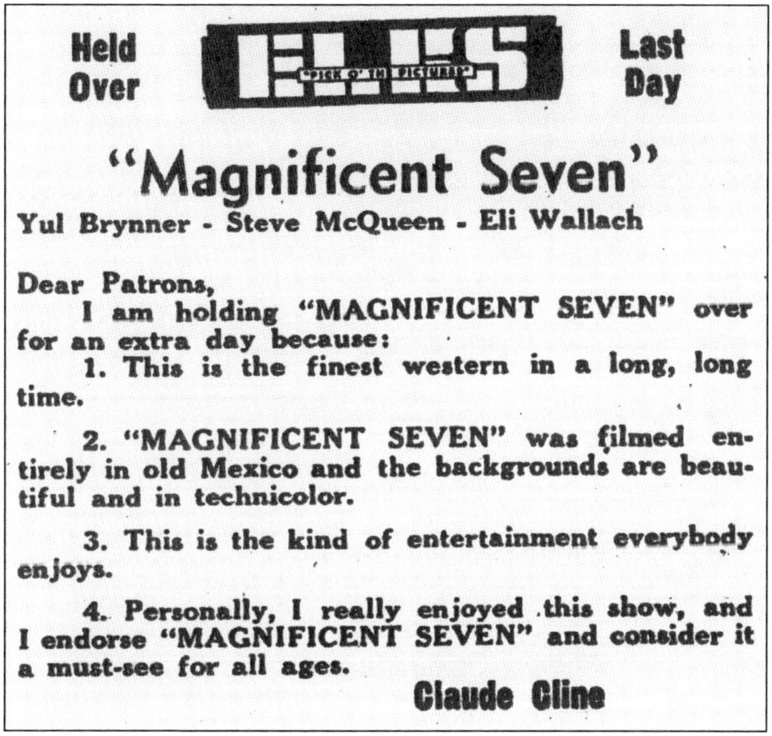

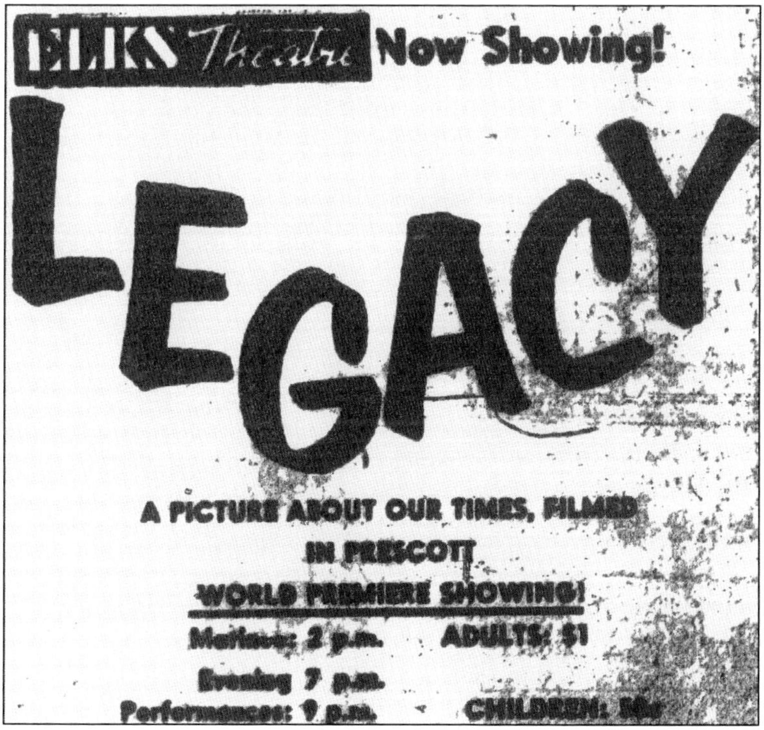

In 1963, a low-budget art film entitled *Legacy* was filmed in Prescott. It attracted quite a bit of attention locally at the time, and it had a "world-premiere showing" at the Elks Theatre. Although it would later be screened at a handful of film festivals, the movie never had an official release nationwide and remains quite obscure today. The only place it can be easily seen is at Sharlot Hall Museum and Archives in Prescott, which retains a video copy. (Parker Anderson collection.)

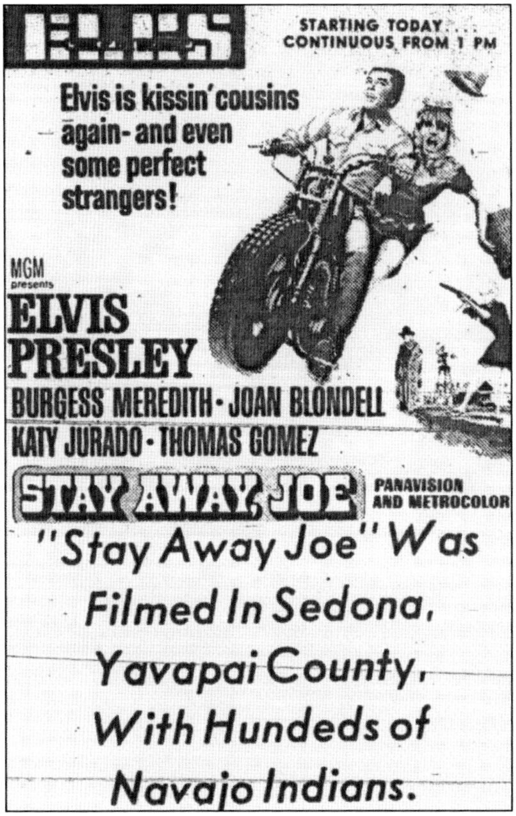

It has always been of interest to filmgoers in the Prescott area when a movie is filmed in nearby areas. In this case, the Yavapai County locations are perhaps the only memorable scenes in the 1969 Elvis Presley film *Stay Away, Joe*. (Parker Anderson collection.)

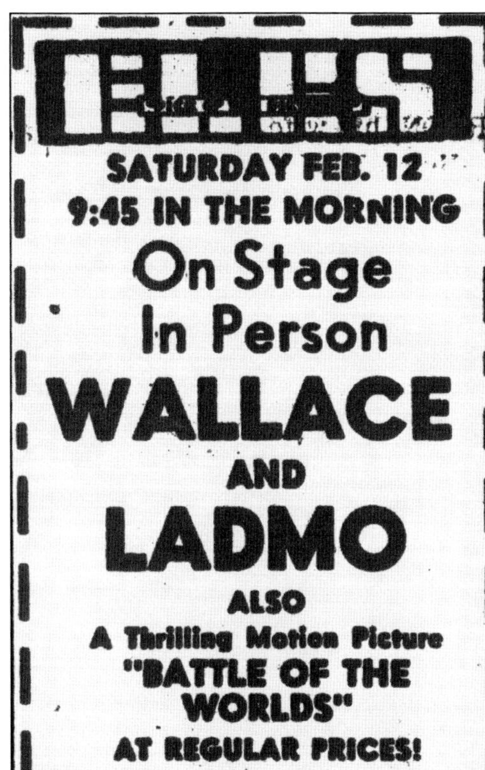

The Wallace and Ladmo Show, a children's television program, ran on KPHO-TV5 out of Phoenix from 1954 until 1989. In the days before home computers and video games, the vast majority of Arizona children watched the show faithfully, and Wallace and Ladmo became Arizona legends. They made many personal appearances around the state and always played to packed houses. (Parker Anderson collection.)

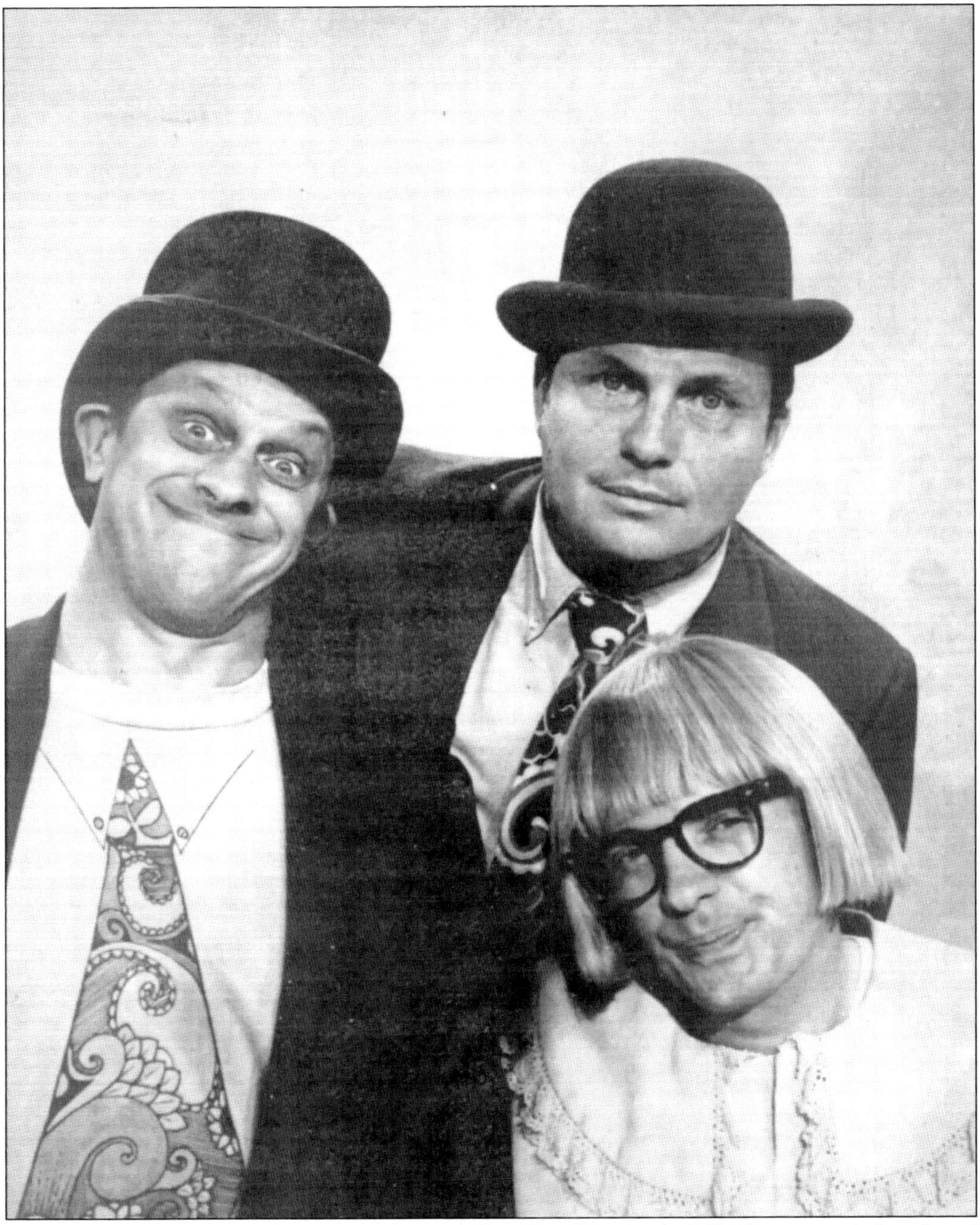

From left to right are Ladimir Kwiatkowsi (who played Ladmo), Bill Thompson (who played Wallace), and Pat McMahon (who played a variety of costumed characters on *The Wallace and Ladmo Show* and is seen here as Gerald). Many long-term Arizona residents still retain happy memories of them, and a permanent display of Wallace and Ladmo memorabilia exists at the Arizona Historical Society at its Papago Park museum in Tempe, Arizona. (Steve Hoza at www.wallacewatchers.com.)

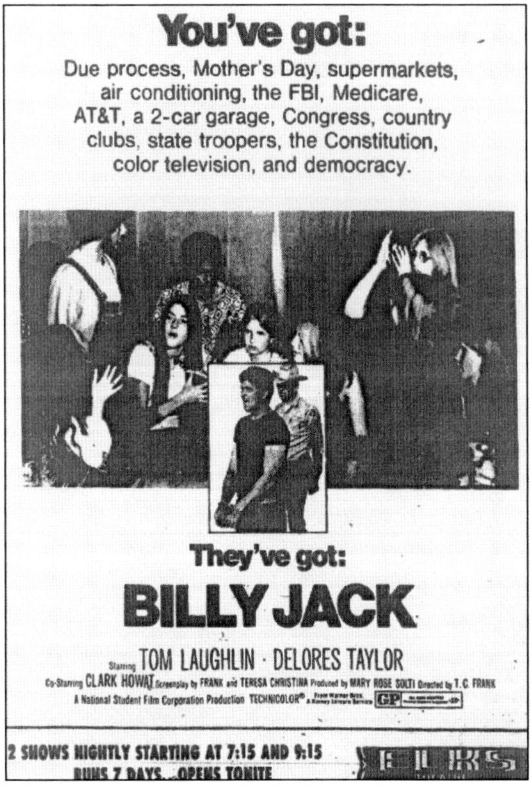

The 1971 grassroots hit *Billy Jack* was partially filmed in Prescott. The first half of the film contains many familiar locations, including the Elks Building, seen in one of the opening shots; however, Prescott residents of the era were none too pleased to see the town depicted as being inhabited by vicious rednecks. (Parker Anderson collection.)

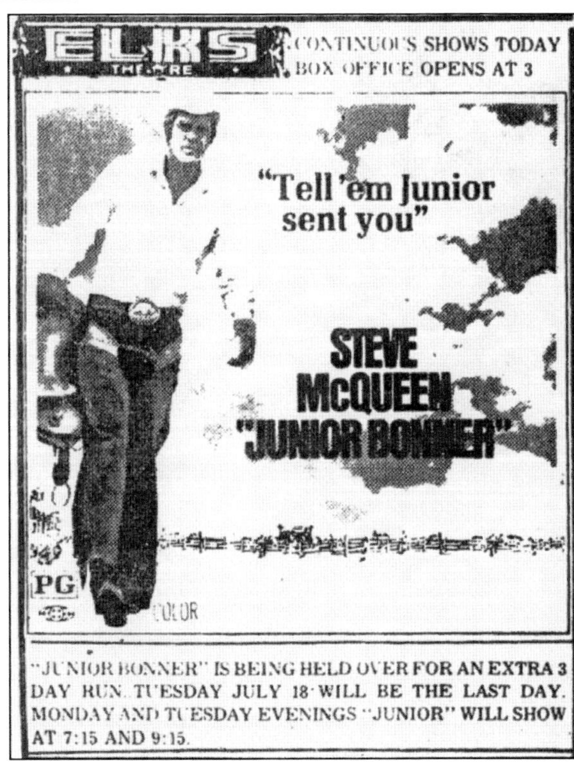

The 1972 film *Junior Bonner*, starring Steve McQueen, directed by Sam Peckinpah, and written by Jeb Rosebrook, was filmed entirely in Prescott, with the story set against the backdrop of Prescott's historic Fourth of July rodeo. The film is still fondly remembered by longtime Prescott residents, particularly because of so many scenes that depict downtown Prescott the way it was long ago. (Parker Anderson collection.)

The film version of Glendon Swarthout's novel *Bless the Beasts and Children* was partly filmed in Prescott and Jerome. The film stirred some controversy among hunters because of its condemnation of so-called "canned hunting." In one scene, the main characters are driving past the Elks Theatre. (Parker Anderson collection.)

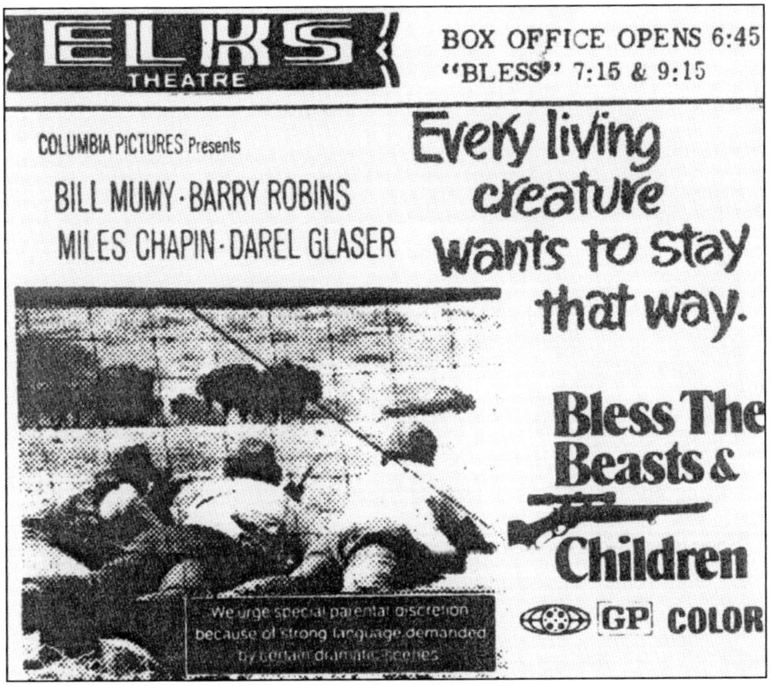

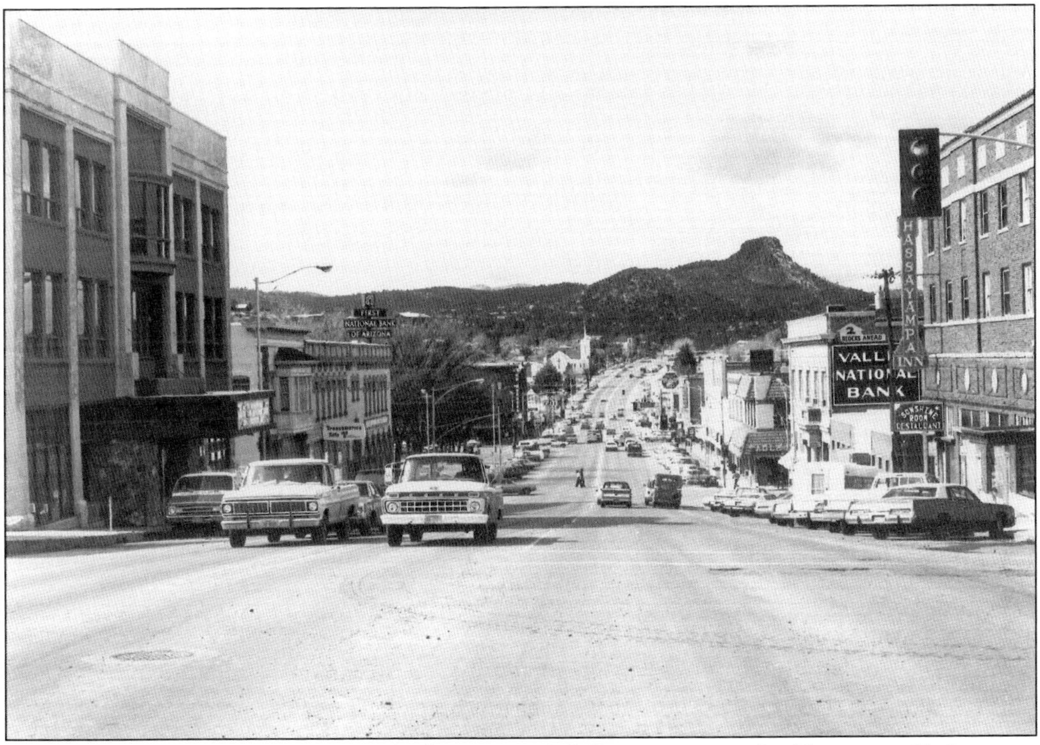

Shown around 1978 is Gurley Street looking west. A different marquee had been installed at some point in the late 1960s or early 1970s. Except for the lighted front, which was replaced several times, this marquee remained until the 2010 Elks Opera House restoration when it was taken down. (Sharlot Hall Museum Library and Archives.)

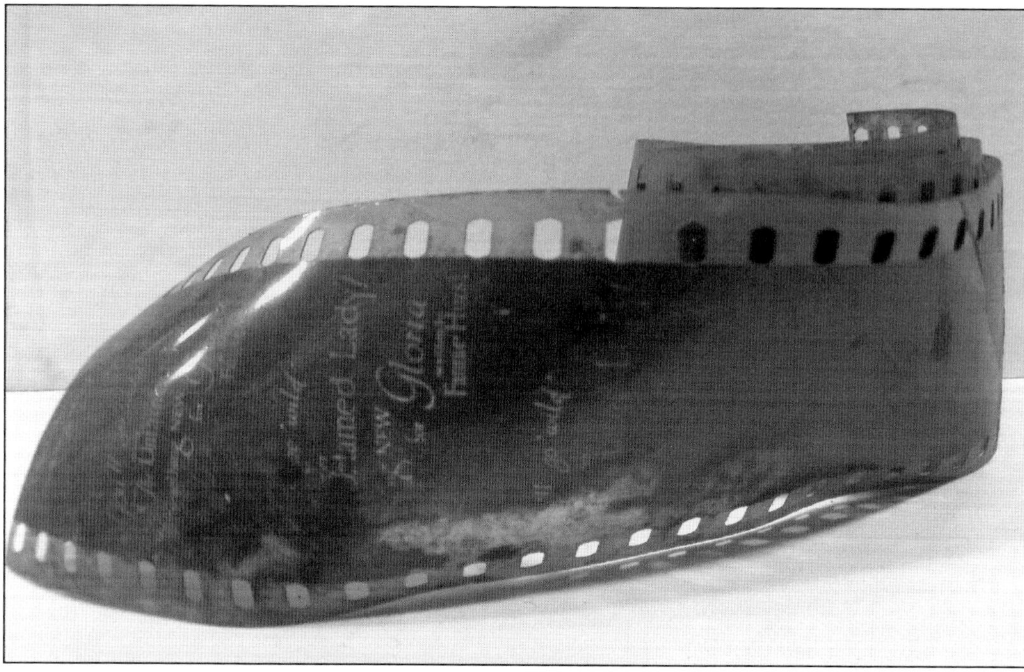

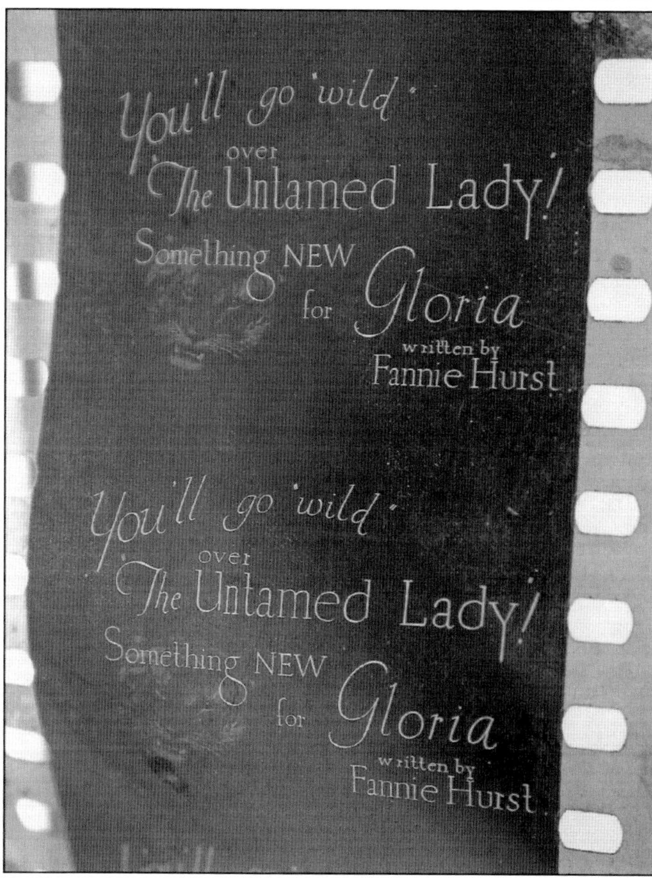

During the 2009–2010 restoration of the Elks Opera House, many small artifacts were discovered, long hidden after many years of falling through cracks and crevices. Perhaps the most interesting is this small nitrate filmstrip from a 1920s-era "Coming Attractions" trailer. (Both photographs by David Schmittinger.)

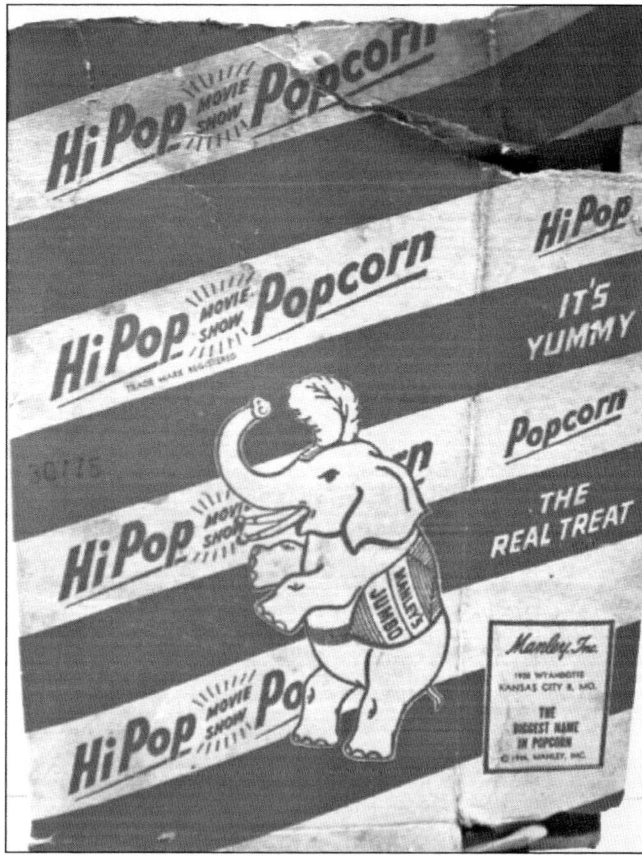

Popcorn boxes like this were common in movie theaters of the 1920s era. Manley, Inc. was a major distributor of popcorn and popcorn products to theaters nationwide. This was also found during the 2010 restoration. (Photograph by David Schmittinger.)

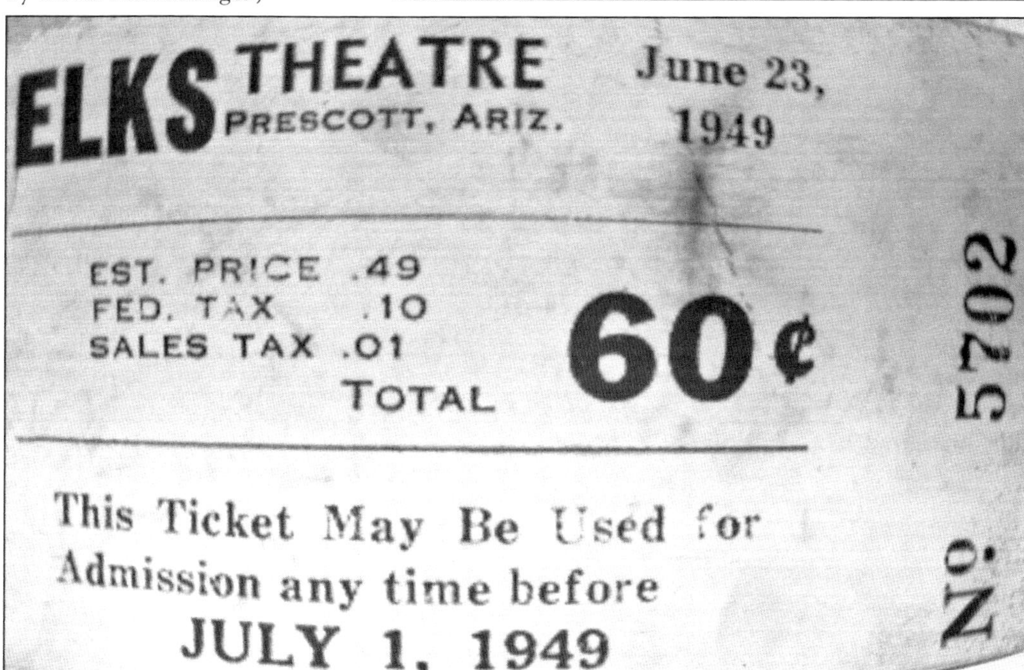

Shown is an old Elks Theatre ticket from 1949, probably unused. This type was sold in advance for people who were planning ahead. It was also found during the restoration. (Photograph by David Schmittinger.)

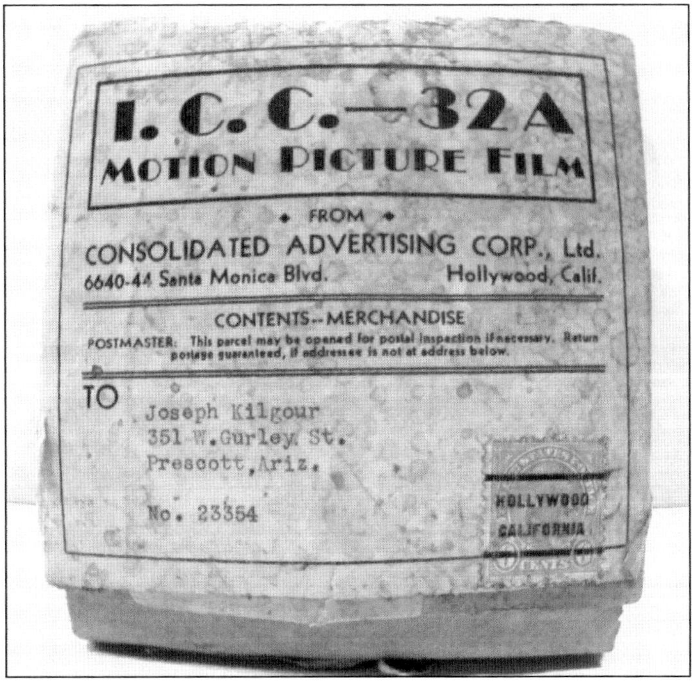

In the days prior to the digital era, light was projected through a moving acetate film with the resultant moving images shown on a screen for patrons to watch. An audio track on the edge of the acetate was synchronized with the individual images and supplied the sound. Once a movie was completed by a studio and ready for theatrical release, copies of the original movie reels were made, and those copies would be mailed to theaters around the country for showing. Found during the restoration was this small mailing container for a film reel. (Photograph by David Schmittinger.)

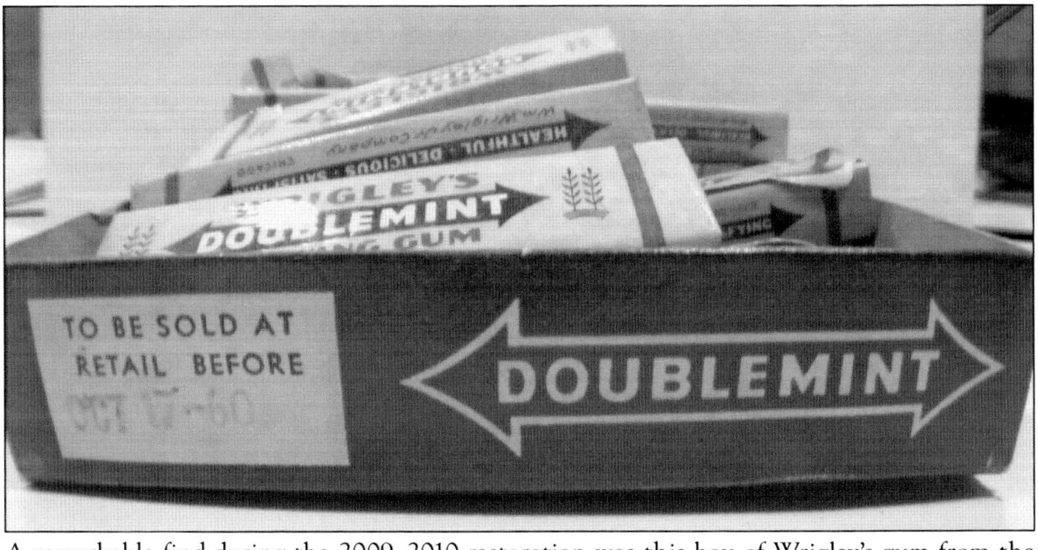

A remarkable find during the 2009–2010 restoration was this box of Wrigley's gum from the theater concession stand with unopened packs sporting a 1960 sale date. (Photograph by David Schmittinger.)

Four

The Modern Era

Prescott BPOE Lodge no. 330 had sold the Elks Building in 1968, and when it found new lodgings, members removed the copper elk from the roof where it had been standing since June 1905. It is no longer known why Prescott BPOE Lodge no. 330 sold the building, but it may have been because of economics, as upkeep on the aging building was likely becoming increasingly expensive. Preservationists refer to such a situation as "demolition by neglect." A law firm headed by Donald Head and Philip Toci ultimately purchased the building and moved its offices upstairs, while Claude Cline kept his lease on the theater.

In 1973, Claude Cline, who still operated the venue as a movie theater, built a two-screen duplex on Marina Street called the Marina Theatres to show first-run movies. At this point, he changed the Elks Theatre to a venue that showed first-run family films and second-run, PG-rated movies. It was the first major shift in Elks Theatre scheduling in decades.

When Claude Cline retired in 1980, Timberline Productions, a group headed by Ronald Swartz and Roger Pearsall, remodeled the theater and continued to operate it as a movie house for a while but then planned to bring in live performances.

Building owners Don Head and Phil Toci formed a nonprofit group called Prescott Center for the Performing Arts (PCPA) to bring in live shows, but Head and Toci would later sell the theater portion to the Arizona Community Foundation. At this time, the building was divided into two separate, condominium-style properties with the theater auditorium as one property and the upper floors, office space, and ground-floor retail as another property.

Yavapai College and, later, Prescott College became lessees of the Elks Opera House and guided the theater through many live shows, both local and touring, during the 1980s and 1990s.

People had been discussing restoring the Elks Opera House to its former glory since the mid-1970s, with Prescott activist Elisabeth Ruffner leading the efforts. In 2000, guided by Prescott mayor Sam Steiger, the City of Prescott purchased the Elks Opera House portion of the building to save it as an active and productive theater.

The Elks Opera House Foundation was formed in 2002 to raise funds to restore the theater, which was still in use but had fallen into disrepair over the decades.

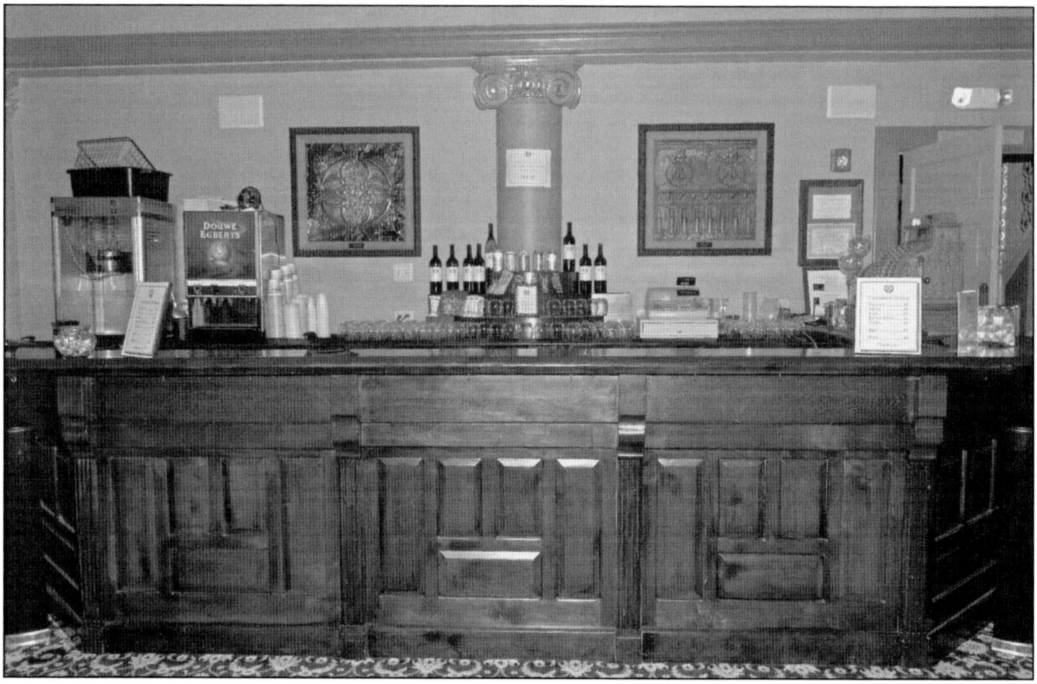

This antique-style bar and concession stand was first installed during the 1980 remodeling. During the Claude Cline era, the lower lobby (about where the photographer was standing) contained a small, rectangular concession stand in the middle of the room, which was removed during the renovation work in 1980. (Photograph by Terry Berrett.)

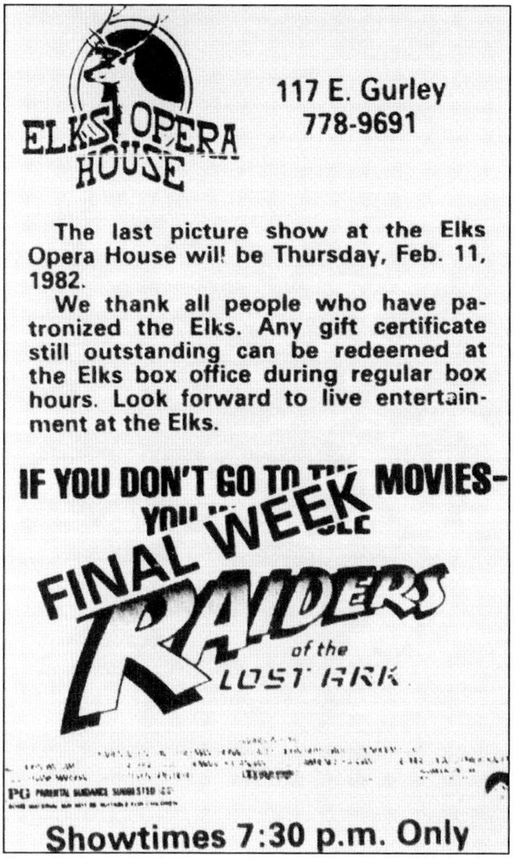

The final film shown during the Elks Opera House's official movie theater years was *Raiders of the Lost Ark* in early 1982. This was a return engagement, as the film had also played at the Elks the previous summer. (Parker Anderson collection.)

PROCLAMATION

Elks Opera House Re-dedication Day

May 8, 1982

Whereas, the Elks Opera House, a National Registry treasure, built in 1904 to function as a center for live entertainment is now being re-dedicated to that purpose, and

Whereas, the Prescott Center for Performing Arts, a non-profit organization, has been created to administer and operate the Elks Opera House as a center for performing arts; and

Whereas, the Elks Opera House will be made available to Prescott's cultural organizations for their presentations; and

Whereas, the re-dedication is being celebrated with a "Gala" evening on May 8, 1982.

Now, therefore, I, Lawrence A. Caldwell, Mayor of the city of Prescott, Arizona, do hereby proclaim and declare May 8, 1982 as Elks Opera House Re-dedication Day in Prescott, Arizona.

In witness whereof, I have hereunto set my hand and caused the Corporate Seal of the City of Prescott to be affixed this 21st day of April, 1982.

Lawrence A Caldwell

Lawrence A. Caldwell, Mayor

Prescott mayor Larry Caldwell proclaimed May 8, 1982, as Elks Opera House Rededication Day. The prospect of the Elks Theatre returning to live entertainment caused great excitement in Prescott. (City of Prescott collection.)

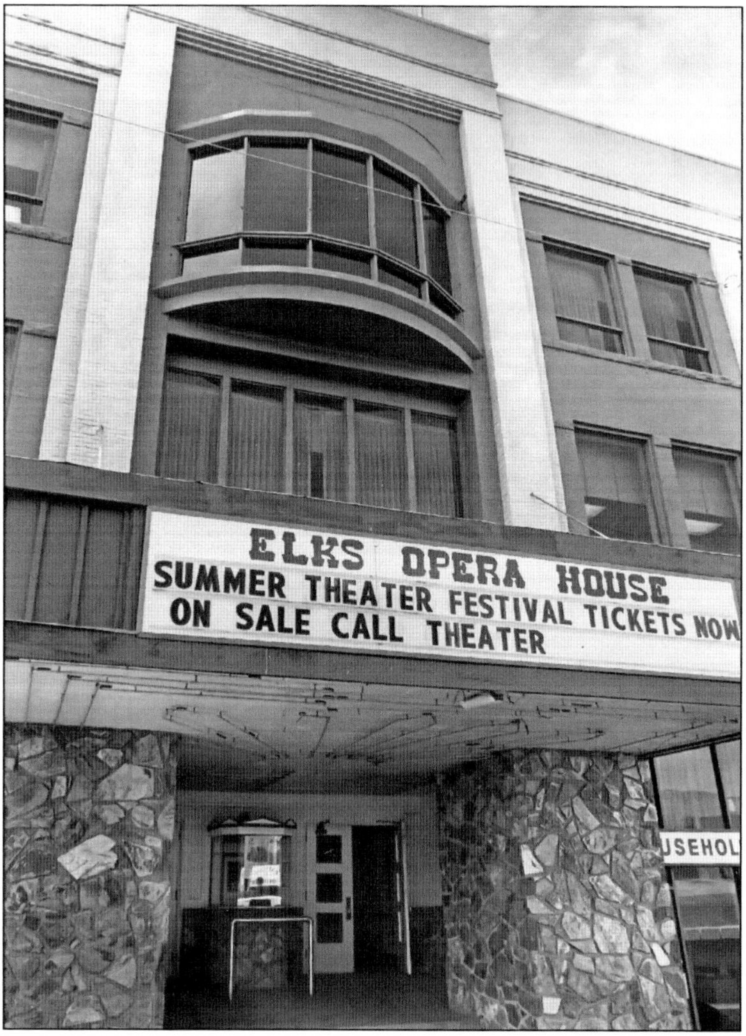

This is the exterior of the Elks Opera House around 1985. The entrance looks considerably different than it had decades earlier, with an exterior rock covering and another marquee. (Sharlot Hall Museum Library and Archives.)

The rededication began with a huge gala in which veteran film actor John Dehner was invited to perform and participate. In this photograph, Dehner chats with two unidentified gala participants. (The *Daily Courier*.)

Elks' Theater reborn in style in star-studded gala program

By GREG FISTER
Courier Staff Writer

They began arriving at the Hassayampa Inn a little before six, the women in their long gowns and finest jewelry, the men in their suits and tuxedos.

A stiff, cooling breeze did its best to raise havoc with the carefully coiffured hair of the guests, but nothing could or would take the edge off of Prescott's fanciest evening in years.

It was billed as the gala rededication of the Elks Theater. Rededicated it was, a gala it certainly was.

After an absence of more than four decades, live theater productions have returned to the theater now known officially as the Prescott Center for the Performing Arts. Almost 500 people turned out Saturday night to be a part of history and show their support for the performing arts in Prescott.

Marvin Pitts, president of the Prescott Chamber of Commerce said, "They've managed to turn out a tremendous crowd. If they can pull this off, it will be a tremendous cultural addition to the community."

The evening got started as any party would, with food and drinks. But this wasn't just any party. Table after table held everything from escargot in mushroom caps to chicken crepes in wine sauce. Add conversation with a senator or a state representative or a Hollywood actor, and the evening could have been judged a success immediately.

As the crowd milled around the inn, Dr. Charles Dockter said, "This is an example of what Prescott has wanted for a long time. Now, we have to get out and make sure we support it."

As the hour drew closer to cross Gurley Street and attend the official rededication ceremonies, mingling among the crowd began in earnest. Senator Dennis DeConcini was spotted caucussing with state Rep. John Hays. U.S. Rep. Bob Stump, retiring state Senator Boyd Tenney and state Rep. Jerry Everall were meeting and greeting old friends. Secretary of State Rose Mofford and the first lady of Arizona Hattie Babbitt also attended the gala. Meanwhile, Jane Russell, who set Hollywood on its ear at one time, sat at a table taking it all in.

She said she was looking forward to getting a glance at the inside of the theater and commented that live theater was needed north of Phoenix.

Even crossing the street was not a simple task Saturday night. Complete with searchlight and red carpet, and accompanied by the horn blowing of Glen Bowling, a prancing jester and several torches, the audience entered the Prescott Center for the Performing Arts in style.

There, Julia Shelley of the San Diego Civic Light Opera began the program with several selections, including such non opera pieces as *Summertime*.

John Dehner, whose face is familiar to millions of Americans through his work in almost 100 films and televison shows, read Dylan Thomas' work *A Story*.

According to Gil Laurence, the center's managing director, Dehner made a special trip to attend the event Saturday night, flying in from New York where he is curently filming another movie.

The audience then got a taste of what is in store this summer during the Prescott Theater Festival '82 when four productions from the Megaw Theater of California will be presented.

Elaine Moe, Rick Rourke and Terrence O'Connor of the theater group performed two scenes from *The Corn is Green*, one of the productions scheduled at the theater this summer.

Three other plays will be presented by the award-winning Megaw Theater this summer, including *Romantic Comedy*, *The Rainmaker*, and *Company*.

The old, grand lady of Prescott is now ready to host its first live performance in years as the Yavapai College drama department presents *Flowers for Algernon*, Thursday, Friday and Saturday.

In a style benefitting the 78-year-old building, the performing arts have returned to Prescott.

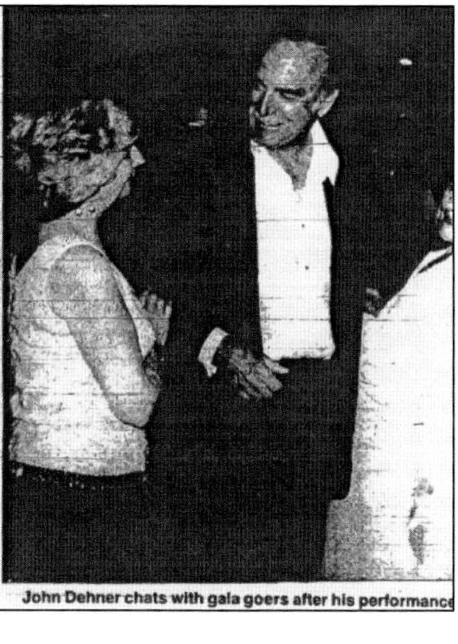

John Dehner chats with gala goers after his performanc

One of the mainstays of the Elks Opera House in the 1990s was the Arizona Jamboree, a large, flamboyant musical variety show that performed in the summertime for many years at the Elks Opera House and had additional shows at Christmas. It starred Patti Bell (third row, center) and a band of talented musicians and performers, including Prescott Valley Chamber of Commerce director Lew Rees (first row) and Melissa Ruffner (fourth row, far right), who opened each show with stories of old Prescott. (Marchettiphoto.com.)

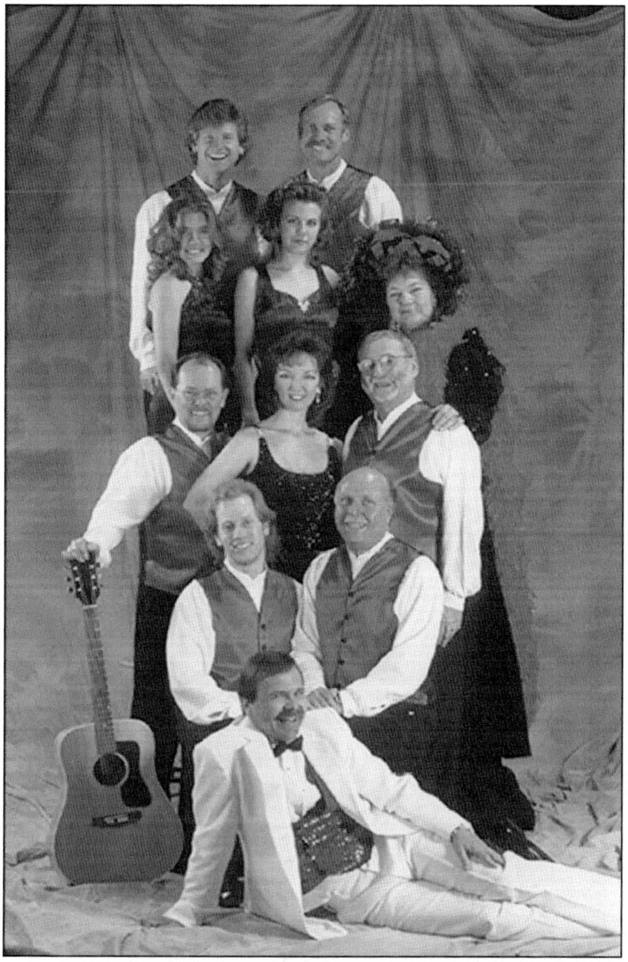

Prescott Fine Arts Association's lavish production of *Camelot* brought a huge cast and a giant-sized set to the Elks Opera House stage in 1992. (Prescott Center for the Arts collection.)

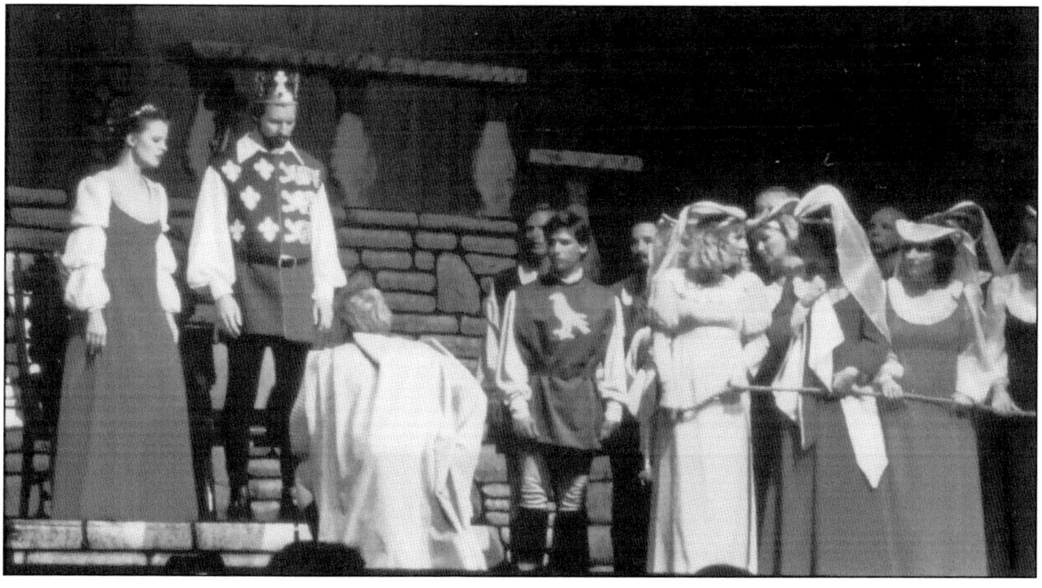

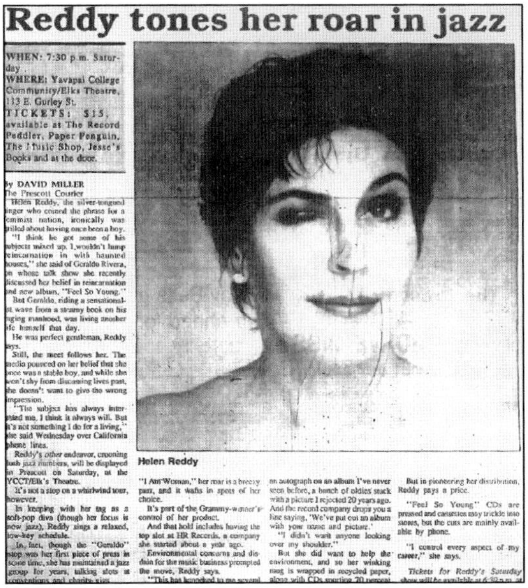

Reddy tones her roar in jazz

WHEN: 7:30 p.m. Saturday.
WHERE: Yavapai College Community/Elks Theatre, 113 E. Gurley St.
TICKETS: $15, available at The Record Peddler, Paper Penguin, The Music Shop, Jesse's Books and at the door.

by DAVID MILLER
The Prescott Courier

Helen Reddy, the silver-tongued singer who coined the phrase for a feminist nation, ironically was grilled about having once been a boy.

"I think he got some of his subjects mixed up. I wouldn't lump reincarnation in with haunted houses," she said of Geraldo Rivera, on whose talk show she recently discussed her belief in reincarnation and new album, "Feel So Young."

But Geraldo, riding a sensationalist wave from a steamy book on his raging manhood, was living another life himself that day.

He was perfect gentleman, Reddy says.

Still, the meet follows her. The media pounced on her belief that she once was a stable boy, and while she won't shy from discussing lives past, she doesn't want to give the wrong impression.

"The subject has always interested me, I think it always will. But it's not something I do for a living," she said Wednesday over California phone lines.

Reddy's *other* endeavor, crooning lush jazz numbers, will be displayed in Prescott on Saturday, at the YCCT/Elk's Theatre.

It's not a stop on a whirlwind tour, however.

In keeping with her tag as a soft-pop diva (though her focus is now jazz), Reddy sings a relaxed, low-key schedule.

In fact, though the "Geraldo" stop was her first piece of press in some time, she has maintained a jazz group for years, talking slots at conventions and charity gigs

Helen Reddy

"I Am Woman," her roar is a breezy purr, and it wafts in spots of her choice.

It's part of the Grammy-winner's control of her product.

And that hold includes having the top slot at HR Records, a company she started about a year ago.

Environmental concerns and disdain for the music business prompted the move, Reddy says.

"This has happened to me several

an autograph on an album I've never seen before, a bunch of oldies stuck with a picture I rejected 20 years ago. And the record company drops you a line saying, 'We've put out an album with your name and picture.'

"I didn't want anyone looking over my shoulder."

But she did want to help the environment, and so her winking mug is wrapped in recycled paper, along with CDs sporting 70 percent

But in pioneering her distribution, Reddy pays a price.

"Feel So Young" CDs are pressed and cassettes may trickle into stores, but the cuts are mainly available by phone.

"I control every aspect of my career," she says.

Tickets for Reddy's Saturday show will be available at 6:30 p.m. at

Among the notable performers who graced the Elks Opera House stage in the 1990s were popular singer Helen Reddy and blues musician Papa John Creach. Papa John, a blues fiddle player, became famous late in his life as a member of Jefferson Airplane and, later, Hot Tuna. (At left, the *Daily Courier*; below, Parker Anderson collection.)

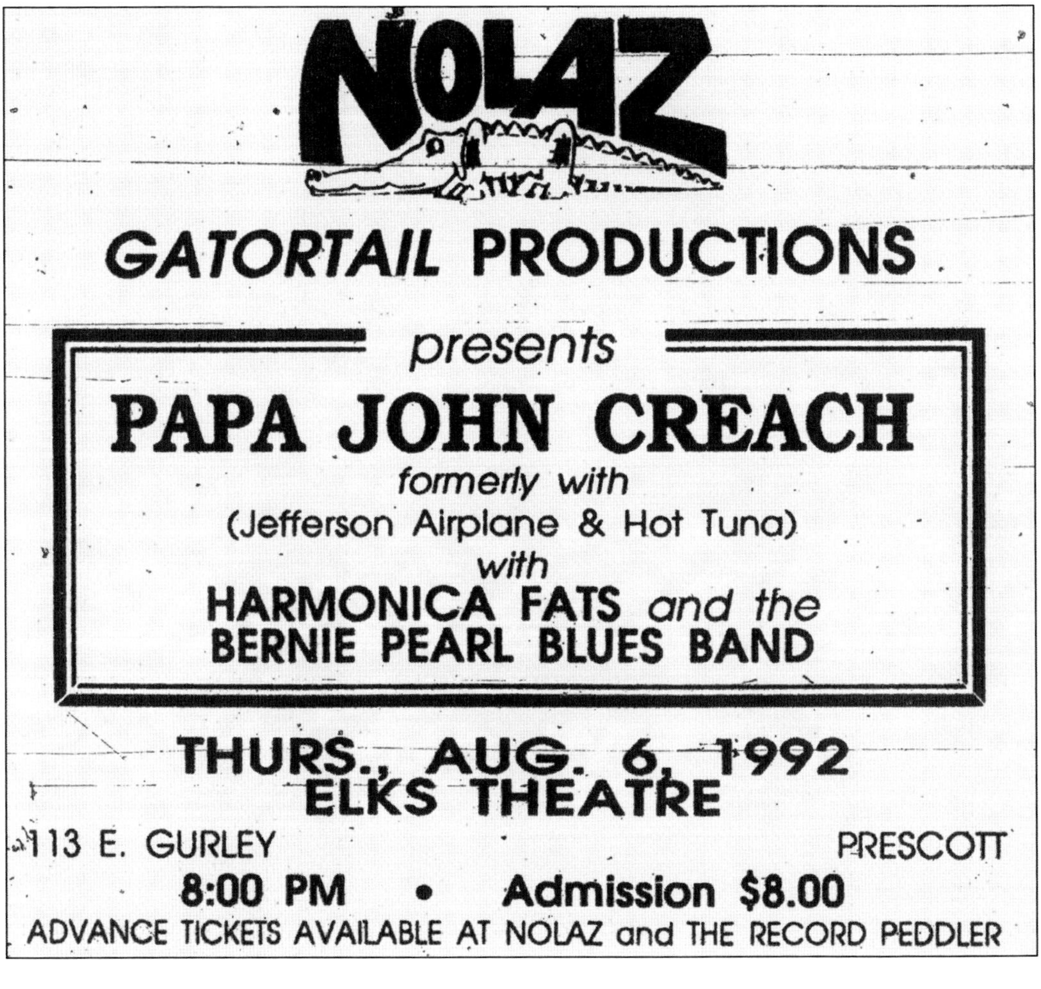

$2,500 donated to Elks Theater

Prescott College Elks Theater general manager Mary Grace Lentz recently accepted a $2,500 donation from Delia Taylor of the Actor's Workshop.

The money, which will be used toward the purchase of a sound equipment system for the historic Elks Theater, was raised from a benefit production staged by the Workshop.

The Jane Martin play, *Talking With*, was presented recently on several different nights at the Elks and female actors from the county-based troupe performed on behalf of the theater project.

"It's not really a restoration project, but rather an effort to raise money for equipment and other things that the Elks really needs," said Lentz in a recent interview.

She added that since Prescott College took over the theater, a mission to make it "one of the finest cultural centers in northern Arizona is on!"

One of the goals of the theater is to provide more alternative art events for the Prescott public.

"I think there is an audience out there that is craving more than traditional theater. That's why we are trying to attract some not-so-ordianry events to try and broaden the city's cultural base," Lentz said.

—Holly J. Wolcott

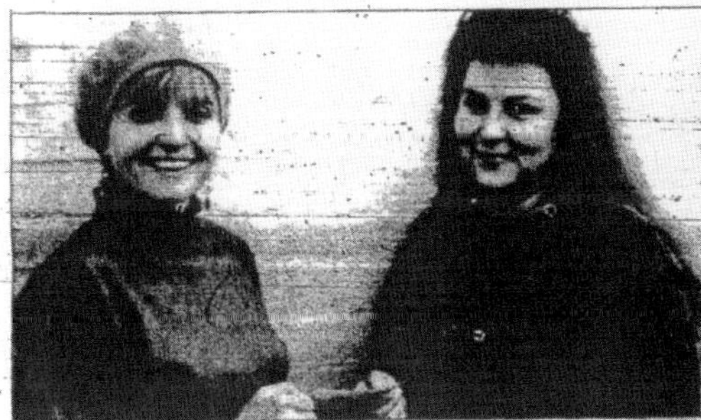

Courtesy Prescott College

Mary Grace Lentz, left, accepts a $2,500 donation from Actor's Workshop member Delia Taylor.

In 1992, a small group of actors led by Mark Duke formed a new theater called the Actor's Workshop, dedicated to bringing more serious theater to Prescott. Here, workshop member Delia Taylor (at right, now Delia Whitehead) gives a $2,500 donation to Elks Theatre manager Mary Grace Lentz (left) during Prescott College's stewardship of the theater. The Actor's Workshop no longer exists. (The *Daily Courier.*)

Once a theater, now a 'Honky Tonk'

Mayor's life now a local production

An original play by Prescott writers Clayton and Patricia Matthews, "Honky Tonk" opens tonight for a two-weekend run at the Prescott College Elks Theater.

The mystery/drama by Caribou Productions is full of song and dance, and stars Prescott Mayor Daiton Rutkowski as bar owner Johnny One-Arm, and teacher Helen Belke as Johnny's long-lost love, Rita.

Directed by Hollywood actor Gary Kirk, the production starts at 8 p.m. tonight, with 8 p.m. shows set for April 17, 23 and 24, and 2 p.m. shows April 18 and 25.

$10 general admission tickets and $8 senior passes are available at Nancy's Hallmark, Smith's grocery store and at the door.

While a majority of the cast is new to the stage, Kirk said four months of preparation has turned the players into entertaining actors and actresses.

The story, reportedly based on the life of Rutkowski, takes place in Johnny One-Arm's Honky Tonk, in Anyplace, Texas, around the Prohibition days of 1935.

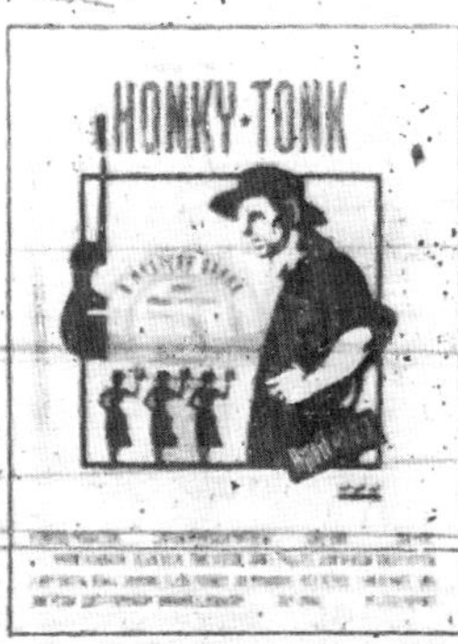

Directed by Hollywood actor Gary Kirk, the production starts at 8 p.m. tonight.

In two acts, cast and crew take viewers through three stories about the love of Johnny and Rita, a con game attempted on Johnny's young helper Kyle (played by film actor Tobe Sexton), and the mysterious deaths of several barmaids.

Key performances are given by Rutkowski, Sexton, John Phillips as Mapes, John Henson as Roland, Grady Hopson as Billy Bob, and Jean Benner as May.

The Elks Theater is located at 113 E. Gurley St. in Prescott.

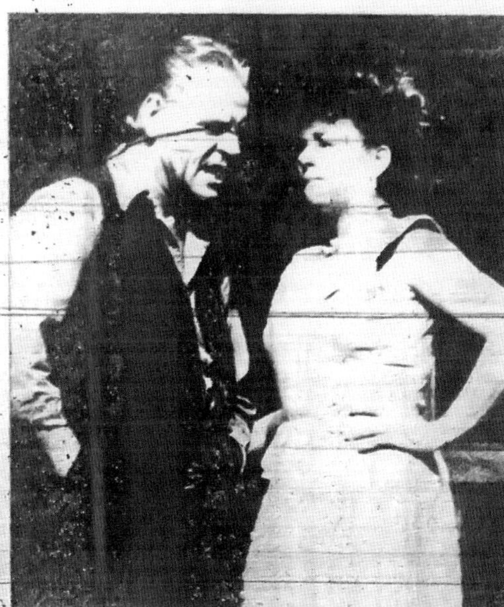

Courier / Marcy Rogers

Johnny One-Arm, played by Daiton Rutkowski and his long lost love Rita, played by Helen Belke, share the Prescott College Elks Theater stage during a recent dress rehearsal of the original play "Honky Tonk." The production opens tonight for a two-weekend run.

Prescott mayor Daiton Rutkowski performs with Helen Rahaley Belke in the locally produced play *Honky Tonk* by Clayton Mathews. Mayor Rutkowski had been a local entertainment performer for some time. Promotion for the show satirically alleged that the play was based on the mayor's life (he portrayed a gangster in the play). Future Prescott mayor Rowle Simmons was also in the cast. (The *Daily Courier.*)

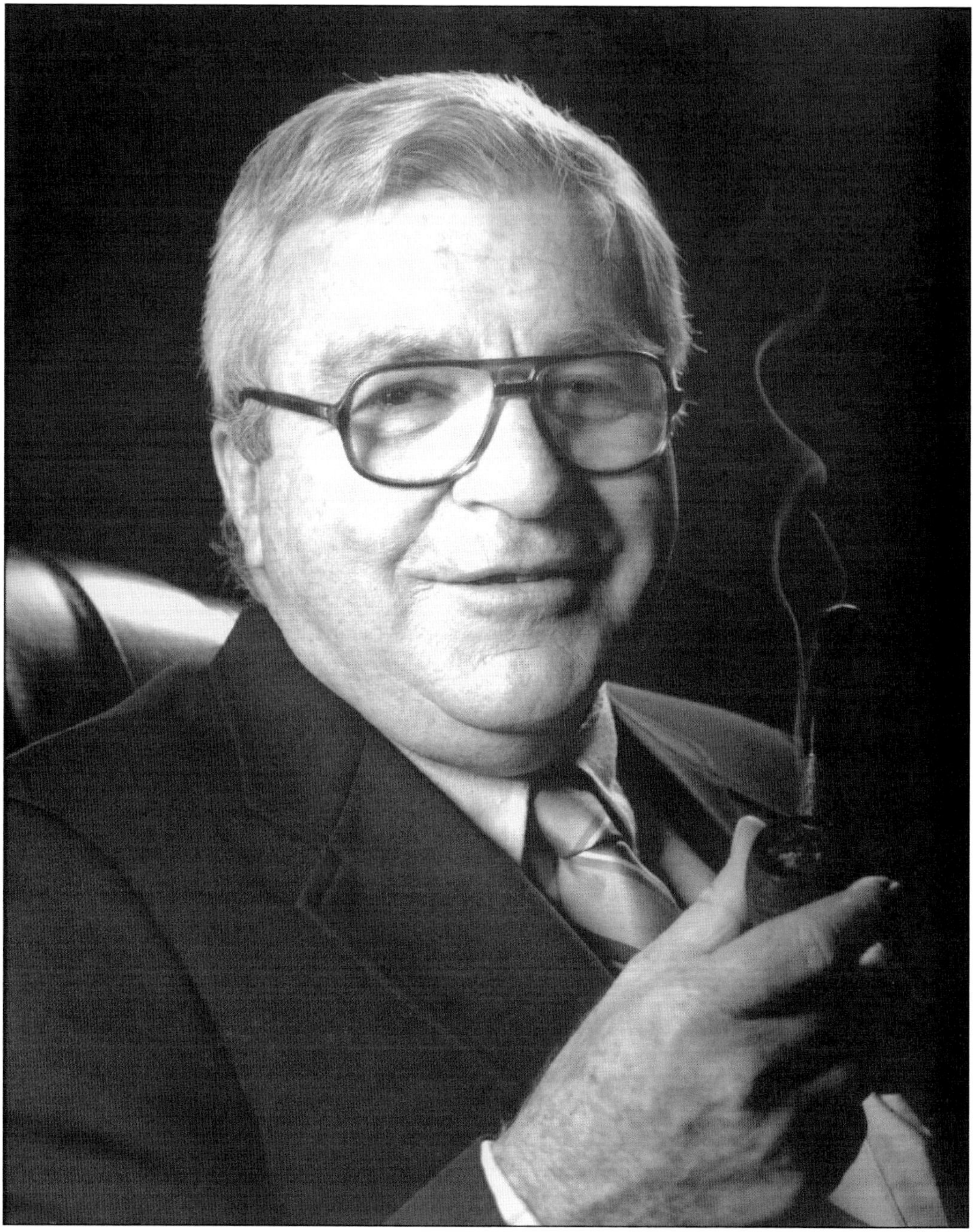

Sam Steiger was an Arizona state senator from 1960 to 1964 and subsequently a member of the US House of Representatives from 1967 to 1977. He became mayor of Prescott in 1999, and during his term, he guided the Prescott City Council to purchase the Elks Opera House (the theater portion of the Elks Building) with the purpose of preserving it as a historic landmark. Shortly after the purchase, the Elks Opera House Foundation was formed to raise funds for restoration of the theater to its former glory. Without the foresight of the mayor and the city council, the theater would not exist in its current renovated state for future generations to enjoy and treasure. (Sam Steiger family collection.)

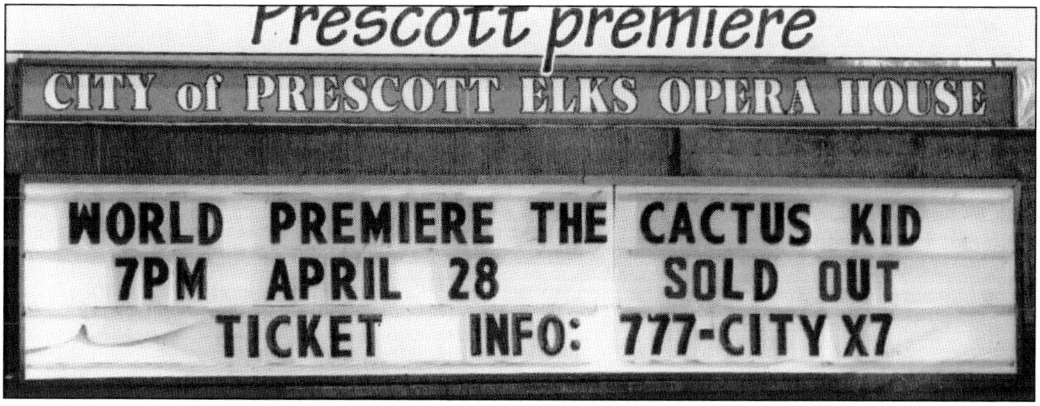

When the City of Prescott purchased the Elks Opera House, the first event to be held was the world premiere of the film *The Cactus Kid*, which had been independently produced, directed, and filmed locally by Don Ashley. The event was a major success, although it is odd that the film has disappeared from circulation as of this writing. (Both, the *Daily Courier.*)

'Cactus Kid' first run brings stars to Prescott

By SANDY MOSS
The Daily Courier

Amid the flash of cameras and cheers of the crowd, movie stars, a director, producer and bigwigs walked the red carpet from the Hassayampa Inn across the street to the historic Elks Opera House Saturday night for the world premiere of "The Cactus Kid."

The historic opera house was packed to the walls with 600 expectant audience members as the movie shot last year in Prescott flickered to life on a stage-sized movie screen.

Many in the crowd experienced dejá vu as they ate popcorn from brown paper bags and waited for the film reels to roll. Several generations of Prescott kids spent hundreds of hours watching movies in the old red plush chairs of the Elks. Built in 1905, the Opera House converted from live shows to a movie theater sometime in the late 1920s.

But Saturday night was even more entertaining. "The Cactus Kid" film was actually a part of Prescott, with dozens of local folks appearing in the movie in bit parts or as extras, and prominent scenes of the Courthouse Plaza, Watson Lake, the old First National Bank building, and other area landmarks as focal points.

Director Don Ashley was on hand to welcome the crowd and introduce his first full-length feature film.

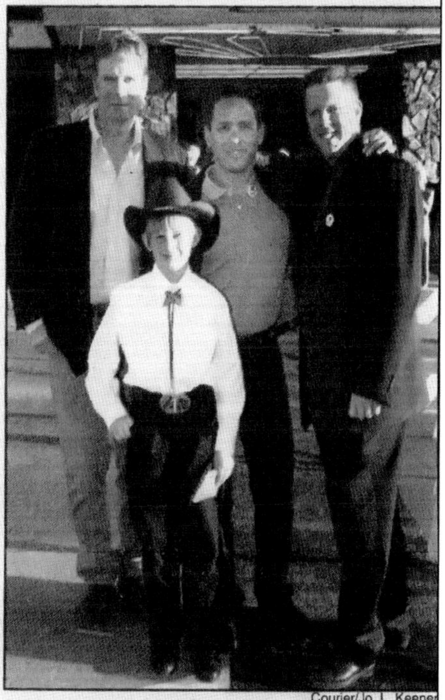

Courier/Jo. L. Keener

'Catcus Kid' stars William Moses, left, and Thomas Curtis, pose with producer/director Don Ashley and studio vice president of production Daniel Wulkan, in front of the Elks Opera House Saturday night

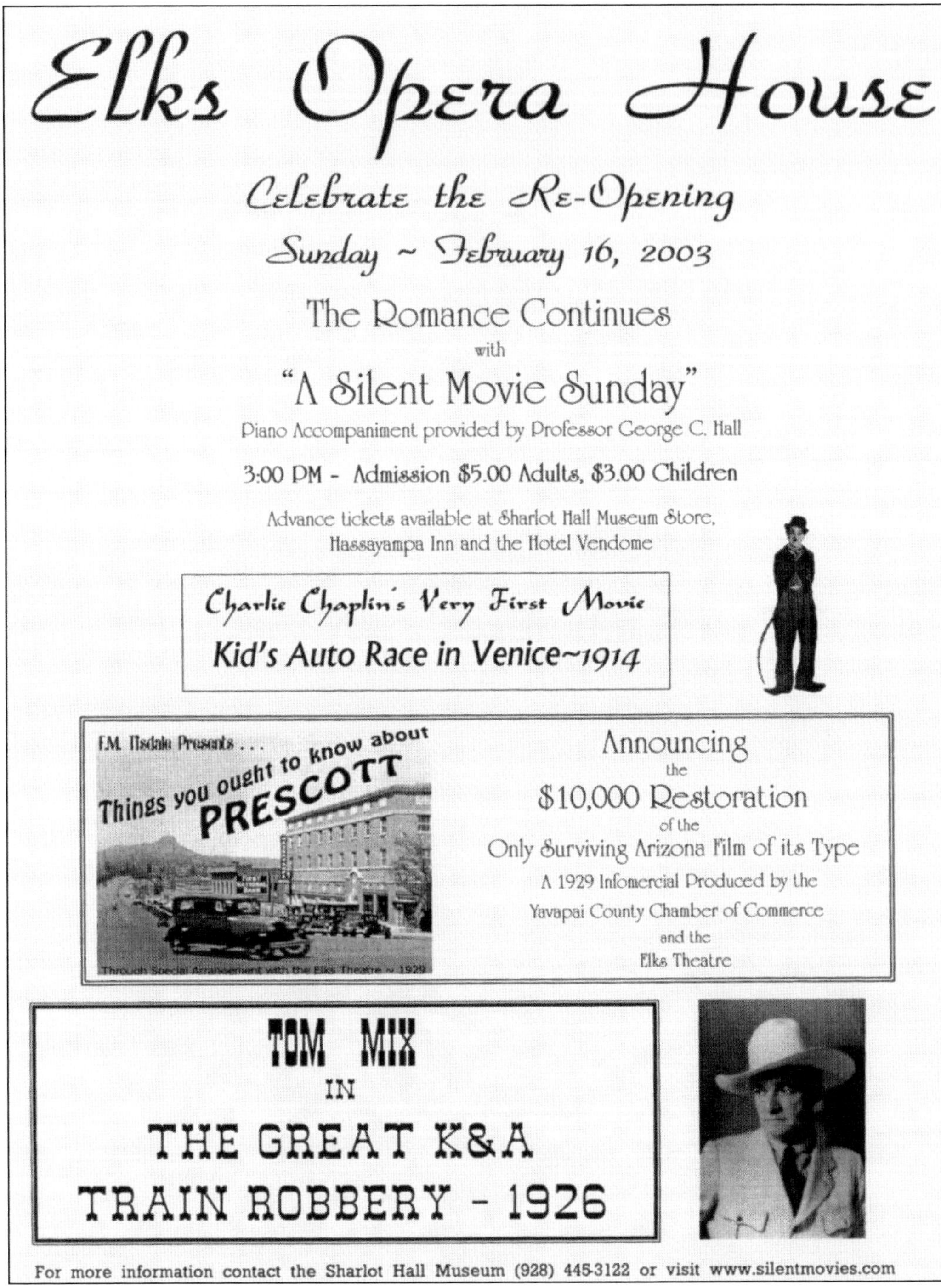

In 1929 with the chamber of commerce, Elks Theatre manager Charles Born coproduced a Prescott promotional film entitled *Things You Ought to Know about Prescott*. A brittle nitrate print had been discovered in the Elks Theatre during the 1970s, and years later in 2003, George Hall (an expert on silent movies) paid $10,000 to create a restored 35mm print of the film, which was screened at the Elks that year along with other silent films. (Parker Anderson collection.)

While various remodeling projects took place over the years, beginning in 2003, directed renovation work had begun on the Elks Opera House. A dropped lobby ceiling was removed to reveal an original higher ceiling and deteriorating decorative canvas (the ceiling had probably been lowered during the 1945 remodeling). In this photograph, city commissioners examine the canvas. This phase of the work was funded by a grant from the Arizona Heritage Fund, which was secured by city historic preservation specialist (retired) Nancy Burgess and matched by the City of Prescott. (The *Daily Courier*.)

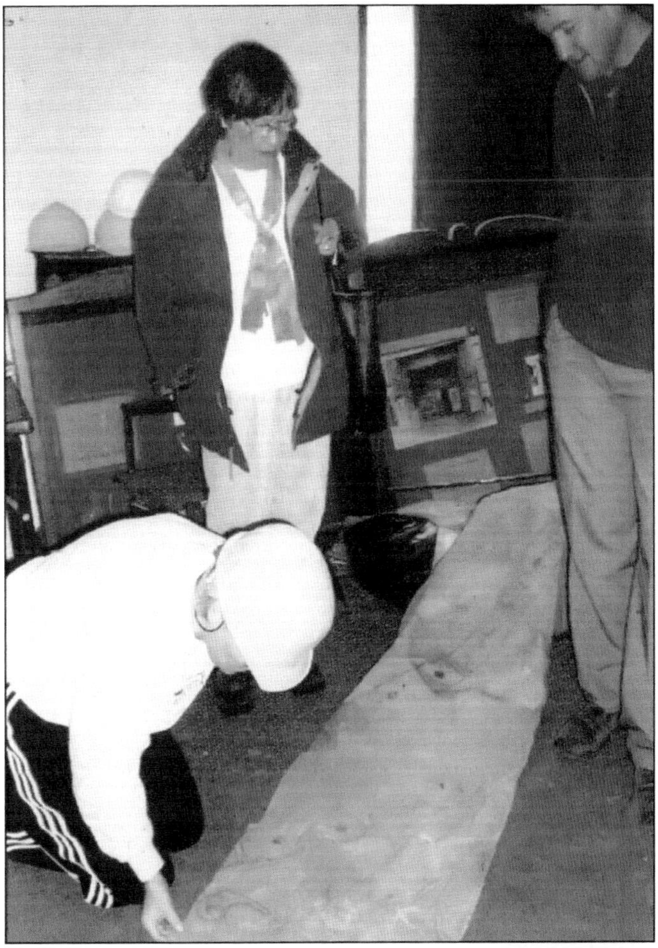

An example of a stencil decoration that was revealed after several layers of paint on the lobby walls was removed. The decoration was determined to date to the 1928 remodeling of the theater. (Elisabeth Ruffner collection.)

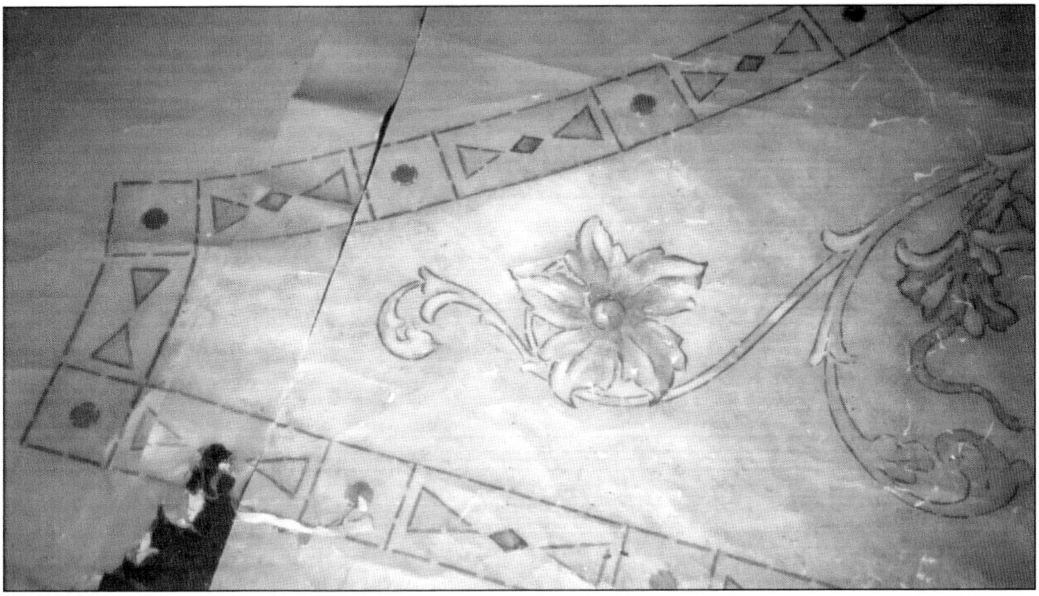

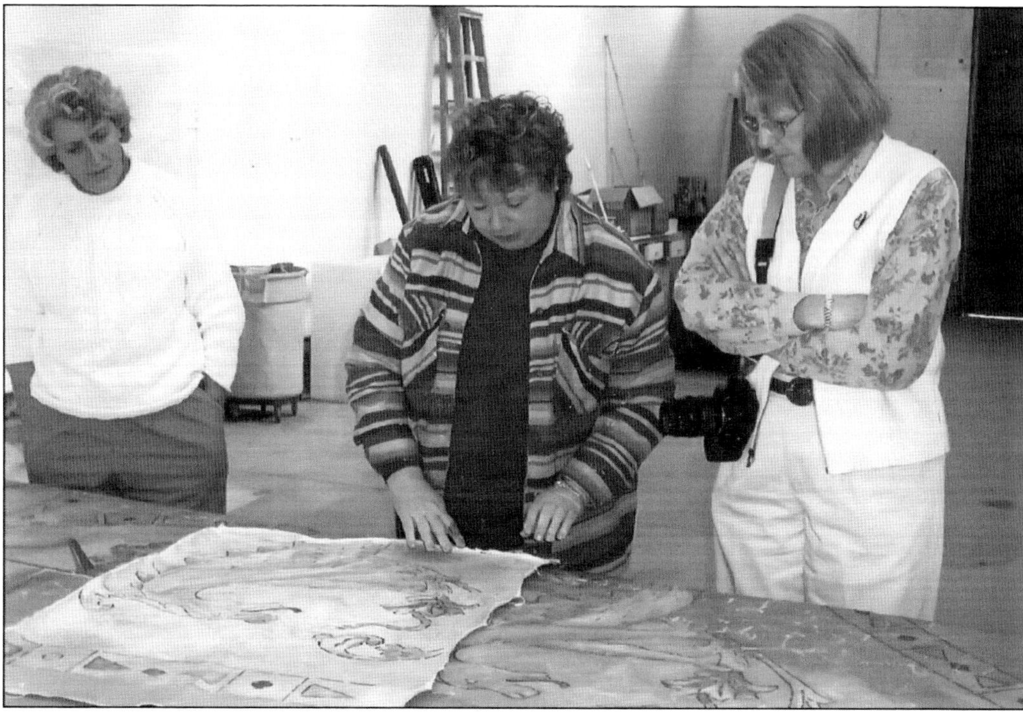

Artist Cheryl Foley (center) is shown continuing the work of restoring the lobby wall design, with Elks Theatre manager Libby Reiman (left) and City of Prescott historic preservation specialist Nancy Burgess looking on. (Elisabeth Ruffner collection.)

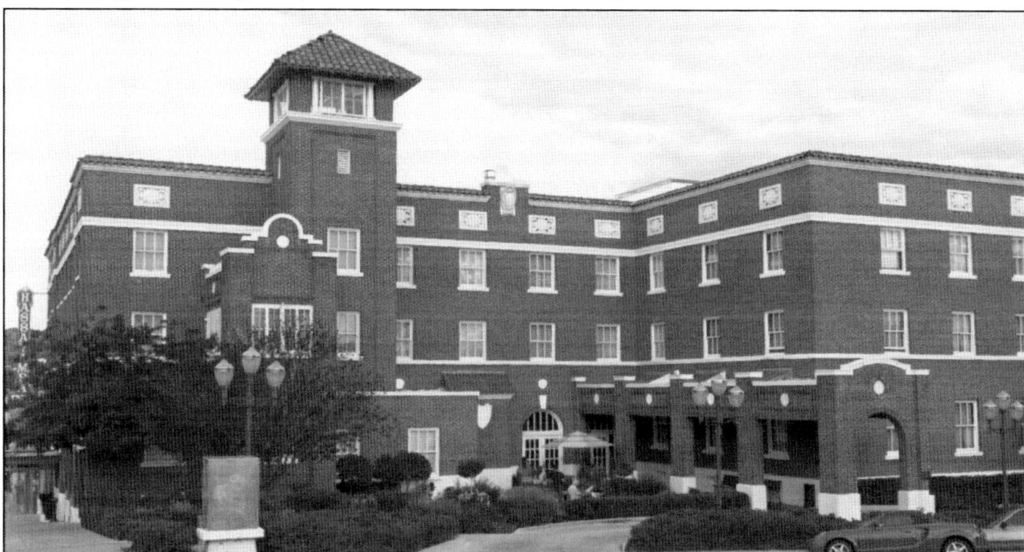

The Hassayampa Inn, located across the street from the Elks Opera House, was built in 1927 and has had a long and close working relationship with the Elks Opera House from its inception. Today, the Hassayampa Inn remains a Prescott landmark, drawing both in- and out-of-state visitors to the historic hotel and its celebrated restaurant. The Elks Opera House restoration fund was the beneficiary of the gala to celebrate the Hassayampa Inn's 75th anniversary in 2002. (Photograph by Terry Berrett.)

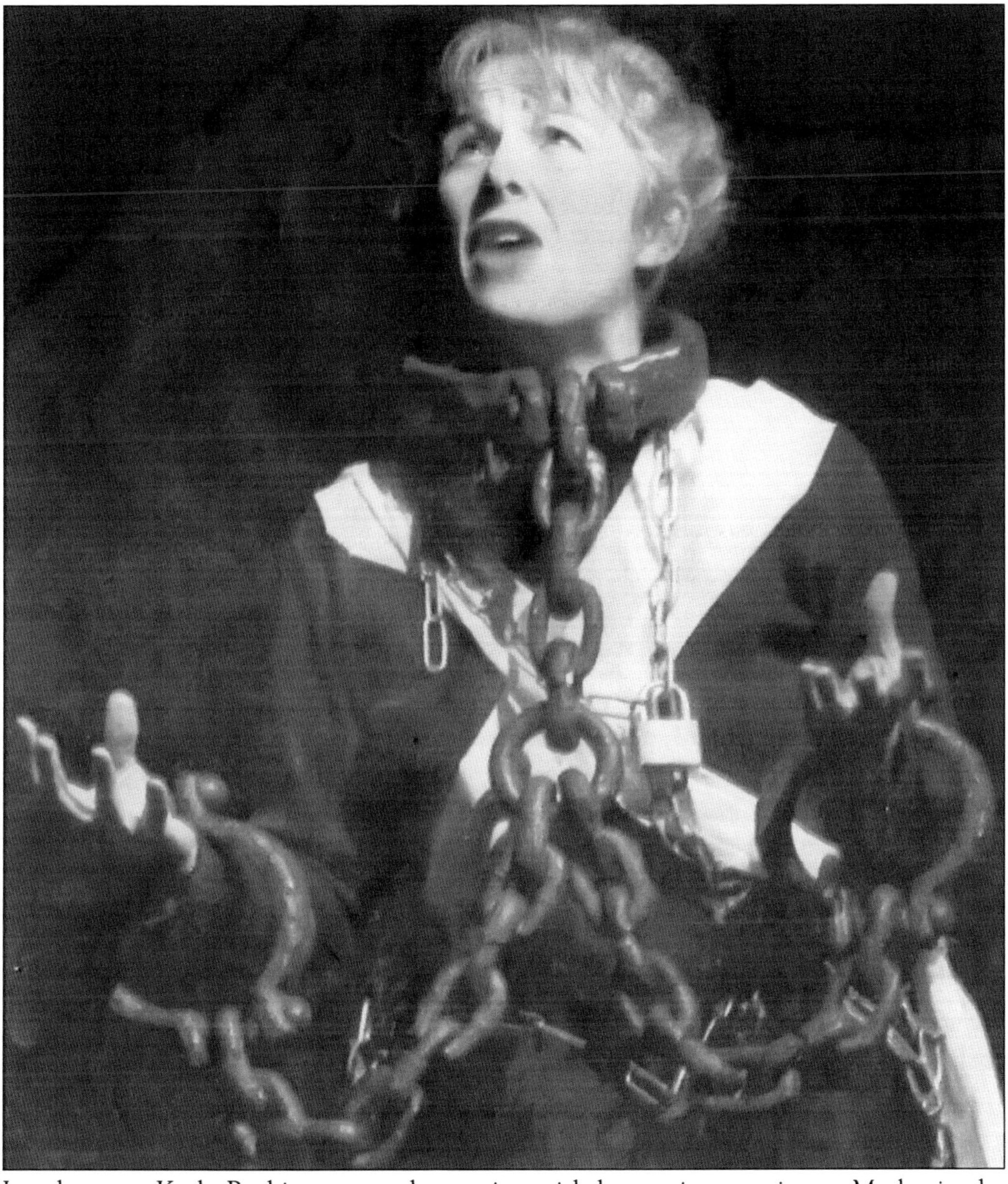

Local actress Karla Burkitt attracted attention with her curious casting as Marley in the Arizona Classical Theater production of *A Christmas Carol* on the Elks Theatre stage in 2004. (The *Daily Courier*.)

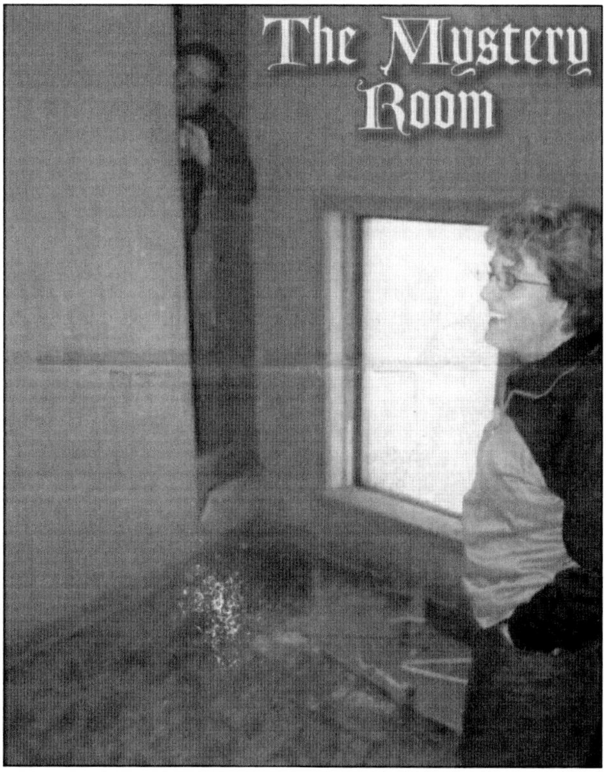

While installing a new heating-and-cooling system, workers discovered a previously unknown walled-off room high above the stage just off the fly loft. When opened, the room was found to contain a table, a chair, a ceiling light fixture, a wall socket, and a window, but there are no records of what the room was used for, or why it was completely sealed off (presumably many years earlier). In the photograph at left, Elks Theatre manager Libby Reiman stands in the room while historian Parker Anderson peers in. The photograph below shows the items found when the room was opened. (At left, the *Daily Courier*; below, photograph by Russell Parker.)

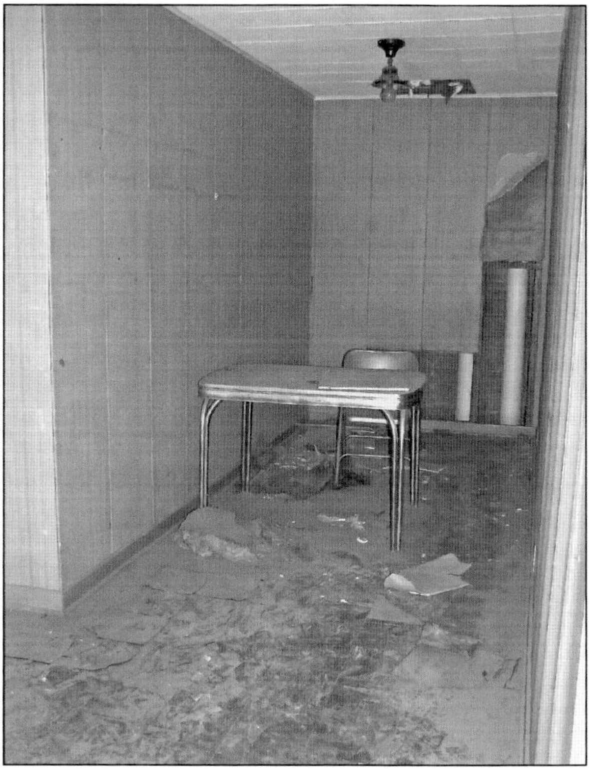

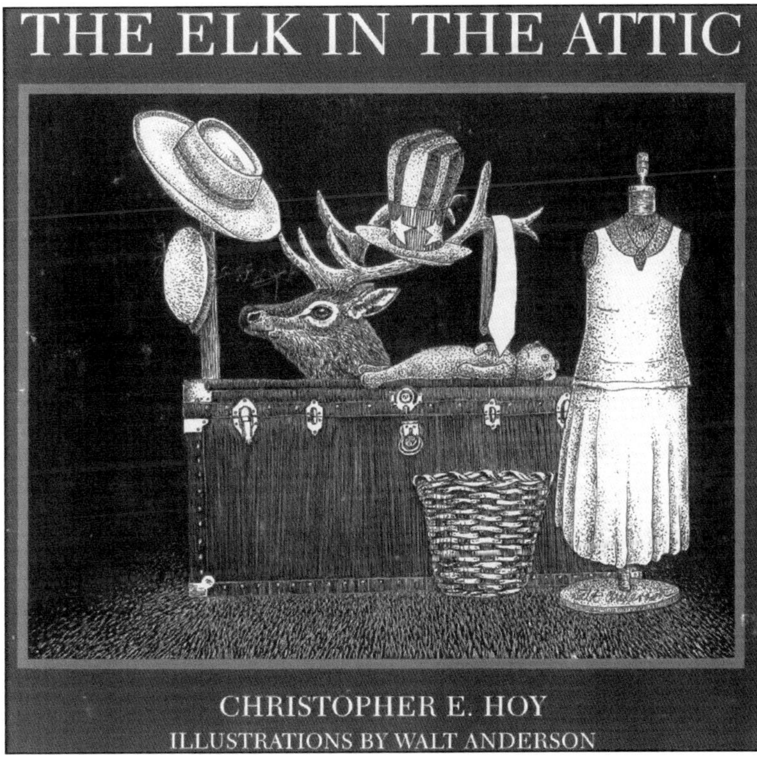

Inspired by the story of the Elks Opera House, Prescott author Chris Hoy wrote a children's book entitled *The Elk in the Attic* for Primrose Press and donated the proceeds to the Elks Opera House restoration fund. The book about a group of animals who take shelter in a child's attic was turned into a stage musical set to be performed in the Elks Opera House in 2012. (Primrose Press.)

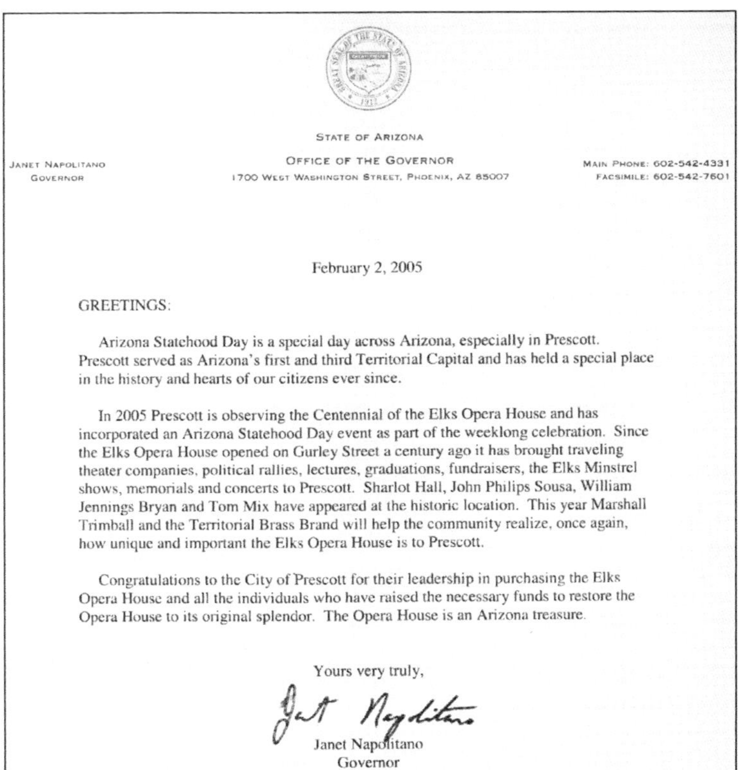

STATE OF ARIZONA

OFFICE OF THE GOVERNOR

1700 WEST WASHINGTON STREET, PHOENIX, AZ 85007

JANET NAPOLITANO
GOVERNOR

MAIN PHONE: 602-542-4331
FACSIMILE: 602-542-7601

February 2, 2005

GREETINGS:

Arizona Statehood Day is a special day across Arizona, especially in Prescott. Prescott served as Arizona's first and third Territorial Capital and has held a special place in the history and hearts of our citizens ever since.

In 2005 Prescott is observing the Centennial of the Elks Opera House and has incorporated an Arizona Statehood Day event as part of the weeklong celebration. Since the Elks Opera House opened on Gurley Street a century ago it has brought traveling theater companies, political rallies, lectures, graduations, fundraisers, the Elks Minstrel shows, memorials and concerts to Prescott. Sharlot Hall, John Philips Sousa, William Jennings Bryan and Tom Mix have appeared at the historic location. This year Marshall Trimball and the Territorial Brass Brand will help the community realize, once again, how unique and important the Elks Opera House is to Prescott.

Congratulations to the City of Prescott for their leadership in purchasing the Elks Opera House and all the individuals who have raised the necessary funds to restore the Opera House to its original splendor. The Opera House is an Arizona treasure.

Yours very truly,

Janet Napolitano
Governor

Excitement grew as the Elks Opera House approached the 100th anniversary of the opening in 2005. Among other things, the City of Prescott and the Elks Opera House Foundation scheduled a weeklong series of events and entertainment to commemorate this milestone. This is a proclamation issued by Arizona governor Janet Napolitano in recognition of the milestone. (State of Arizona.)

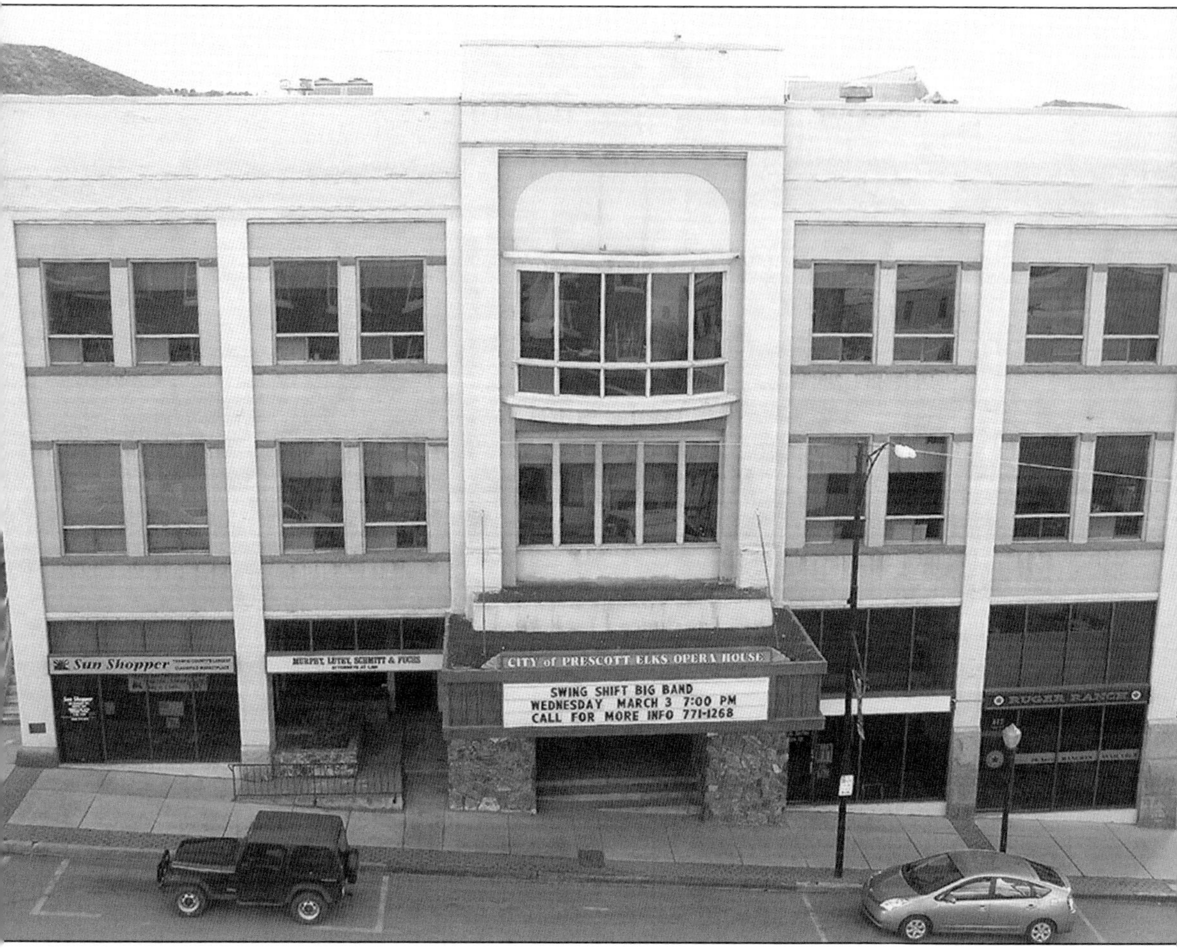

The Elks Building appears around 2006 prior to the exterior restoration and the return of the copper elk to the roof. (Photograph by Russell Parker.)

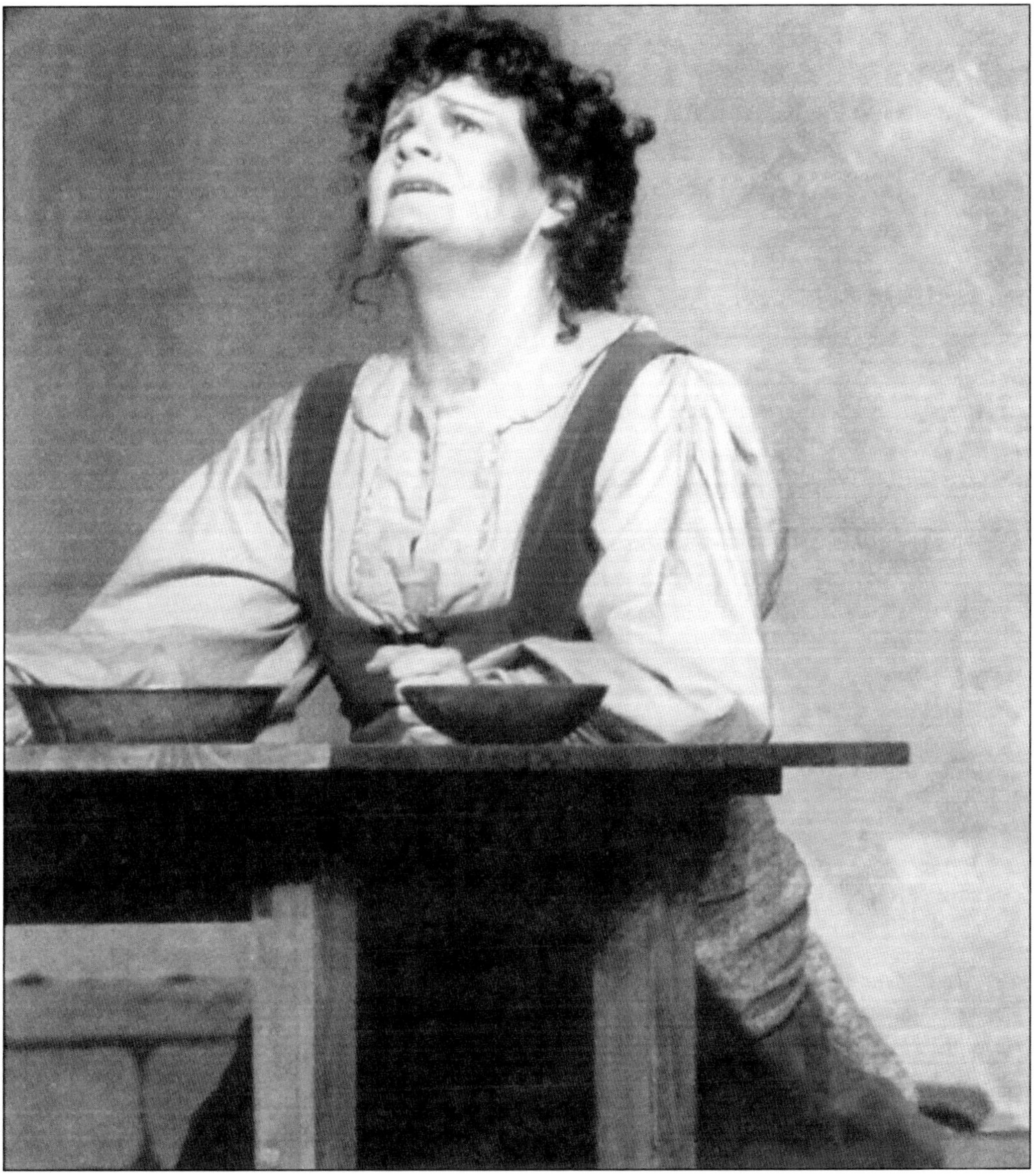

On February 20, 2005, Sharlot Hall Museum and Archive's Blue Rose Theatre, in connection with the City of Prescott, performed Angel Guimera's *Marta of the Lowlands* on the Elks Theatre stage 100 years to the date and time from when the play had first opened the theater. In this photograph, Jody Drake plays Marta, the role Florence Roberts had played at the Elks Opera House at the grand opening. (The *Daily Courier.*)

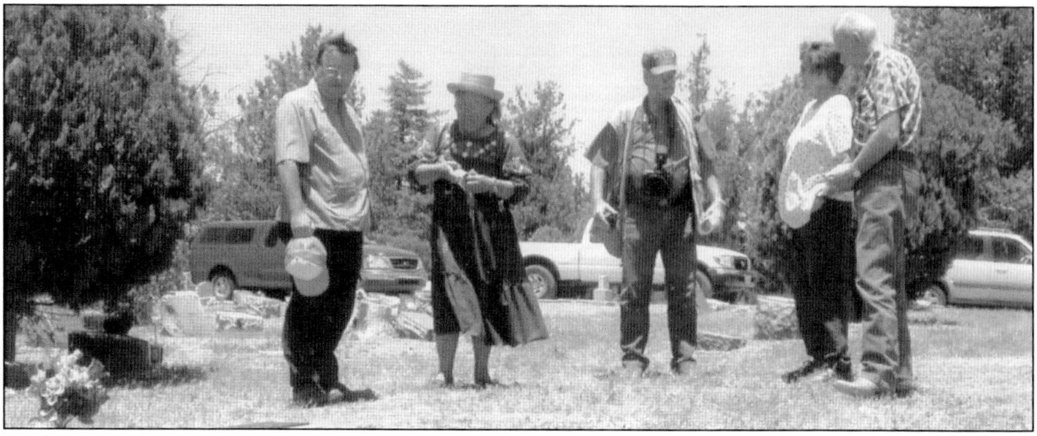

Prof. Stanislaus Scherzel, a violinist who regularly performed at the Elks Opera House in 1912, committed suicide and was buried in an unmarked grave in Mountain View Cemetery. In 2005, a group of local historians got together and secured a tombstone for Professor Scherzel. From left to right are Parker Anderson, Darla Anderson, an unidentified photographer for the *Daily Courier*, Yavapai Cemetery Association president Pat Atchison, and George Goodwin. (Photograph by David Schmittinger.)

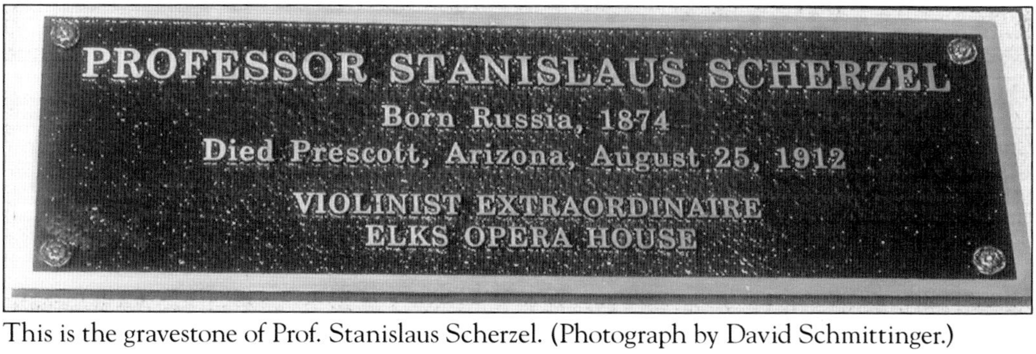

This is the gravestone of Prof. Stanislaus Scherzel. (Photograph by David Schmittinger.)

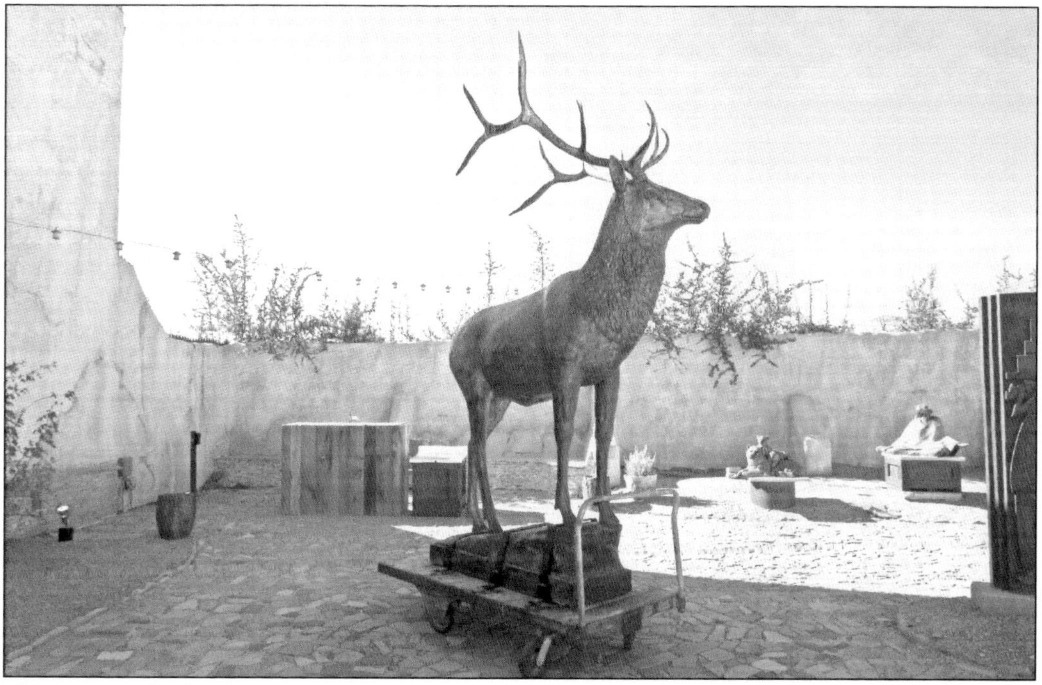

The copper elk that had stood on the Elks Building from 1905 until 1971, when the Elks Lodge moved it to its new building in Prescott Valley, was returned to the Elks Building in 2007 thanks to the efforts of historic preservation specialist Nancy Burgess and financing from Jack D. Wilson. Prior to its return, the elk was first taken to bronze smith Ed Reilly for extensive repair and restoration. (Nancy Burgess collection.)

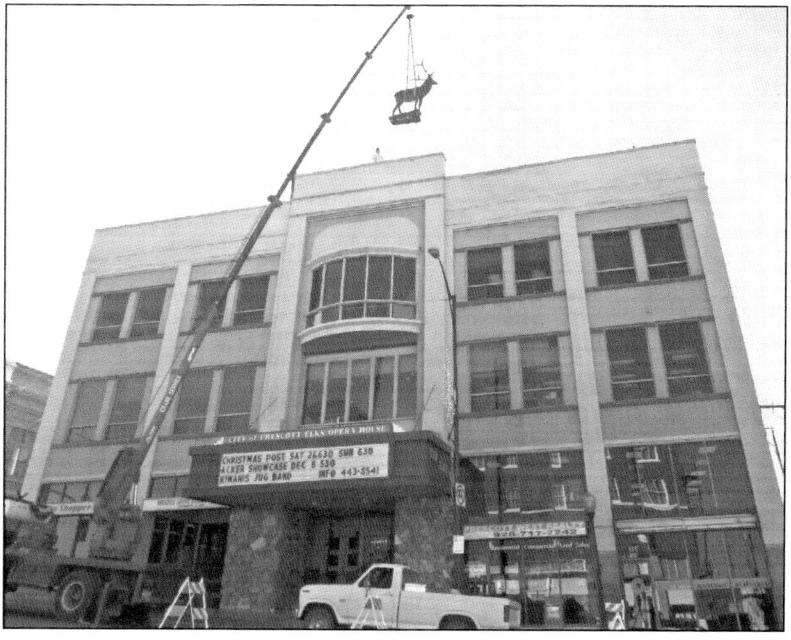

The elk is hoisted back on top of the Elks Building in 2007 by A&B Sign, the same company that had removed the elk in 1971 and taken it to Prescott Elks Lodge no. 330's new quarters in Prescott Valley. (Nancy Burgess collection.)

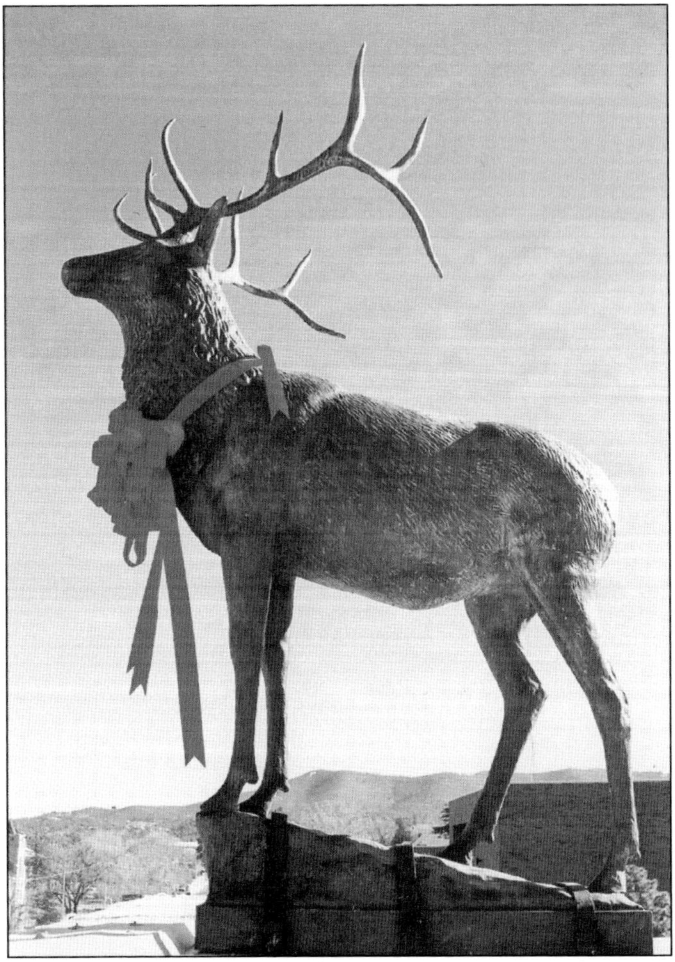

Back in its rightful place on the Elks Building, the elk is decorated with a red bow every Christmas season by city staff. (Nancy Burgess collection.)

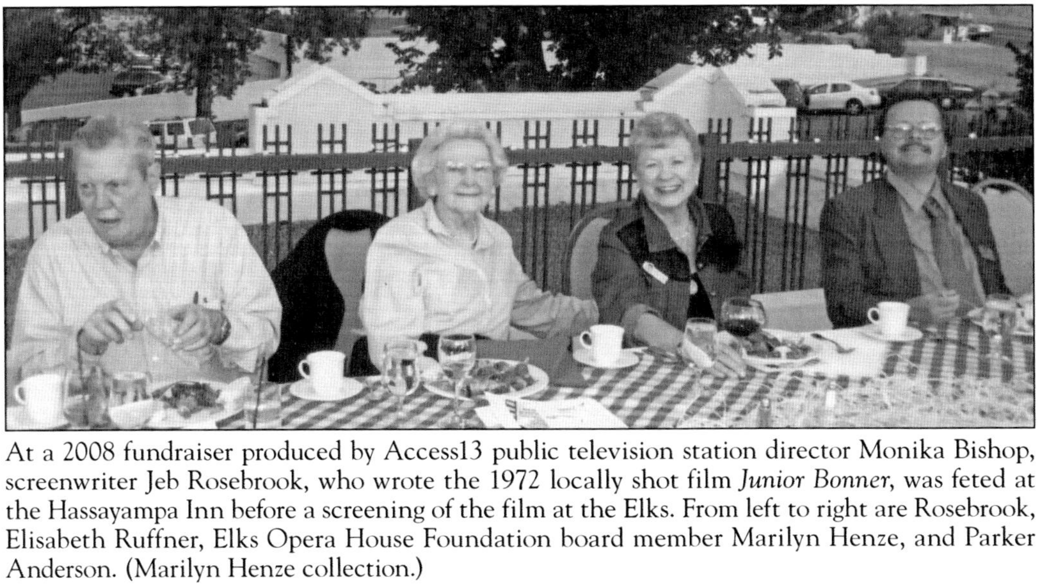

At a 2008 fundraiser produced by Access13 public television station director Monika Bishop, screenwriter Jeb Rosebrook, who wrote the 1972 locally shot film *Junior Bonner*, was feted at the Hassayampa Inn before a screening of the film at the Elks. From left to right are Rosebrook, Elisabeth Ruffner, Elks Opera House Foundation board member Marilyn Henze, and Parker Anderson. (Marilyn Henze collection.)

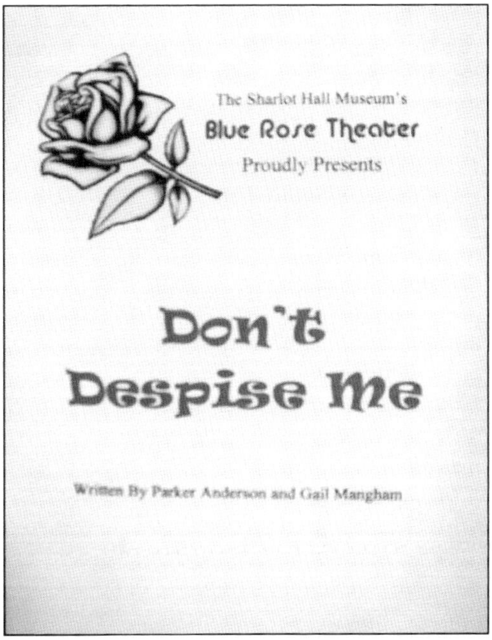

Local actress and drama teacher Gail Mangham starred in a one-woman show about the life of Florence Roberts entitled *Don't Despise Me* at Sharlot Hall Museum and Archive's Blue Rose Theatre in 2006. Mangham later re-titled the show *Tea with Zuzu* and has performed it at the Elks Theatre and a number of other locations. (Both photographs by David Schmittinger.)

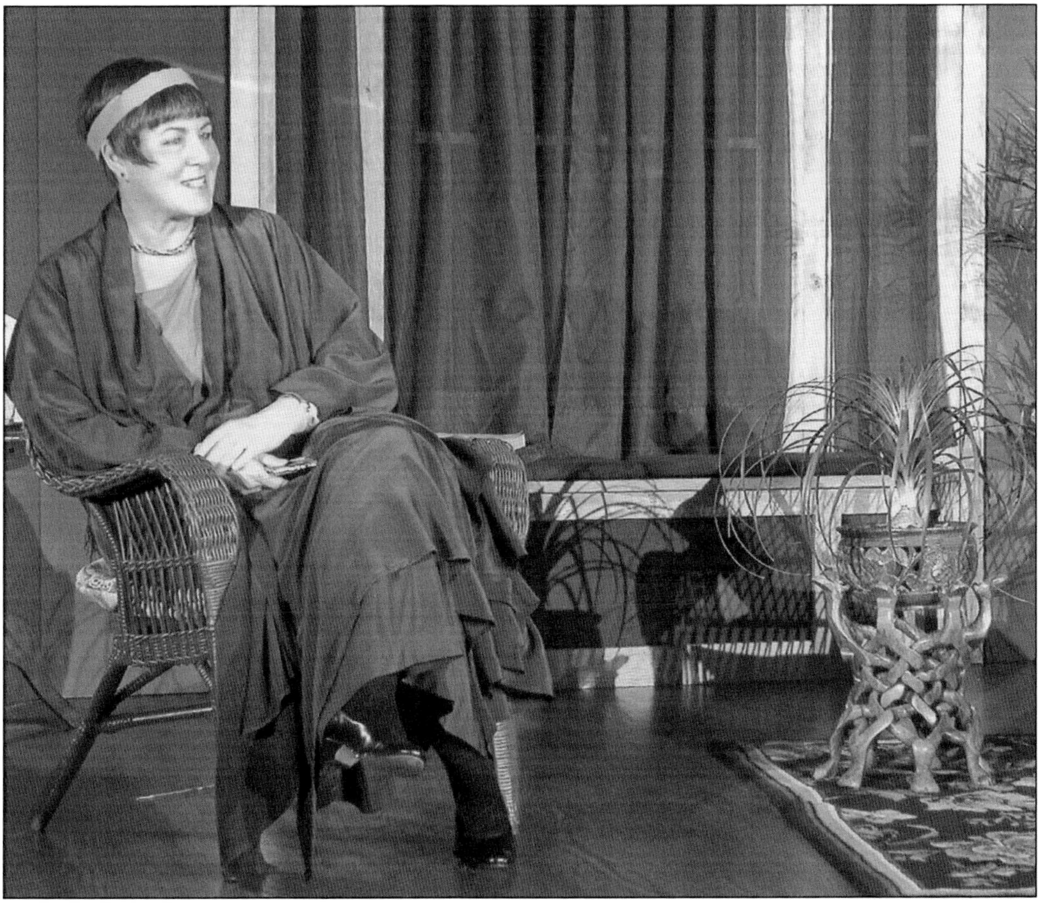

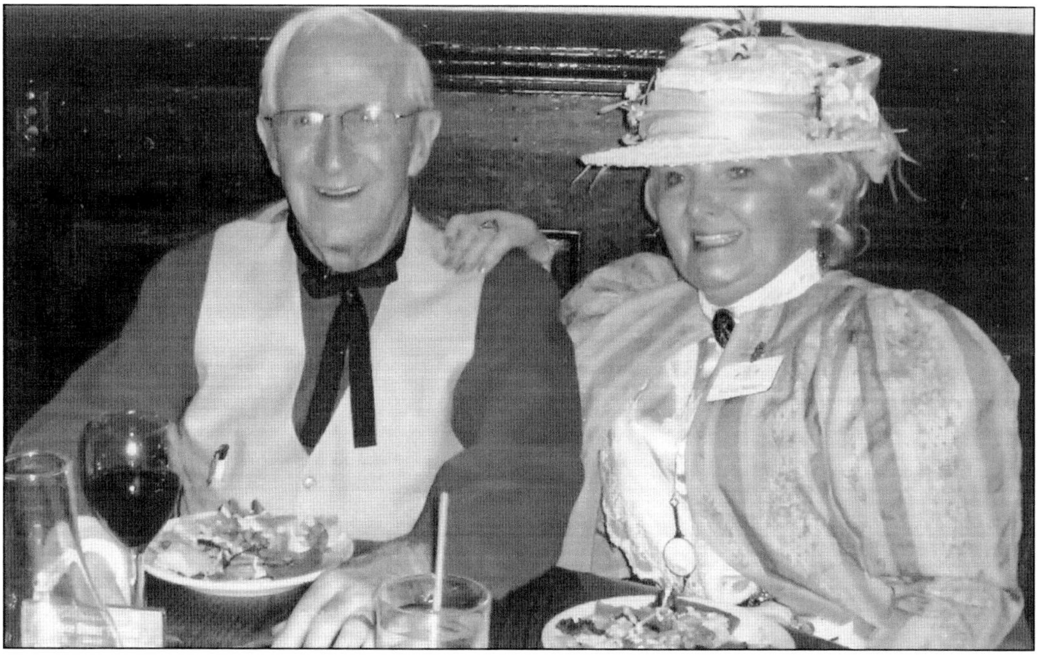

On February 20, 2009, at the 104th anniversary of the opening of the Elks Opera House, a number of prominent supporters held a banquet at the Palace Restaurant hosted by the Elks Opera House Guild. Above are Carl and Alicia Bauer, longtime benefactors of the Elks Opera House; below are, from left to right, Jody Drake, Parker Anderson, Elisabeth Ruffner, and Carl Bauer. (Both, Elks Opera House Foundation Collection.)

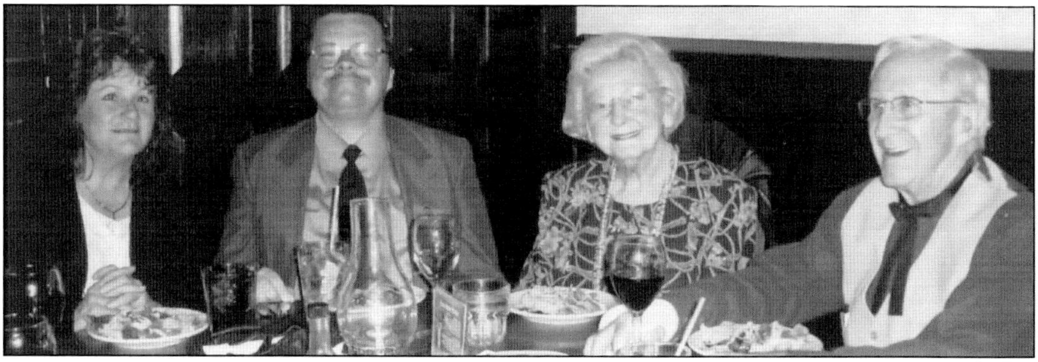

Five

The Restoration

After several years of fundraising, the Elks Opera House Foundation was given a $1.25 million grant by the Harold James Family Trust to restore the theater to its 1905 grandeur. Plans were drawn up, contractors hired, and supporters of the Elks Opera House waited in anticipation. In late 2009, restoration began under the auspices of architects William Otwell & Associates, Haley Construction Company, Evergreene Architectural Arts, E&M Rigging, Custom Service Innovations, Paul Lester, and others.

The first step was to remove the various structures that had been added over the years. The different teams then began the process of identifying the original 1905 condition of the theater. Using historical records, reviewing surviving period photographs, performing chemical analysis of the original paint chips that were found behind walls, finding pieces of original plaster moldings behind old structures, pulling away old paint layers to find original stencils underneath, and using any other sources at their disposal, the teams developed a comprehensive plan for the monumental task of renovating the theater as closely as possible to its 1905 condition.

The opera boxes were rebuilt, plaster decorations were reproduced, and elk-head molds were formed to reproduce those that hung on the boxes and walls. Gold leaf was added to columns and structures, decorative stencils were added, and the original ceiling tins were taken down, repaired, and reinstalled. The old seats were removed and replaced and paint colors were selected and applied to the walls and stage. The original fireproof stage curtain was removed because of its asbestos content, and a replica was produced and installed. Theatre stairways, walkways, and the lobby were all redone. A state-of-the-art sound system was installed, and the heating-and-cooling system was updated to modern requirements and technology.

The theater reopened in grand style on July 24, 2010, with a gala celebration and a promise of continuous service to Prescott for generations to come. Entering the theater today is a spectacular walk back in time to 1905, expressing a tribute to all that contributed to its formation, restoration, and use through the years.

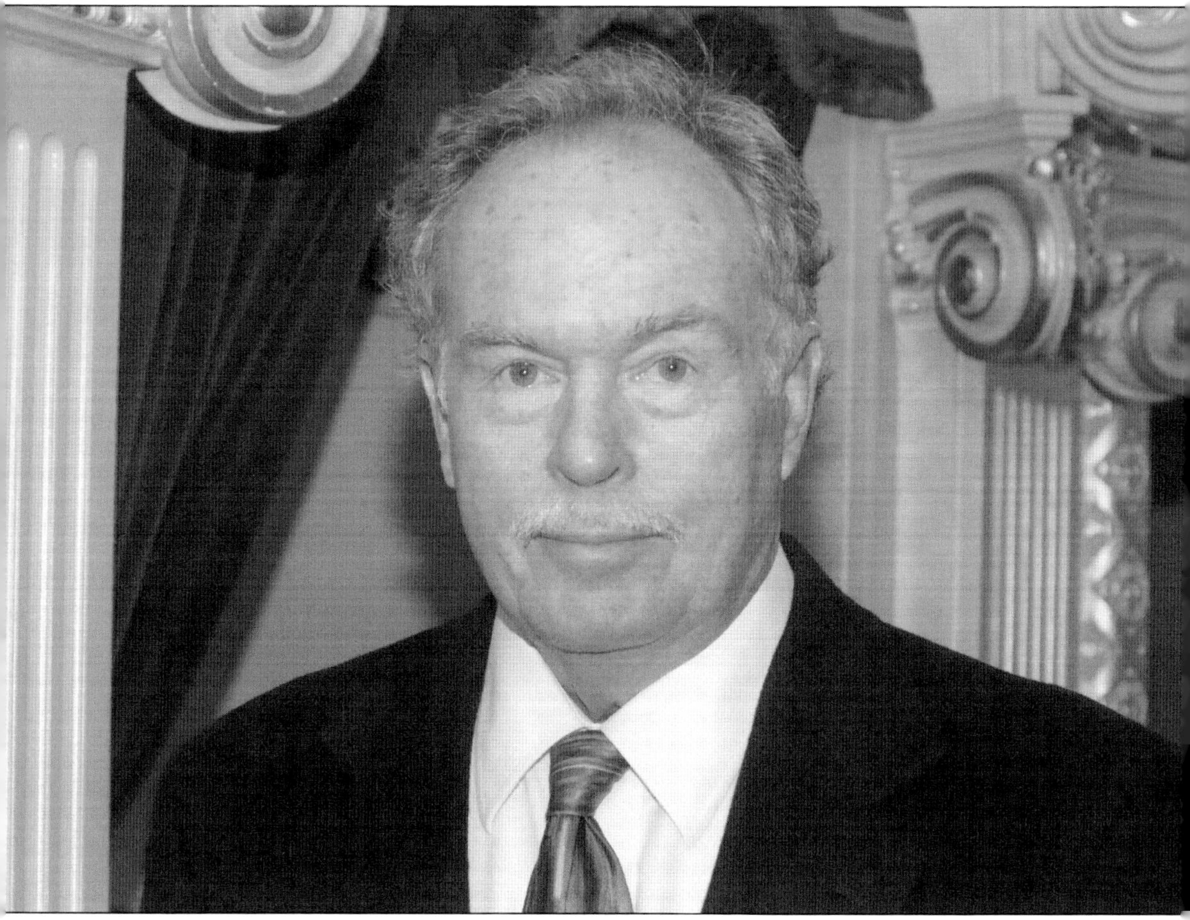

Architect William Otwell, AIA, designed and supervised the 2009–2010 restoration of the Elks Opera House. For his efforts, he was given an Arizona Culturekeepers Award in Phoenix in 2011, an honor bestowed to only 100 individuals in advance of the Arizona statehood centennial in 2012. (Photograph by Terry Berrett.)

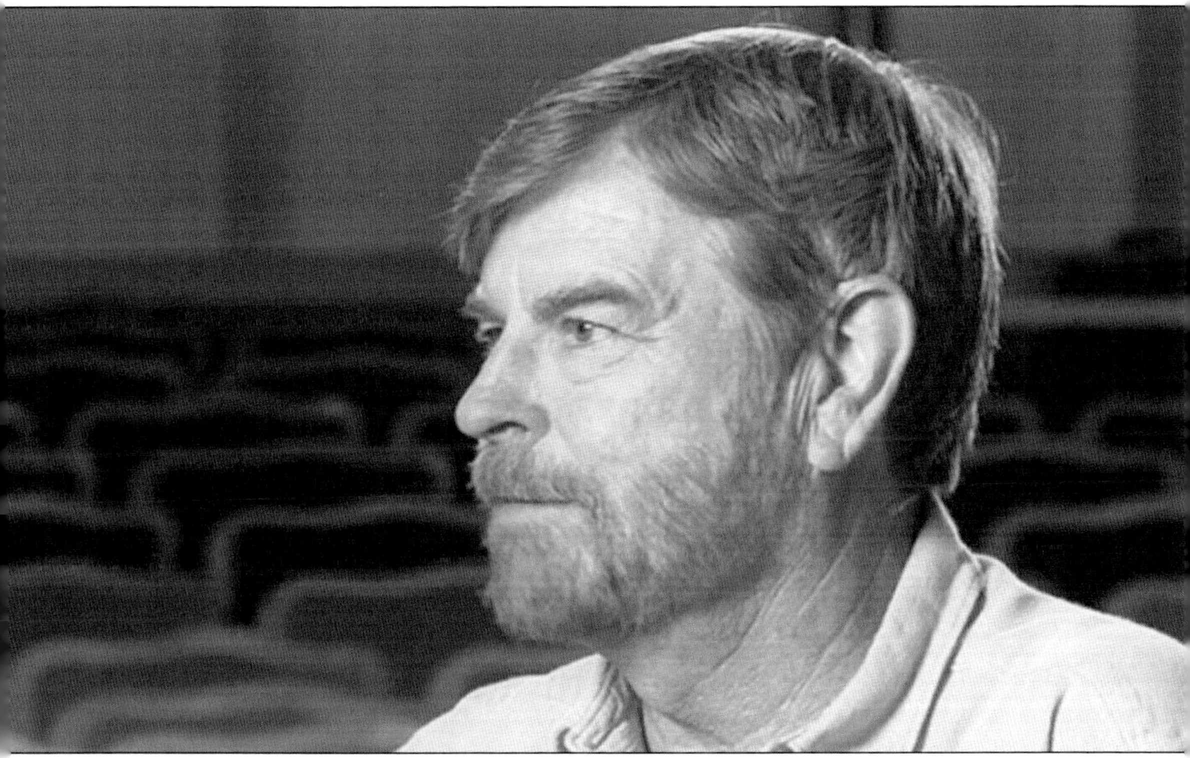

Tom Haley led the construction team on behalf of Haley Construction Company. The company was started as a residential developer by C.J. and Frances Haley in 1955 in Globe, Arizona, and moved to Prescott, Arizona, in 1960. In addition to commercial and residential construction, the company today also specializes in historic restorations. Tom is president of Haley Construction Company and has served on numerous boards and professional organizations, including four terms as president of the Yavapai County Contractors Association and as the president of the Prescott Chamber of Commerce in 1985. (City of Prescott.)

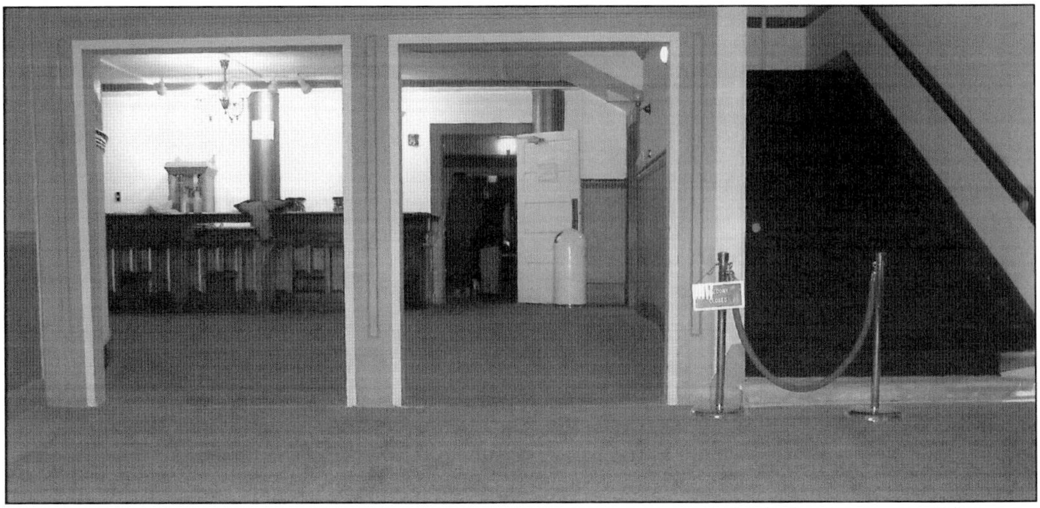

This is the lobby of the Elks Opera House, including the stairway to the balcony. Most of this area had been renovated in the early 2000s. When the theater was new, the lobby contained steps up to the auditorium, but the steps were replaced by a ramp during a 1928 remodeling. (Photograph by Russell Parker.)

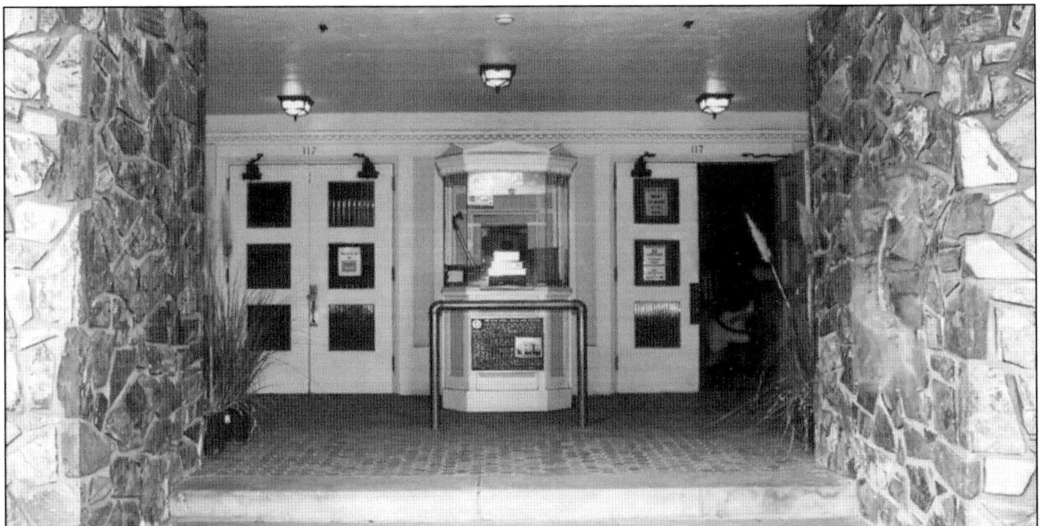

The entrance to the Elks Opera House is shown prior to the restoration. A rock covering similar to that on the sidewalls had already been removed from the lower part of the box office. (Photograph by Russell Parker.)

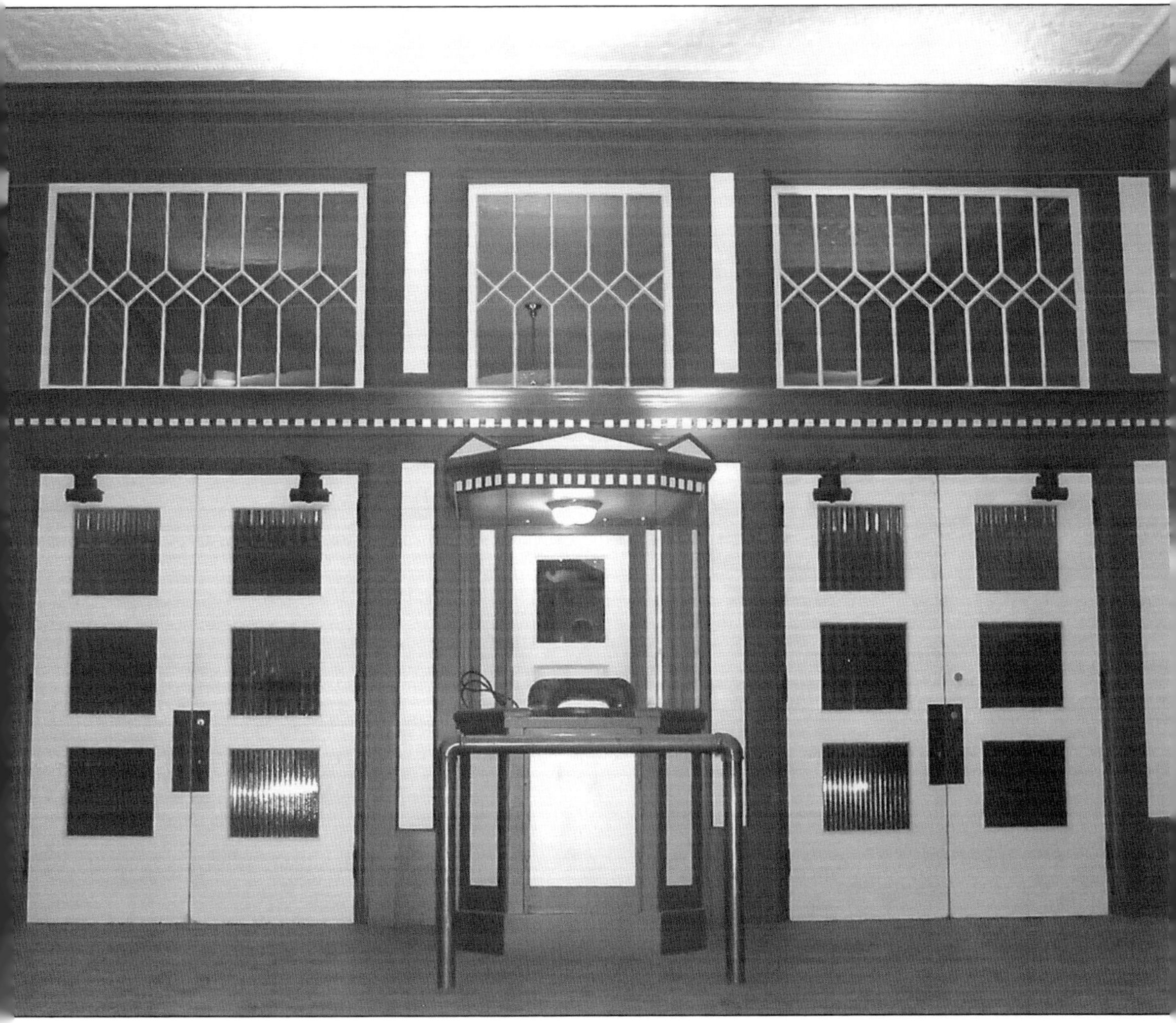

The entrance to the Elks Opera House is shown after the restoration. The dropped ceiling, which was probably installed during the 1945 remodeling, has been removed, revealing transom windows that had not seen the light of day for many years. Although not visible in this photograph, the sidewall rock covering was removed, revealing the original entrance structure. (Photograph by Russell Parker.)

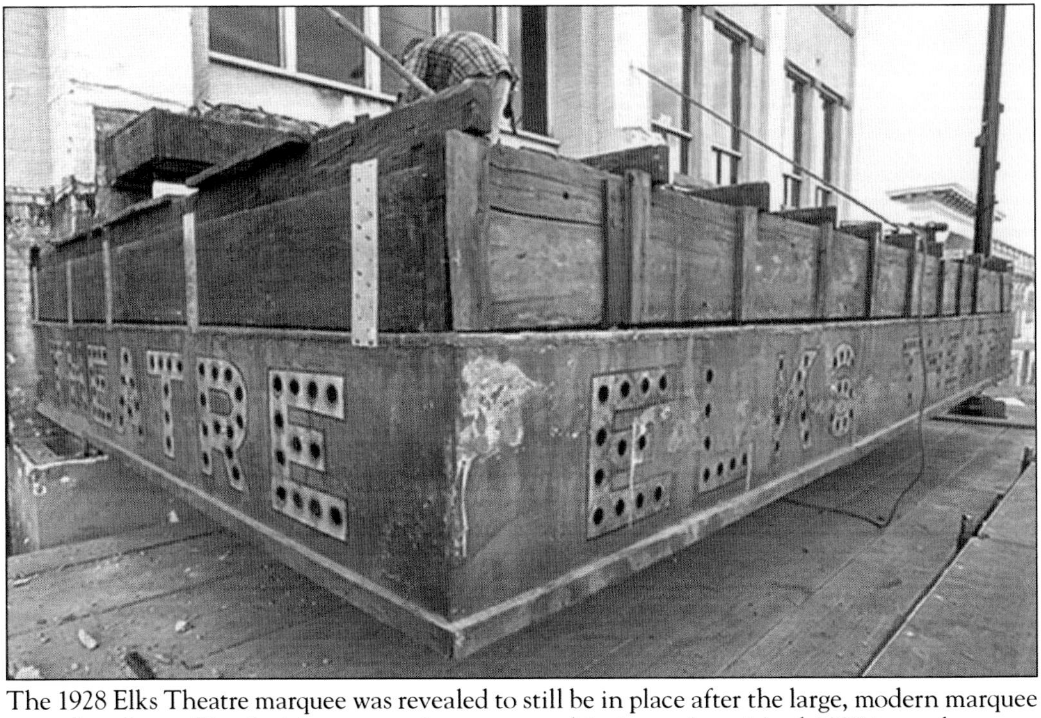

The 1928 Elks Theatre marquee was revealed to still be in place after the large, modern marquee was taken down. The decision was made to restore this sign to its original 1928 incandescence. (Both photographs by Russell Parker.)

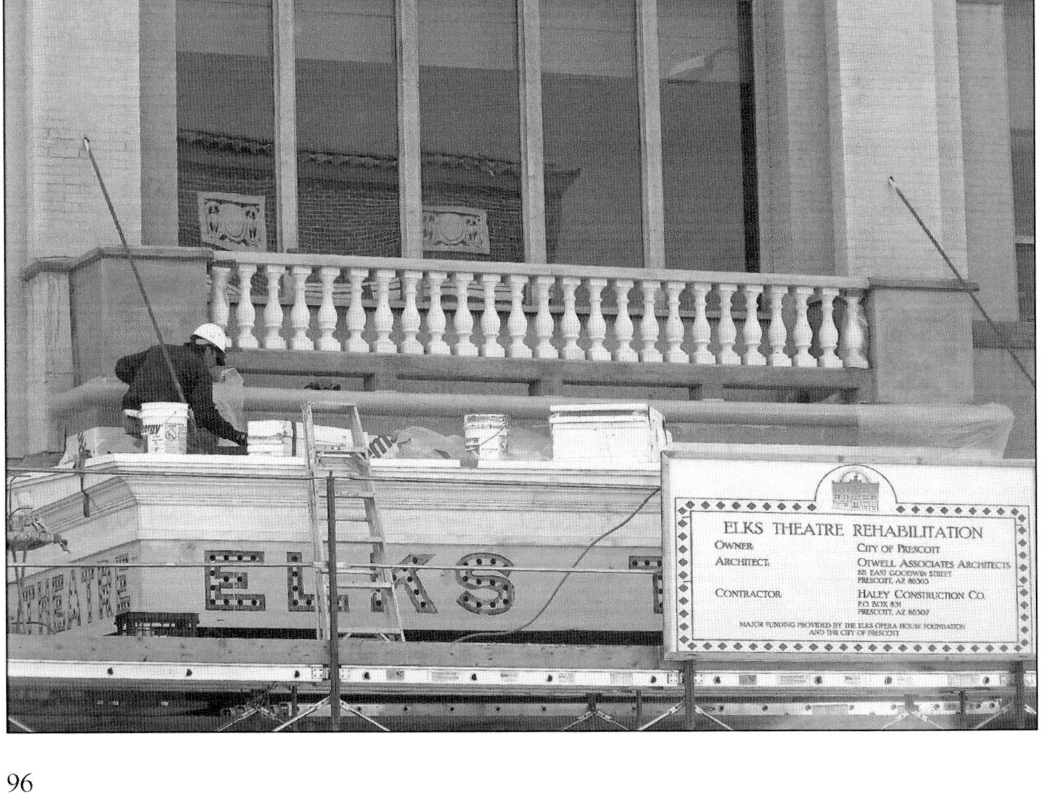

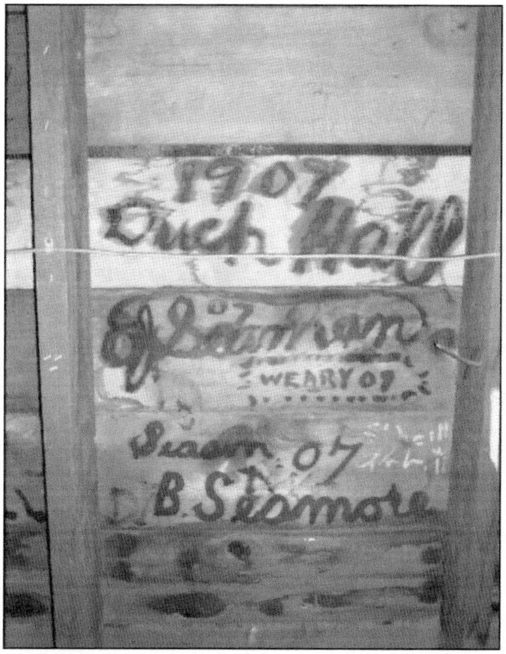

High above the stage in the fly loft, various theater hands wrote their names and other graffiti from the early days up to the present. (Photograph by Russell Parker.)

When the Elks Opera House opened in 1905, it was equipped with a fire curtain made of asbestos. Shortly before the renovation, it was realized that the curtain was still hanging above the stage after over a century, as no fire requiring the lowering of the curtain had occurred. The fire curtain was removed and put in storage in a biohazard container. Longtime Prescott resident John Helvig reports that the curtain was taken down once in the early 1980s, examined, and returned to its position because knowledge about the dangers of asbestos were not prevalent at that time. (Photograph by Russell Parker.)

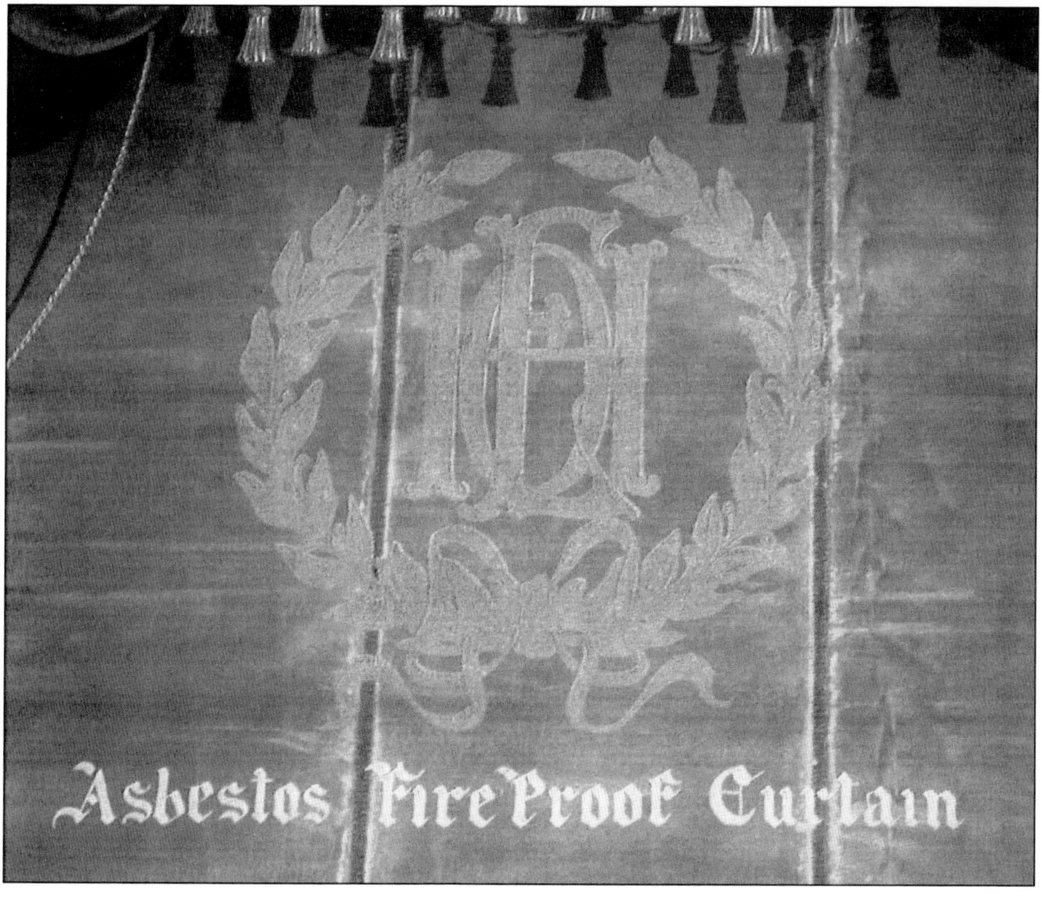

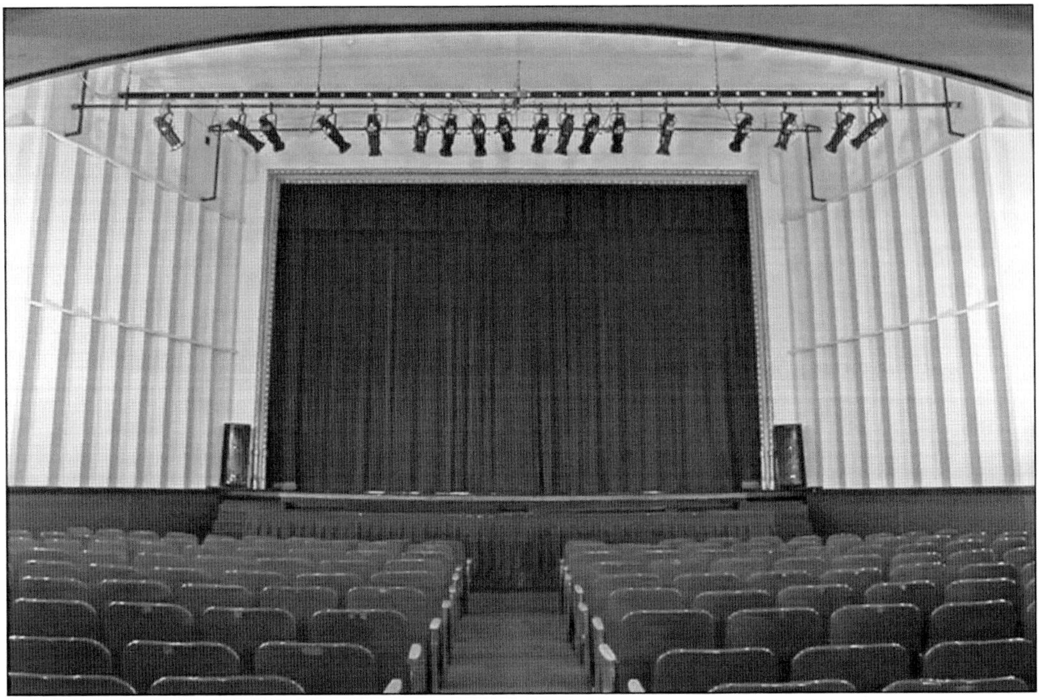

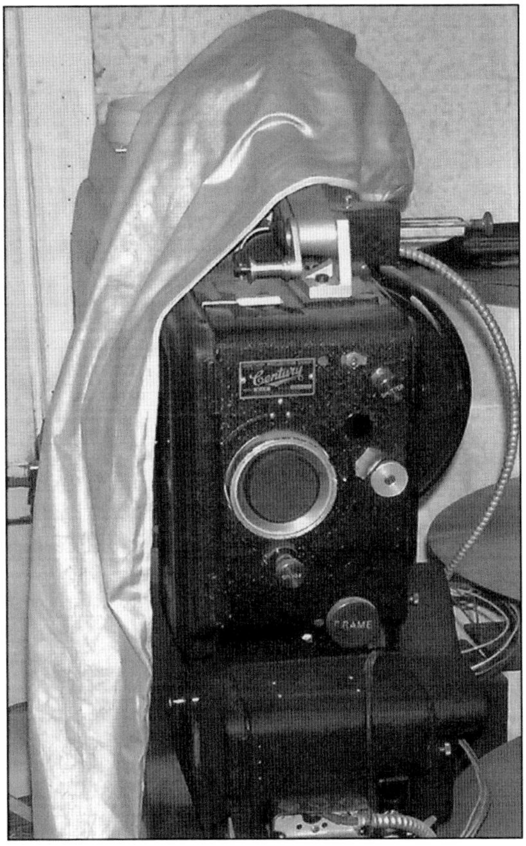

The auditorium of the Elks Opera House appears prior to restoration with Claude Cline's 1945 wood paneling (used to optimize movie showings) still in place where the original opera boxes had been. This photograph is illustrative of the changes from a performing theater to a movie theater. The light grid had been added in 1999 with a grant from the Prescott Area Arts and Humanities Council (PAAHC) funded by Warren Miller's Save The Elks Committee. (Photograph by Russell Parker.)

This old movie projector, which probably dates to at least the 1950s, was sitting in the Elks Theatre projection booth and was likely in use up until the end of the motion picture era in 1982. During the restoration, the projection booth was converted to the manager's office and the projector placed in storage. (Photograph by Russell Parker.)

As all of the theater seats were being replaced, an open house was held for members of the public to come and take the old seats as souvenirs. They all went very quickly, with the new owners of the seats making contributions toward the purchase of new seats. (Parker Anderson collection.)

Take A Seat From The Historic Elks Opera House!

First dates, first kisses, favorite movies, treasured memories have all happened in this great old theater! Now is your chance to own a piece of Prescott history as the red theater seats find new homes...If you can haul it you can have it!

Come and take your seats before they're gone.

"The Take Your Seat Event"

will be 6/29—7/2 from 10am –5pm

No Returns

Donations accepted but not necessary

For information please call (928)777-1366.

The Elks Opera House restoration is in progress. The wood paneling that had been added for movie projections has been removed, revealing the frames where the box seats once had been. (Photograph by Russell Parker.)

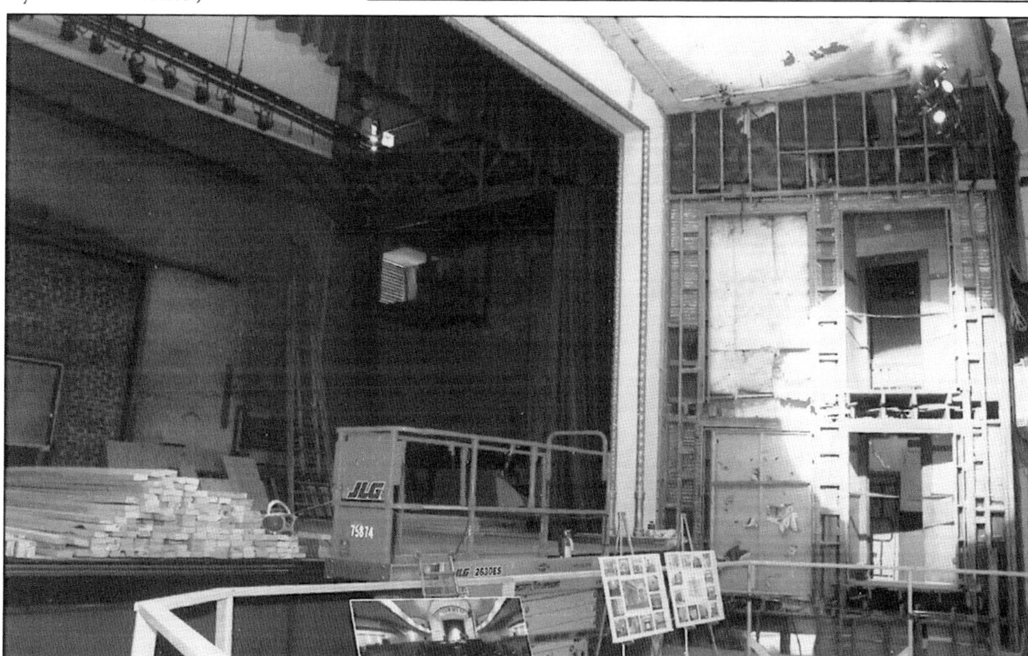

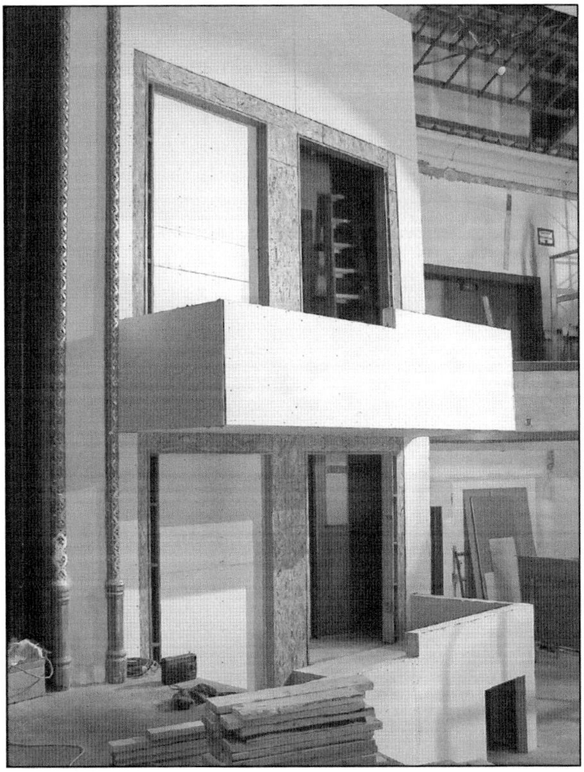

The new opera boxes start to take shape. Because of newer building code restrictions, each box now contains two chairs for a total of 16 seats in the opera boxes. Smaller gold-finished chairs purchased by the Elks Opera House Foundation may be used three to a box for weddings and special occasions. In 1905, each box remarkably held six seats apiece for a total seating of 48 in the boxes. (Both photographs by Russell Parker.)

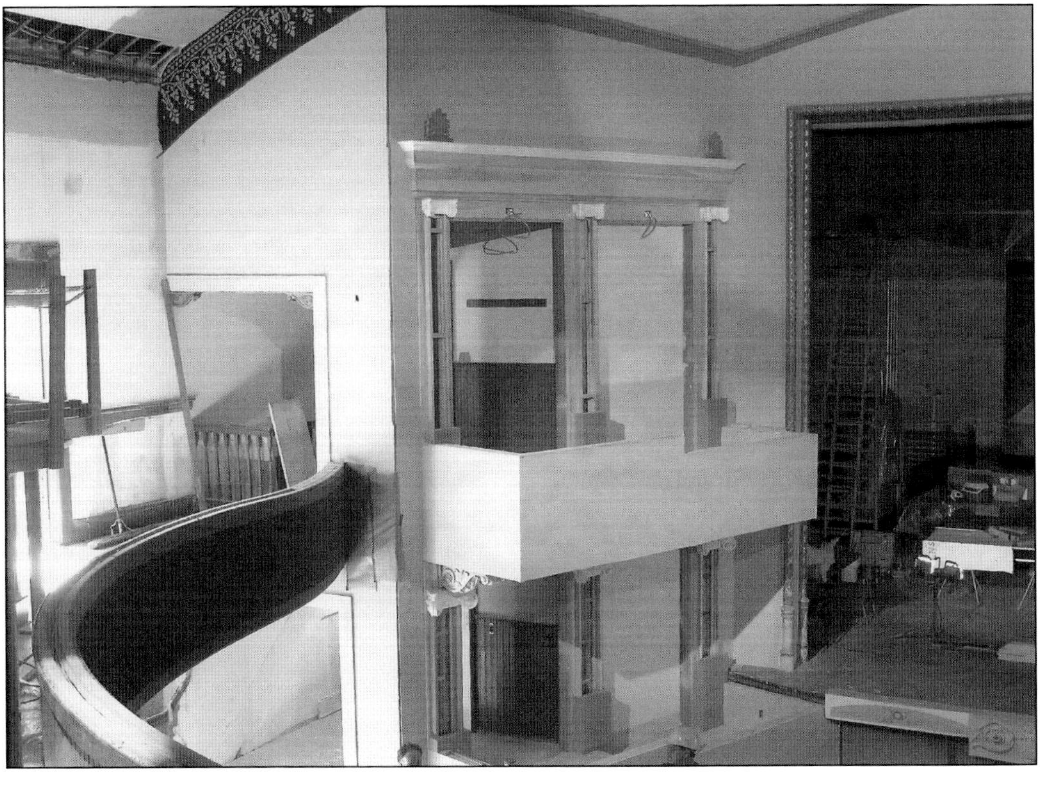

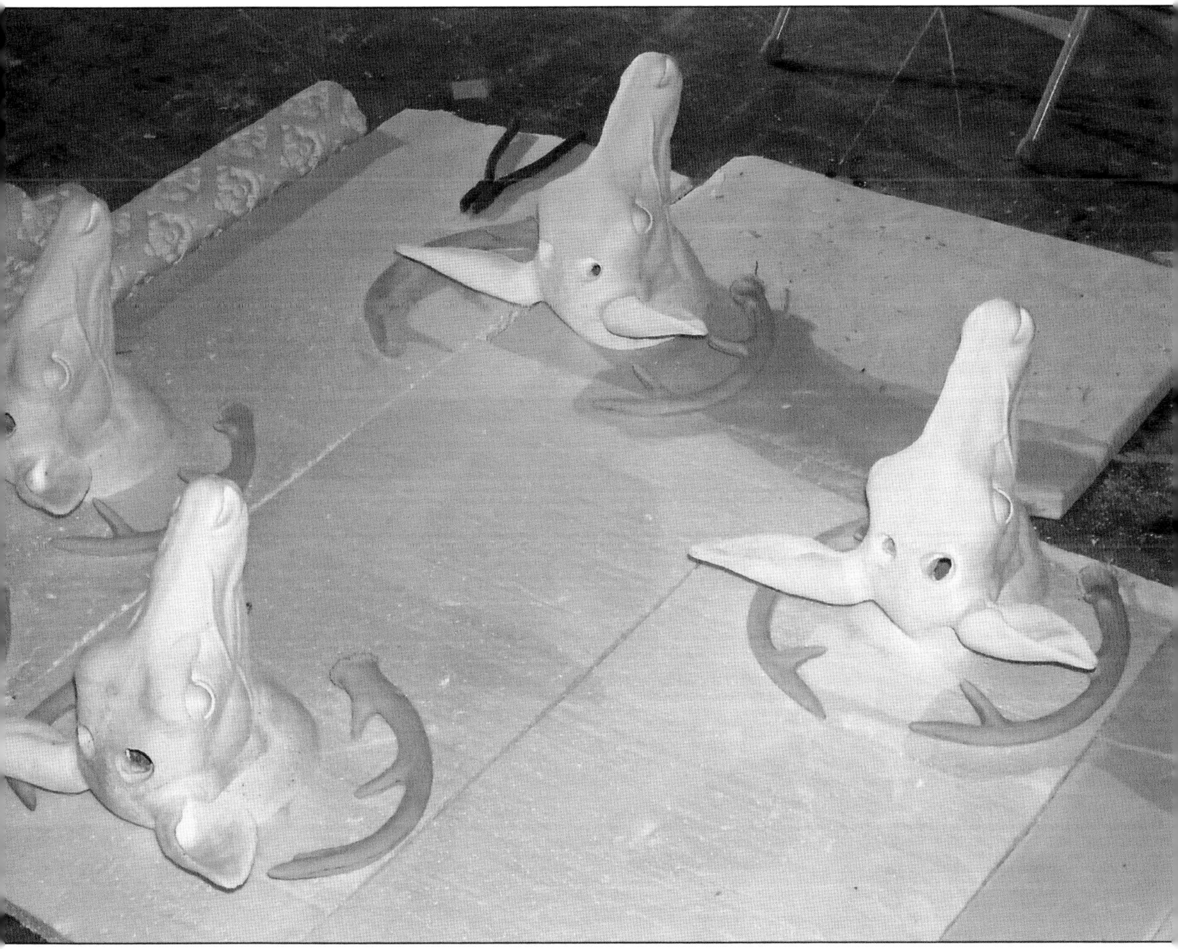

Among the unique features of the original Elks Opera House were the elk heads that adorned the opera boxes. Evergreene Architectural Arts, a nationally renowned restoration company, was able to create molds that replicated, as close as possible, the original elk heads. Using these molds, replica elk heads were cast on the opera house stage during restoration. (Photograph by Russell Parker.)

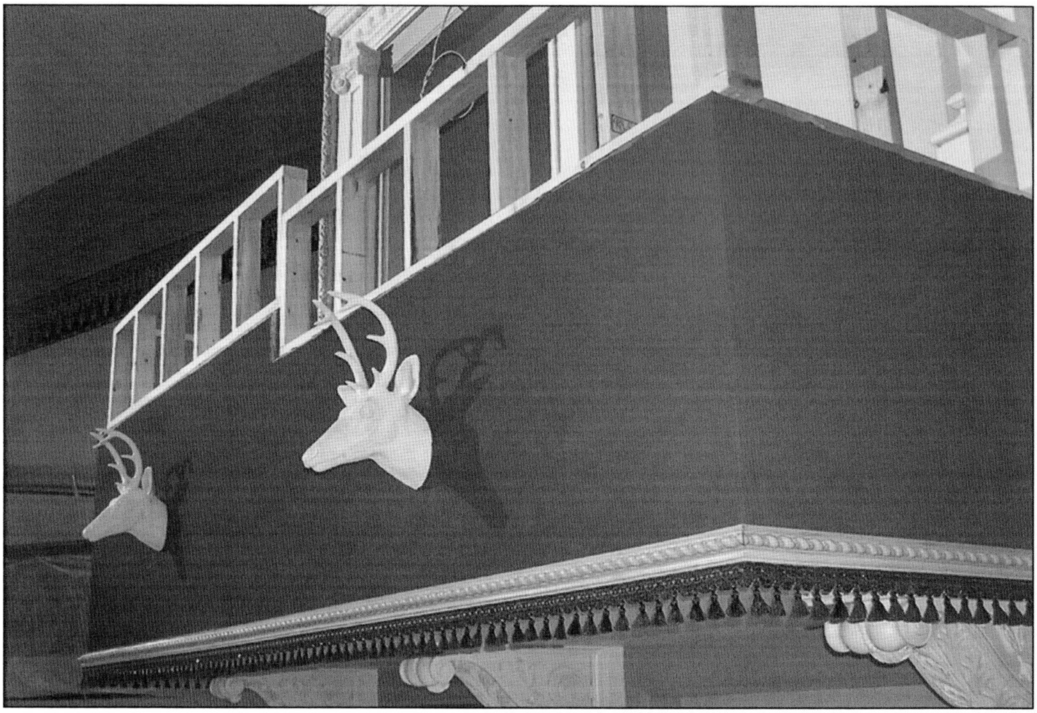

The elk heads are attached to the box seats, which are still under construction. During the initial stages of restoration, when non-original building elements that had been added over the years were being removed, workers were fortunate to have found remnants and pieces of original cast plaster moldings. These pieces allowed workers to duplicate the moldings as closely as possible to those from 1905. (Both photographs by Russell Parker.)

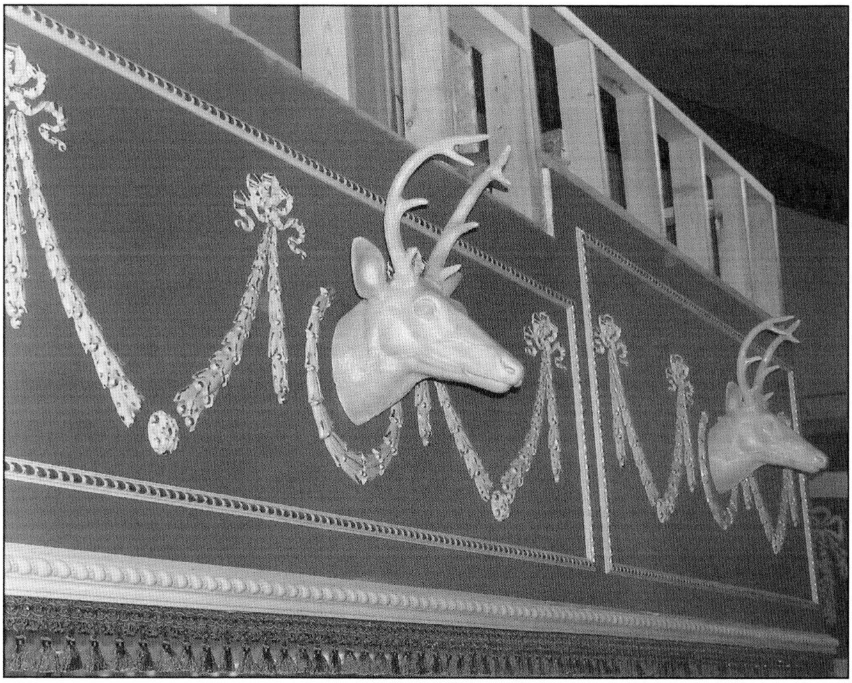

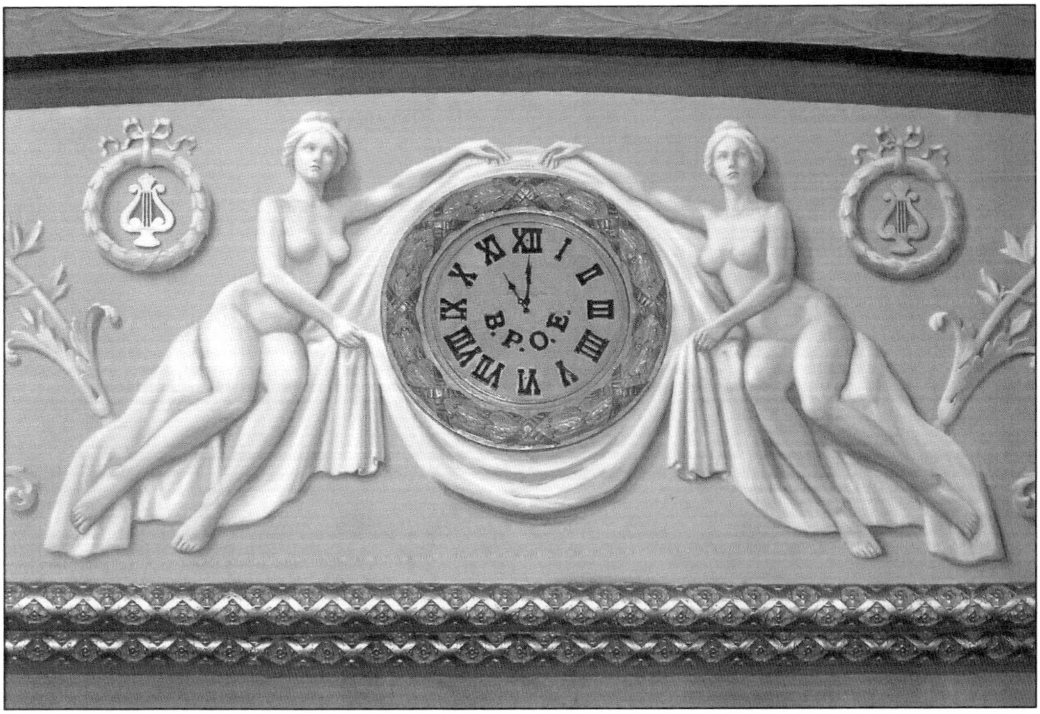

Although the original was formed from plaster, a decision was made during restoration to re-create the proscenium arch with a Trompe L'oiel rendering. This labor-intensive artist's technique effectively uses shadow and light to give a three-dimensional appearance to an object. The proscenium arch, including a clock that always stays at 11:00 (a time that has significance in the ritual of the Elks Lodge) was replicated by Evergreene Architectural Arts of New York City. (Photograph by Russell Parker.)

With a grant from the Arizona Department of Commerce's Main Street Program, the Elks Opera House Foundation ordered a new ceiling light ring, replicating the one believed to have adorned the opera house in 1905. Here, it is in place to be winched by a new motor to the ceiling where it remains except when the lightbulbs need to be changed. (Photograph by Russell Parker.)

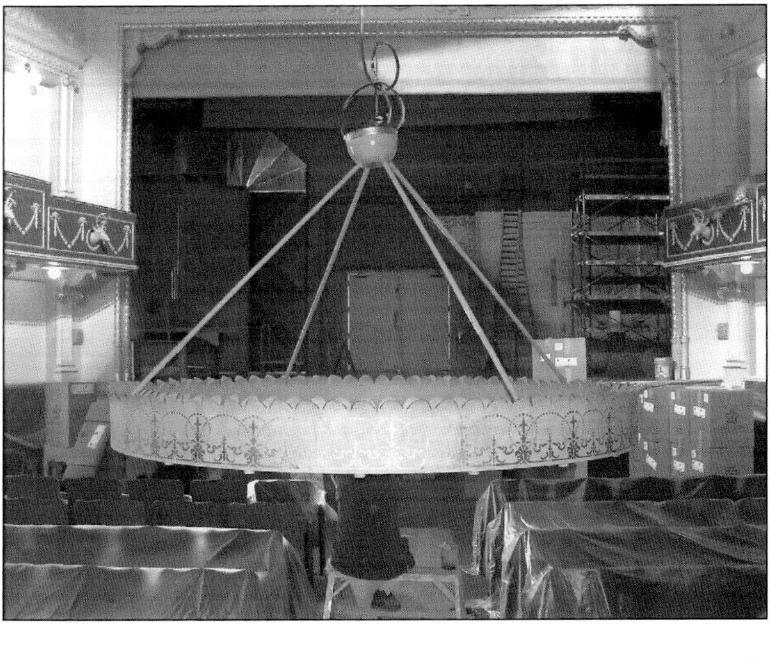

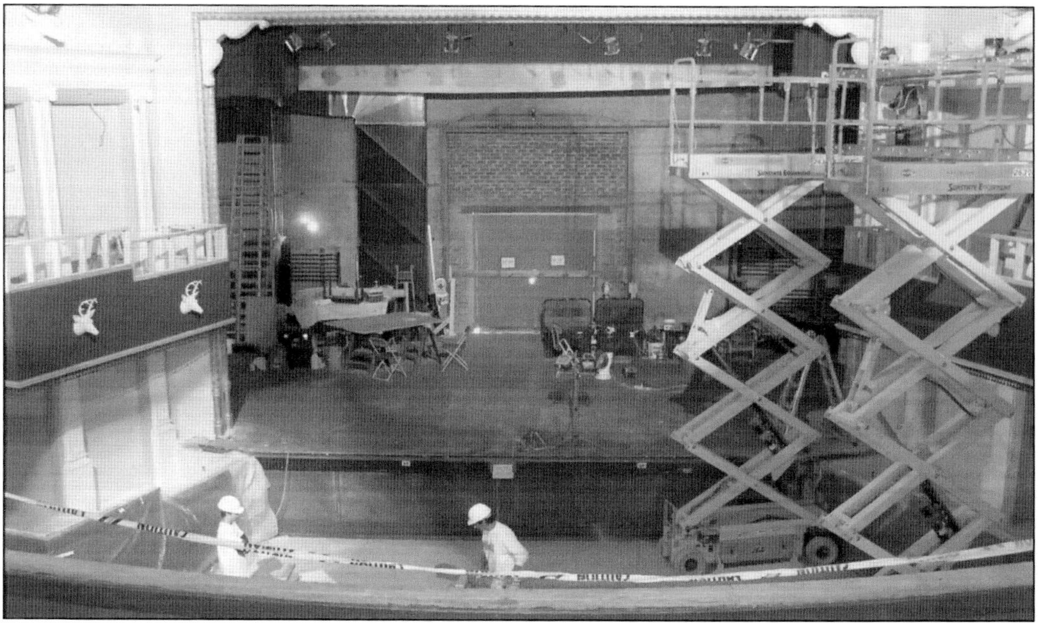

The construction moves ahead full steam. The backstage area is visible in these photographs with the large double doors in the direct center. These open out high above an alley and were used to hoist heavy theater set pieces inside during the early days. Reportedly, an assistant to the hosts of the television children's show *The Wallace and Ladmo Show* fell out of these doors and landed on his head during their 1967 appearance at the Elks Theatre; he survived. (Both photographs by Russell Parker.)

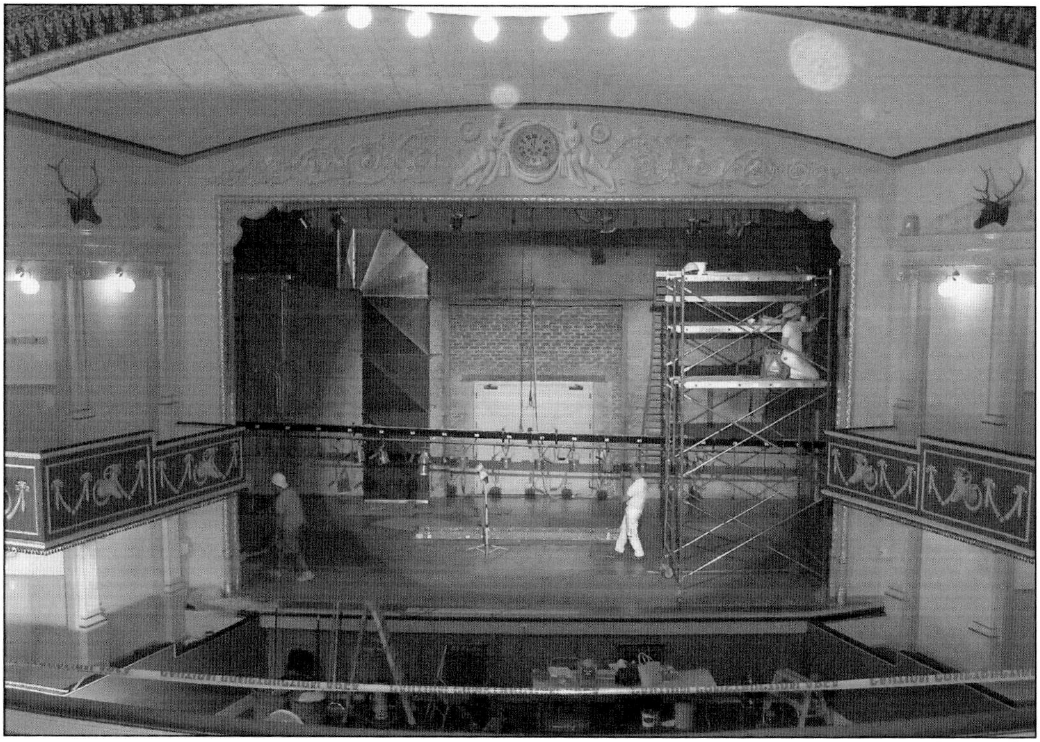

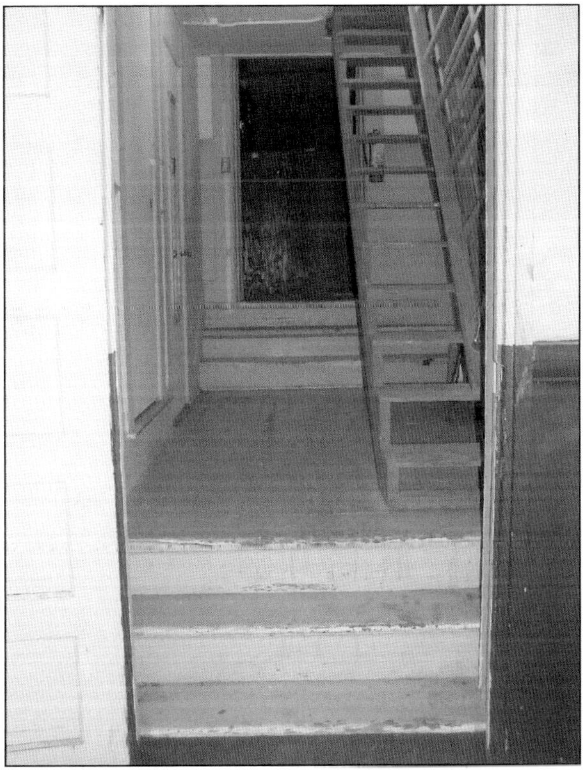

An entrance to the backstage from the auditorium appears before the restoration. Shown on the right are the old wooden steps that once led to the upper box seats. Below, the steps have been removed as this area goes under construction. (Both photographs by Russell Parker.)

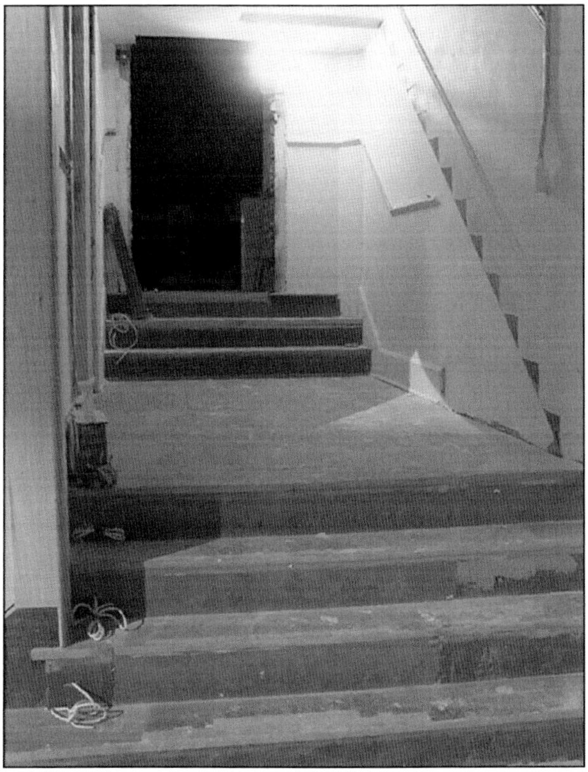

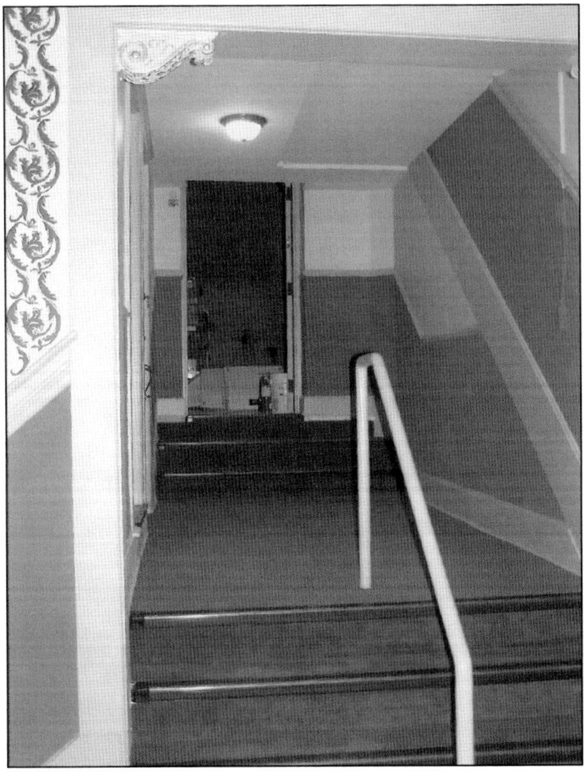

The same backstage entrance appears after restoration. The lower opera boxes are now accessible from this entrance. Current building codes did not allow the restoration of steps to the upper boxes, which today can only be accessed from the balcony. (Both photographs by Russell Parker.)

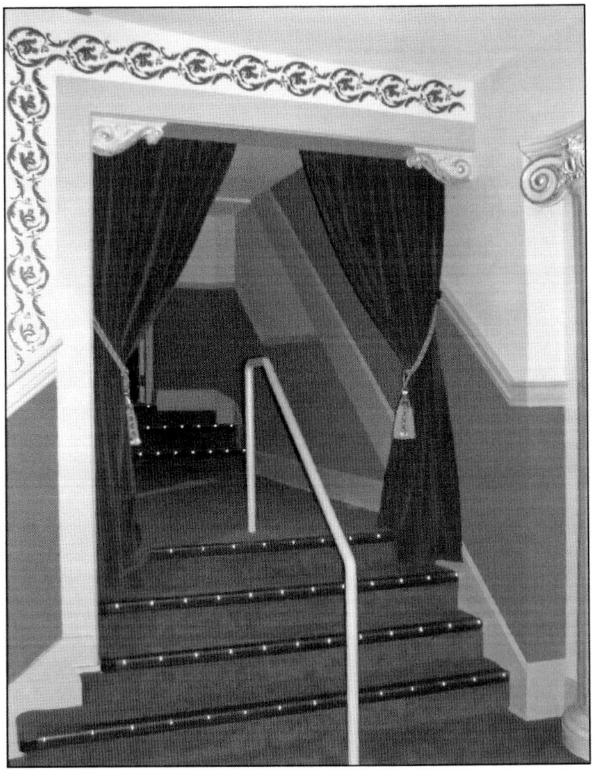

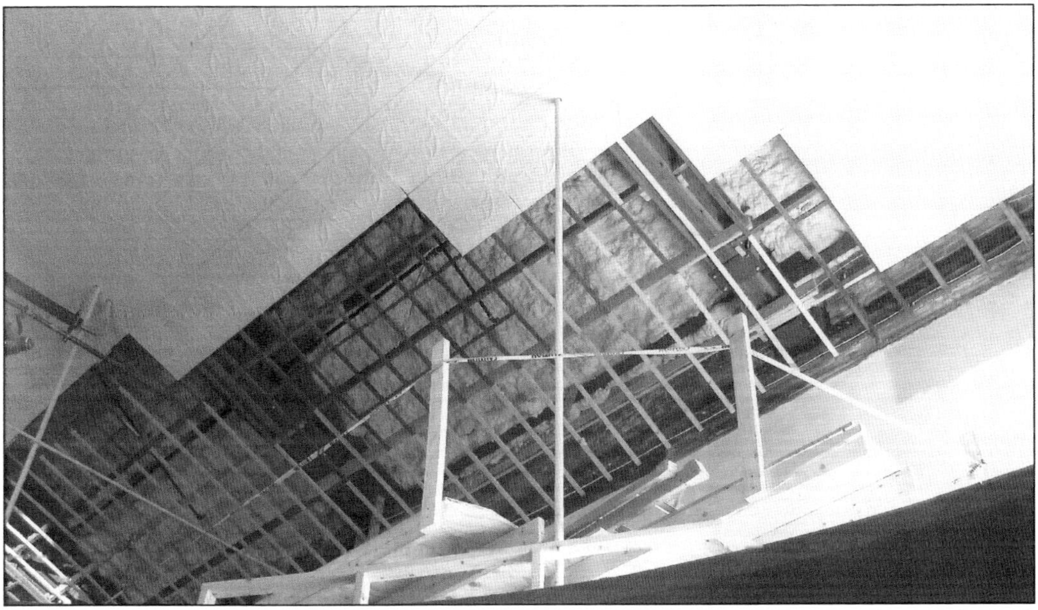

The original pressed metal ceiling panels were all removed and either restored or replicated. Such panels had once existed all through the building in the upper stories. (Photograph by Russell Parker.)

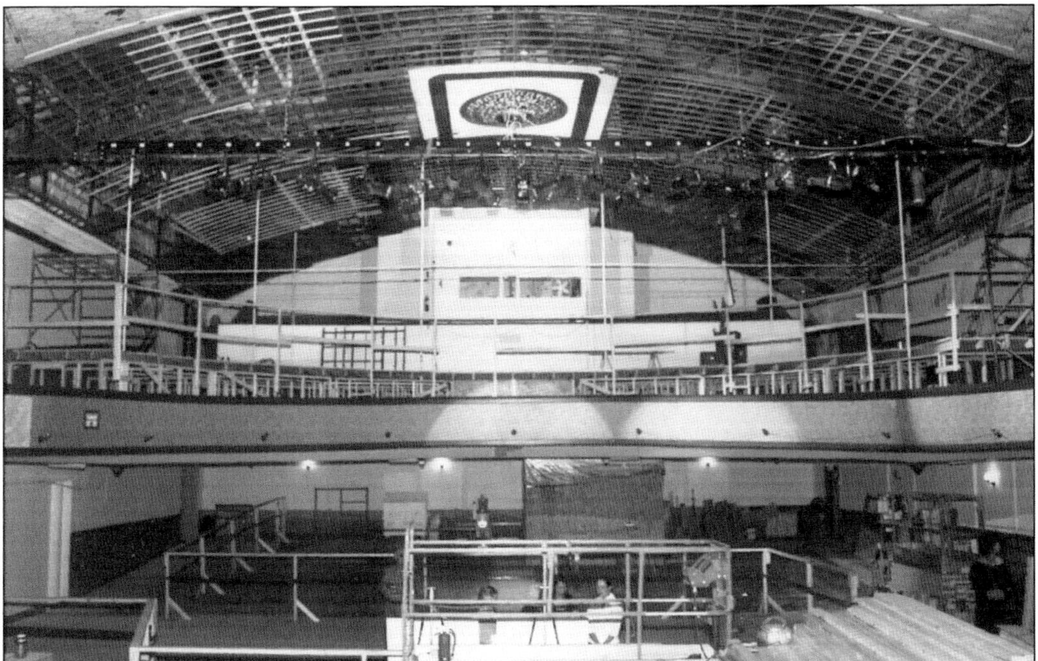

Taken from the stage looking out into the audience, the interior of the Elks Opera House is shown during the restoration. All of the ceiling panels have been removed, as have all of the seats. Construction scaffolding is visible in the balcony. (Photograph by Russell Parker.)

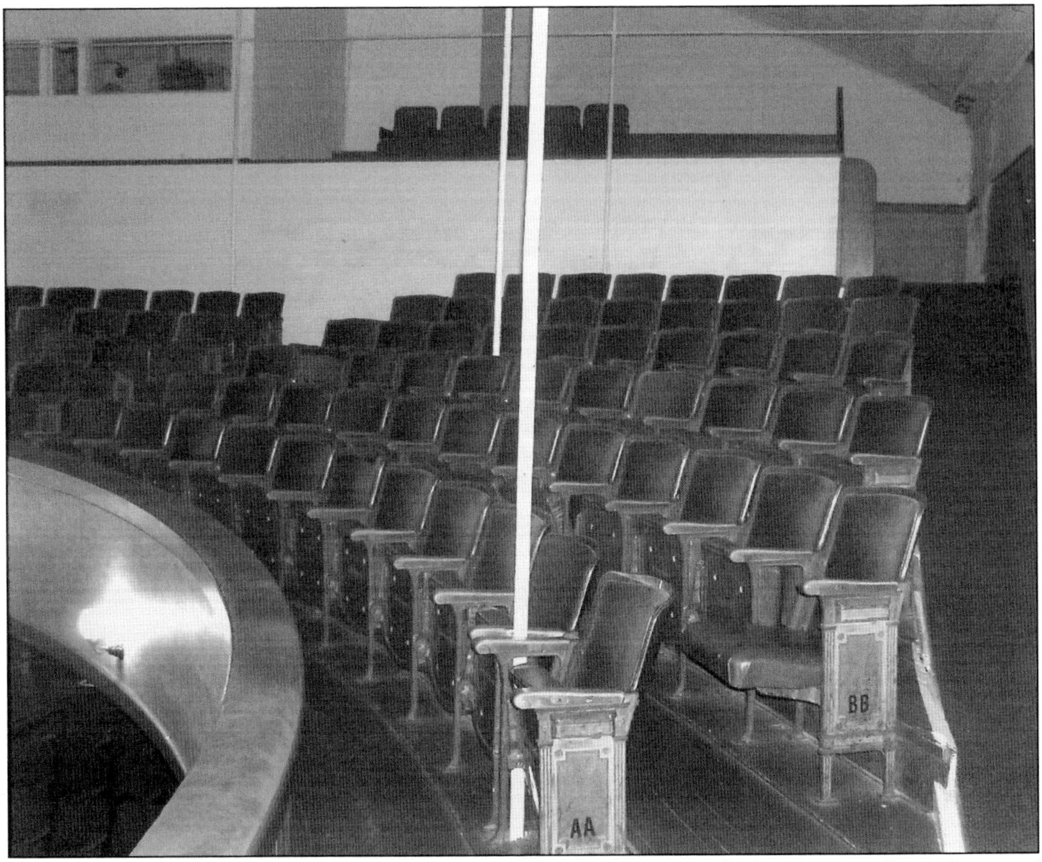

These images show the balcony with the old seats that were installed in 1928 still in place and the balcony with the seats removed. During the renovation, workers discovered evidence of a fire having once occurred in the northeast corner of the balcony, but to date, there is no known documentation as to when this happened. (Both photographs by Russell Parker.)

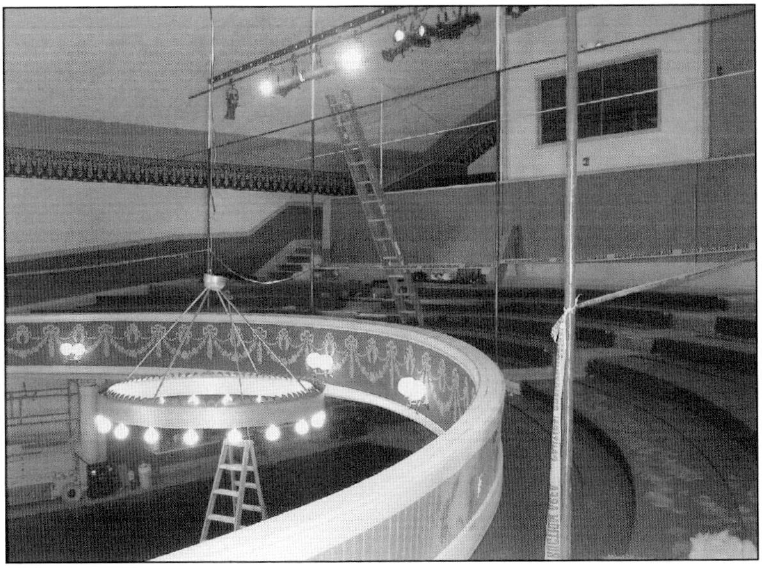

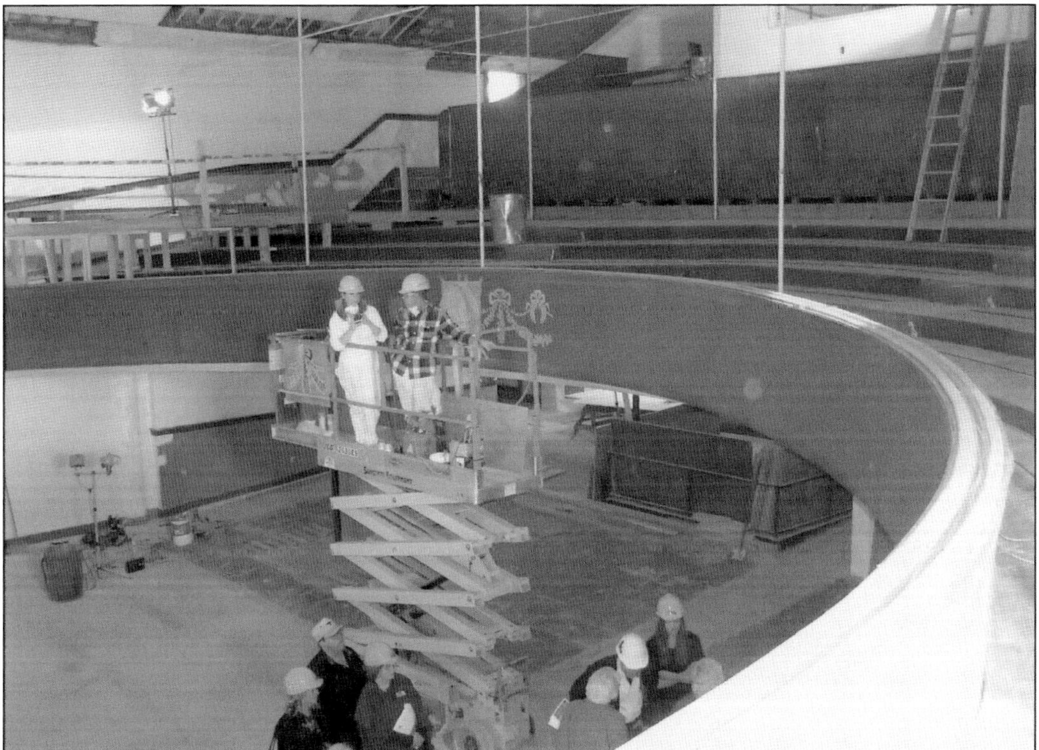

The Elks Opera House interior and balcony appears with all of the seats removed. Atop the scaffolding are award-winning artists Shari Stura and Luis Sanjurjo, who did all the gold-leaf and decorative painting during restoration. (Photograph by Russell Parker.)

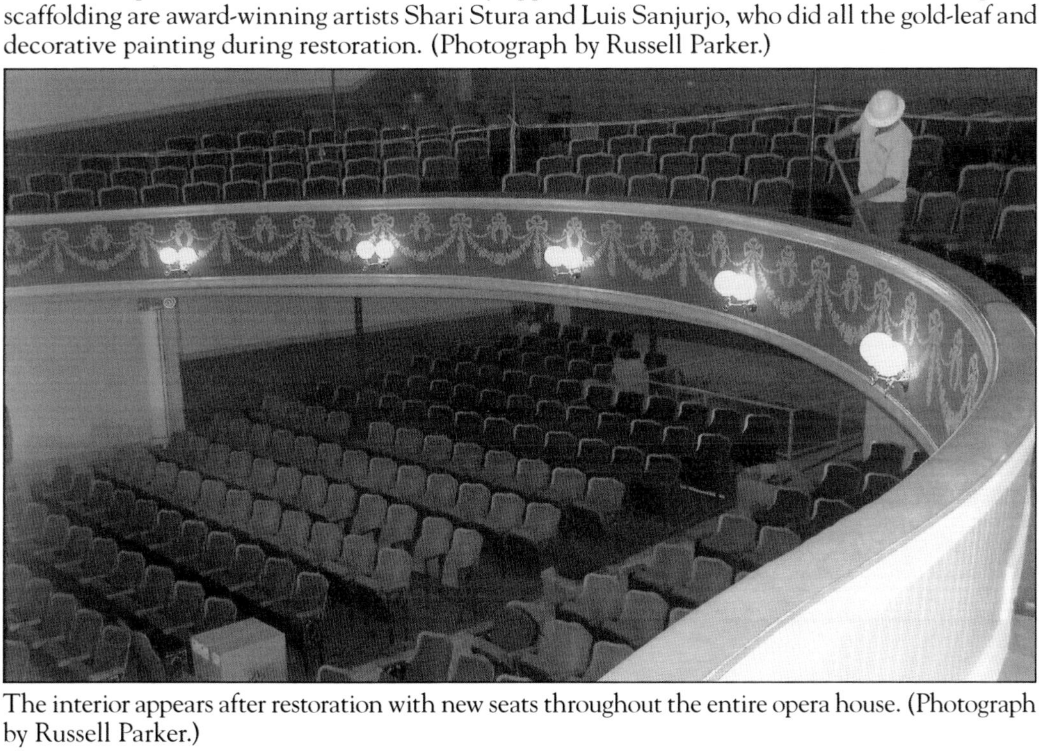

The interior appears after restoration with new seats throughout the entire opera house. (Photograph by Russell Parker.)

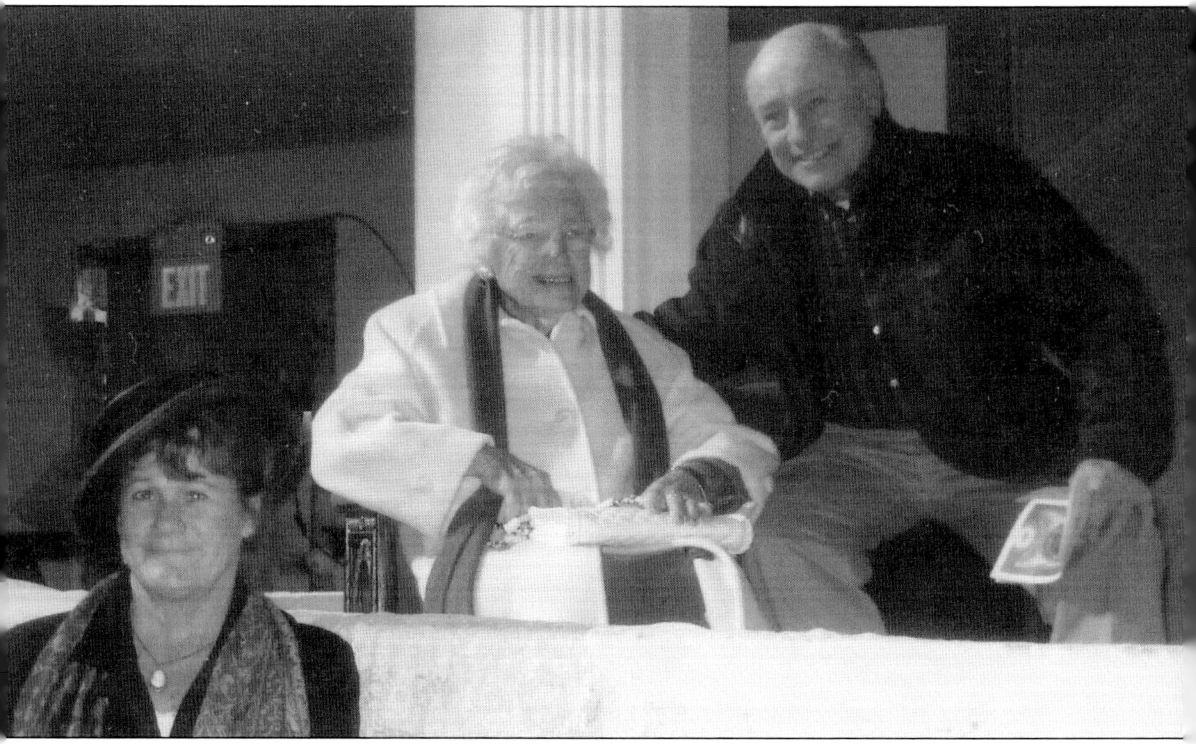

The guest of honor at the 105th Elks Opera House anniversary show was Hazel Deming (seated in the center in an unfinished box seat), who had graduated from Prescott High School on the stage of the Elks Opera House in 1929 and is the last surviving member of that class. She also is probably the last person still living who attended Sir Harry Lauder's performance at the Elks Opera House. Sitting beside Hazel is Dr. Taylor Hicks Jr., a Prescott native and retired orthodontist, and standing in front of the box on the left is Jody Drake from Sharlot Hall Museum and Archive's Blue Rose Theatre. (Elisabeth Ruffner collection.)

Warren Miller (left), who initiated the drive to raise funds to restore the Elks Opera House in 1998 (by organizing the Save the Elks committee of the Prescott Area Arts and Humanities Council), chats with Kurt Vogel before the 105th anniversary show. Kurt, owner of Batterman's Auction Gallery in Prescott, acted as master of ceremonies for the 105th anniversary show. (Photograph by Russell Parker.)

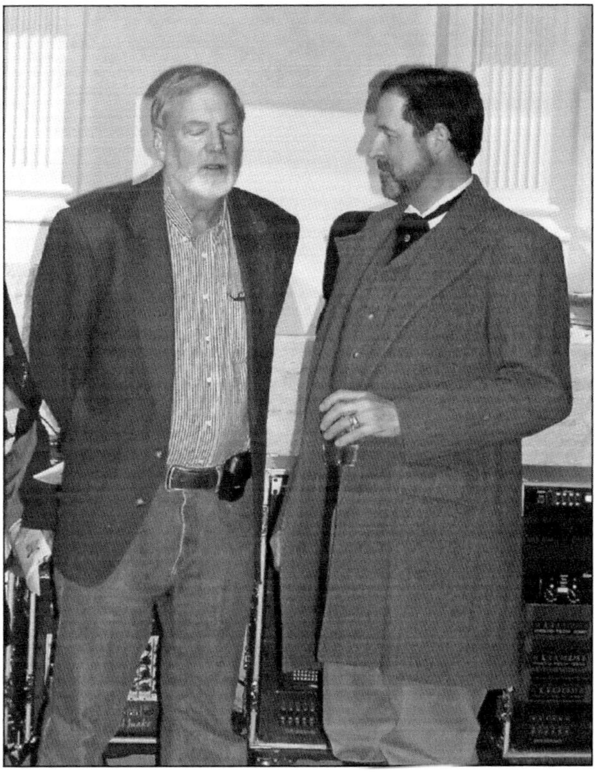

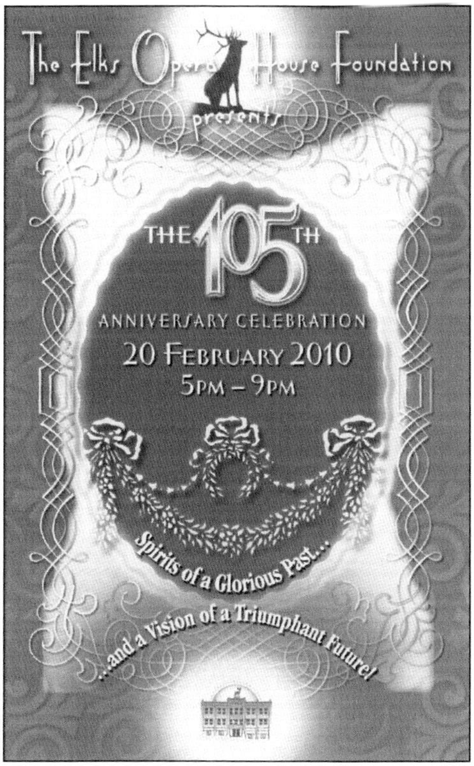

During the restoration, a live show was held in the theater for the 105th anniversary of the opening despite the fact that there were no seats. This show featured local performers portraying notable people who had once appeared live or in a film shown at the Elks Opera House. (Elisabeth Ruffner collection.)

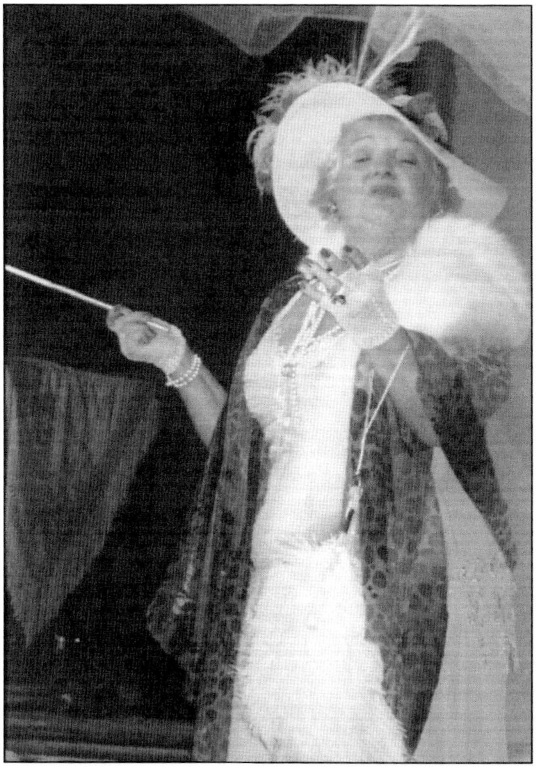

Longtime Elks Opera House benefactor Alicia Bauer portrayed Sophie Tucker during the 105th anniversary "ghost" show. Tucker's movies had played at the Elks Theatre during the 1930s. (Elisabeth Ruffner collection.)

Shown is the completed interior of the Elks Opera House with a replicated forest backdrop courtesy of the James Family Trust. The oldest known photograph of the interior, shown in chapter one, depicts the original forest scene. (Photograph by Russell Parker.)

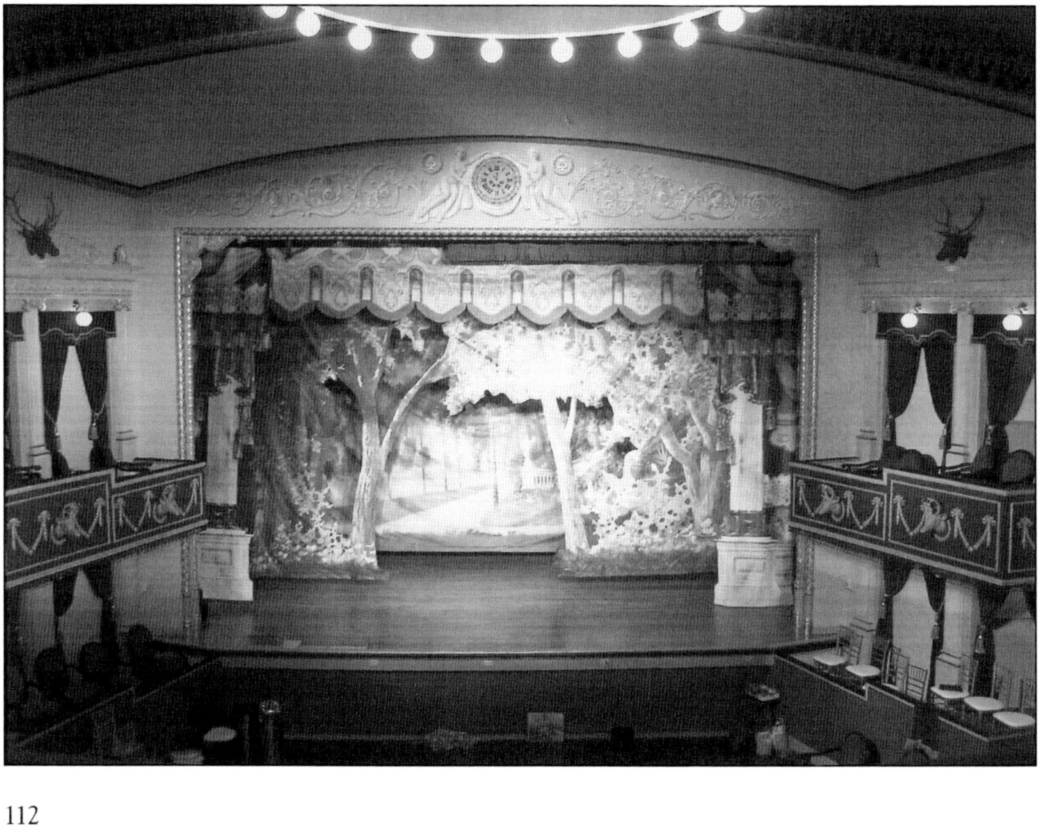

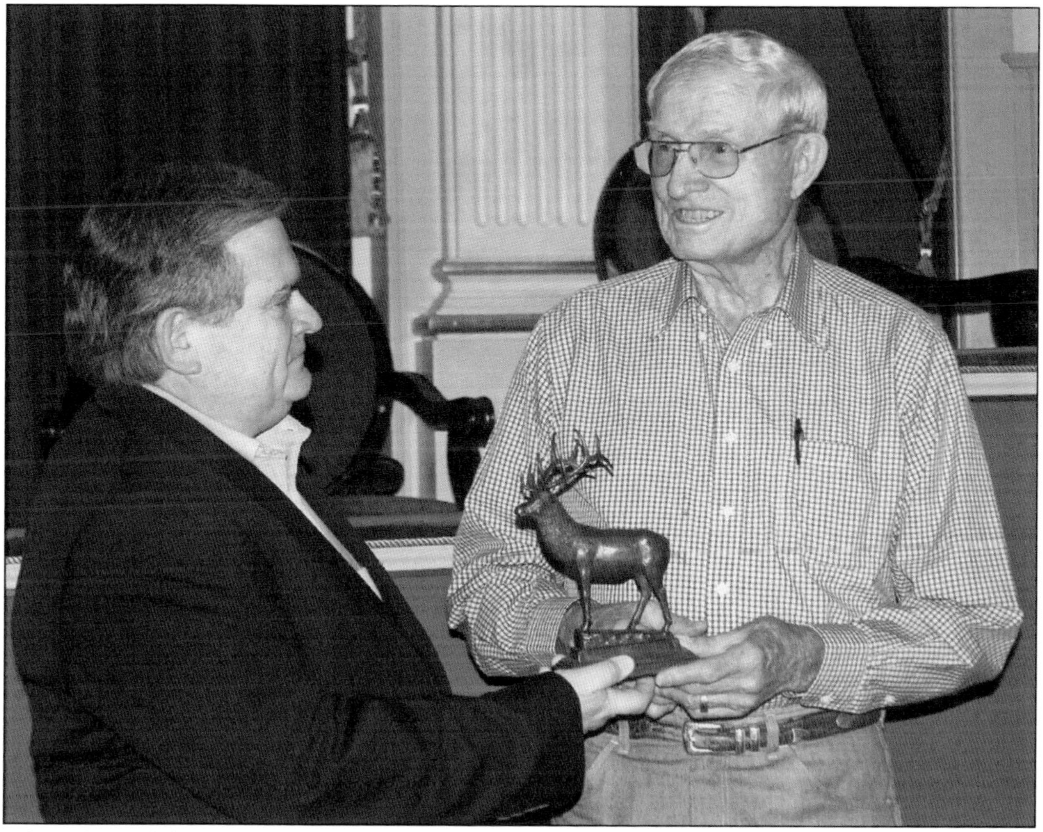

John Olsen (left), president of the Elks Opera House Foundation, presents a bronze replica of the copper elk gracing the building to John Sullivan, associate general manager of the Salt River Project and donor to the restoration. (The *Daily Courier*.)

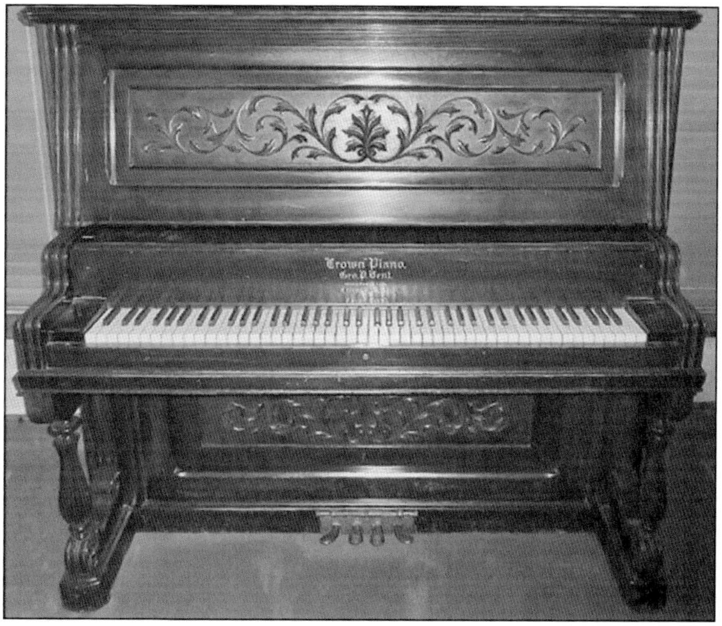

This is probably the original piano used in the Elks Opera House that is visible in the early interior photographs. It is owned today by Prescott resident Jill Tetreau, who has kept it in pristine condition. It had been given to her by longtime Prescott resident Emma Andres many years earlier. (Alan and Kathy Krause collection.)

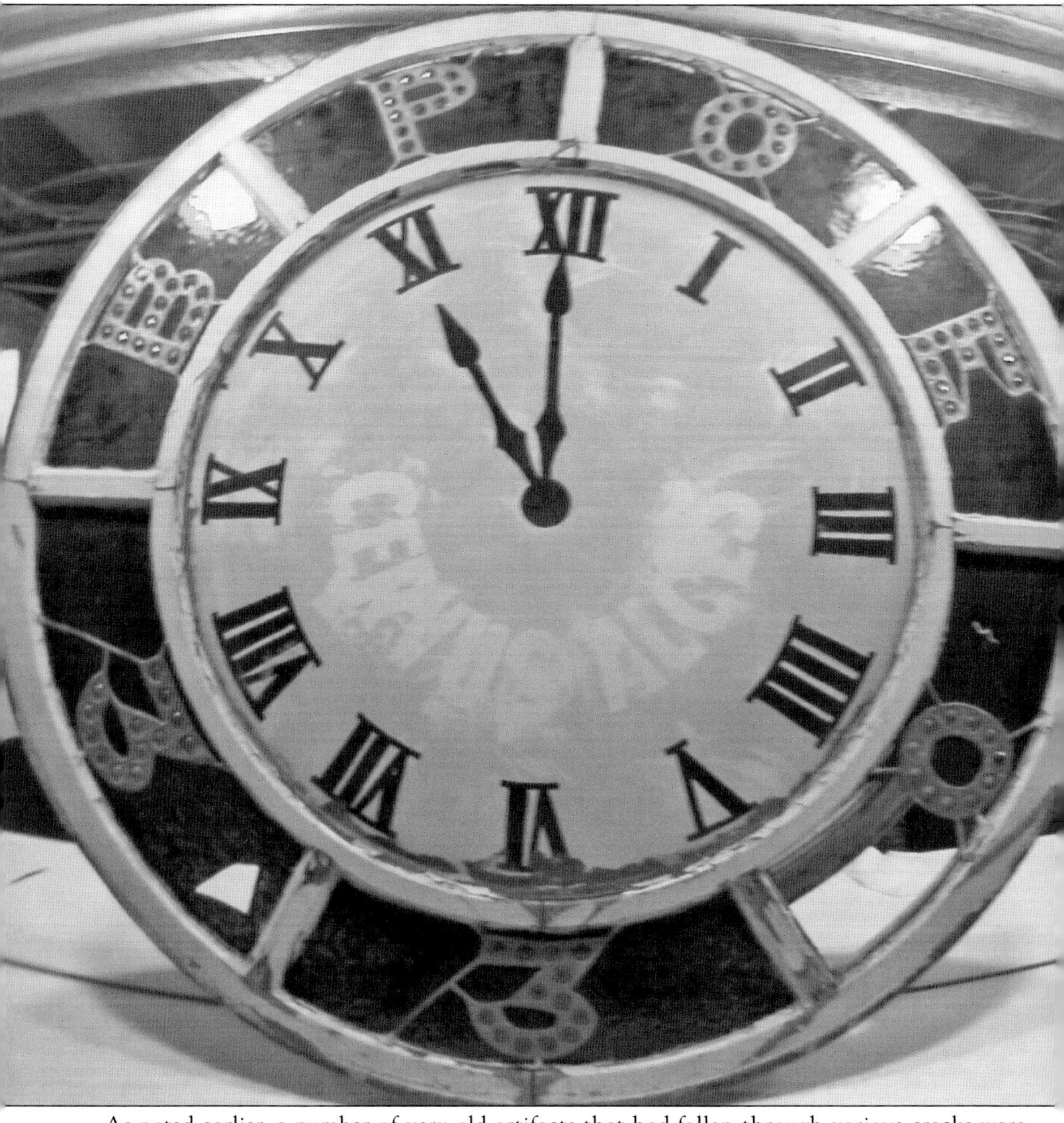

As noted earlier, a number of very old artifacts that had fallen through various cracks were discovered during the 2009–2010 restoration. This old Elks clock with partial stained glass was probably used in the upstairs lodge rooms. (Photograph by David Schmittinger.)

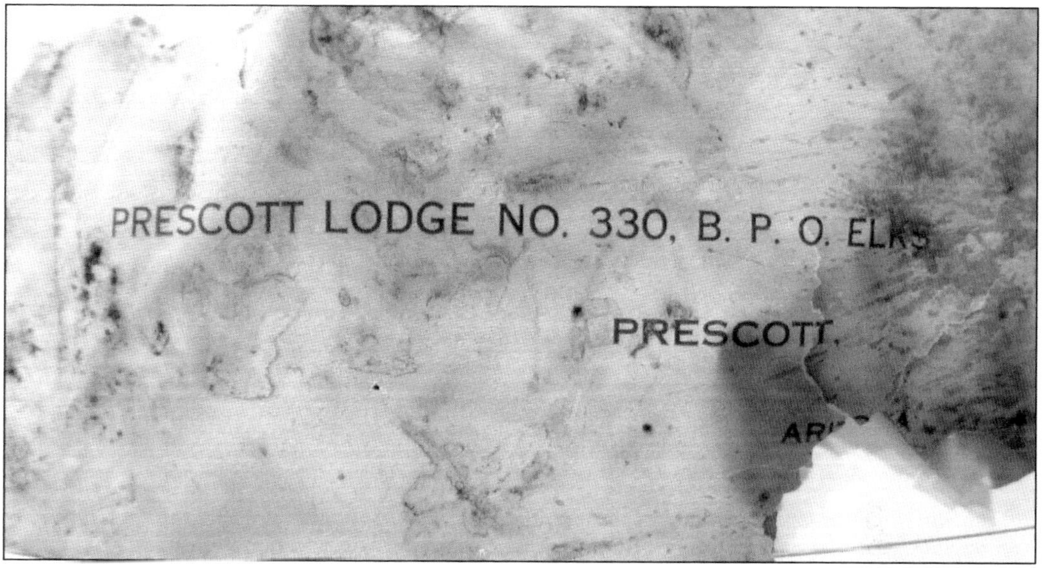

This unused, water- and age-stained envelope addressed to Prescott Lodge no. 330 is difficult to date, but it is definitely from pre–zip code days. (Photograph by David Schmittinger.)

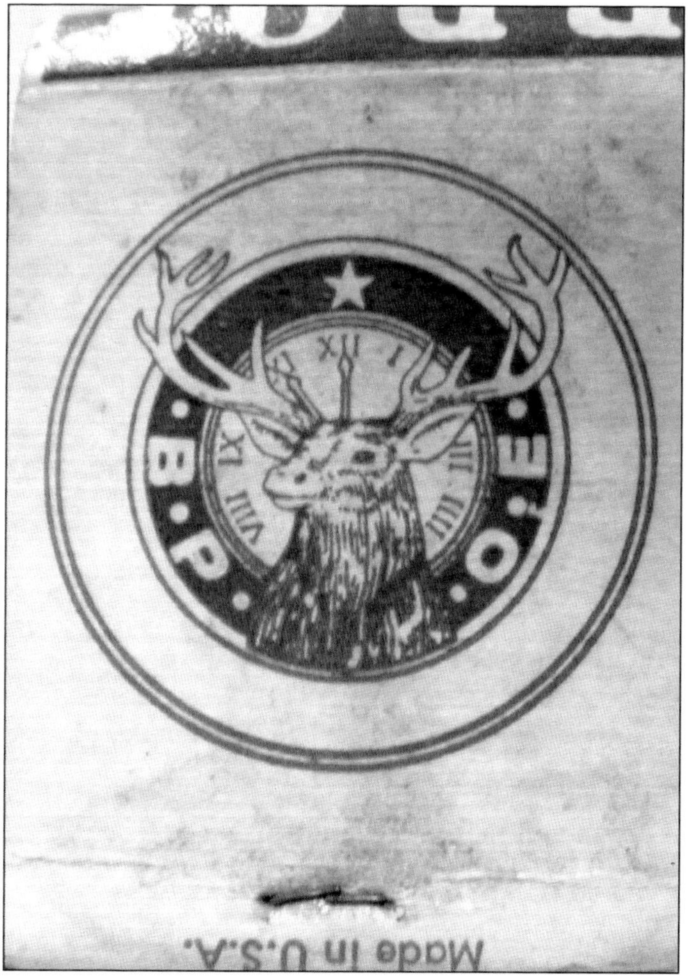

Shown is an Elks Lodge matchbook cover. Smoking was common in this era, and along with the various forms of tobacco came the matchbook. Matchbooks were commonly available in all conceivable forms: as marketing tools with advertising information and logos, unlabeled, or in this case as a memento of the Elks Lodge. This one was most likely available in a canister in the upstairs rooms of the Elks Lodge. (Photograph by David Schmittinger.)

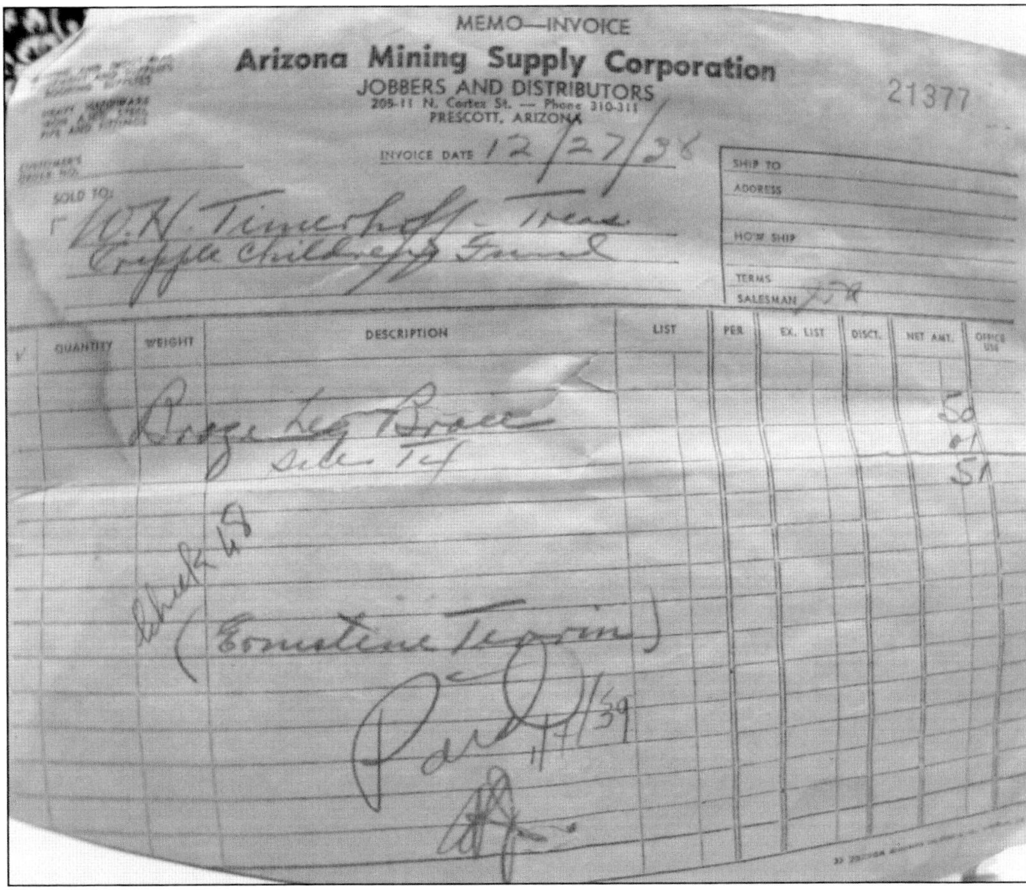

MEMO—INVOICE

Arizona Mining Supply Corporation

JOBBERS AND DISTRIBUTORS

205-11 N. Cortez St. — Phone 310-311

PRESCOTT, ARIZONA

21377

INVOICE DATE 12/27/38

SOLD TO: W.H. Timerhoff Treas

SHIP TO

ADDRESS

HOW SHIP

TERMS

SALESMAN

QUANTITY	WEIGHT	DESCRIPTION	LIST	PER	EX. LIST	DISCT.	NET AMT.	OFFICE USE

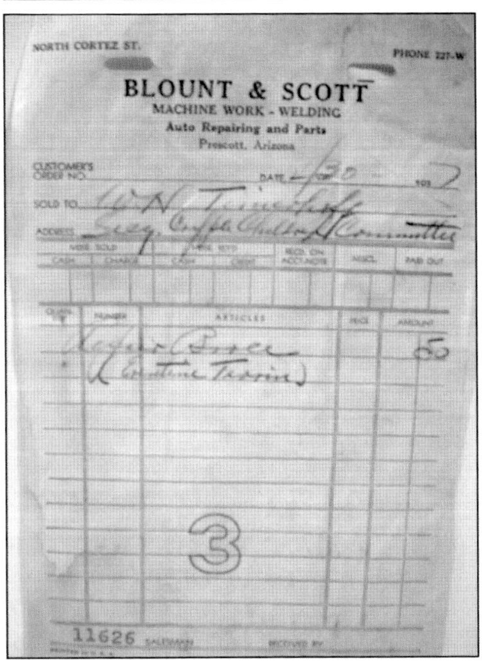

NORTH CORTEZ ST.

PHONE 227-W

BLOUNT & SCOTT

MACHINE WORK - WELDING

Auto Repairing and Parts

Prescott, Arizona

CUSTOMER'S ORDER NO.

DATE

SOLD TO W.H. Timerhoff

ADDRESS

QUAN.	NUMBER	ARTICLES	PRICE	AMOUNT

11626

A sheaf of receipts, apparently lost in the theater by Prescott mayor W.H. Timerhoff in the 1930s, was discovered in 2009 during the restoration. How they ended up in the Elks Opera House is open for speculation. Notable are the two different companies: the Arizona Mining Supply Corporation and Blount & Scott Machine Work–Welding. (Both photographs by David Schmittinger.)

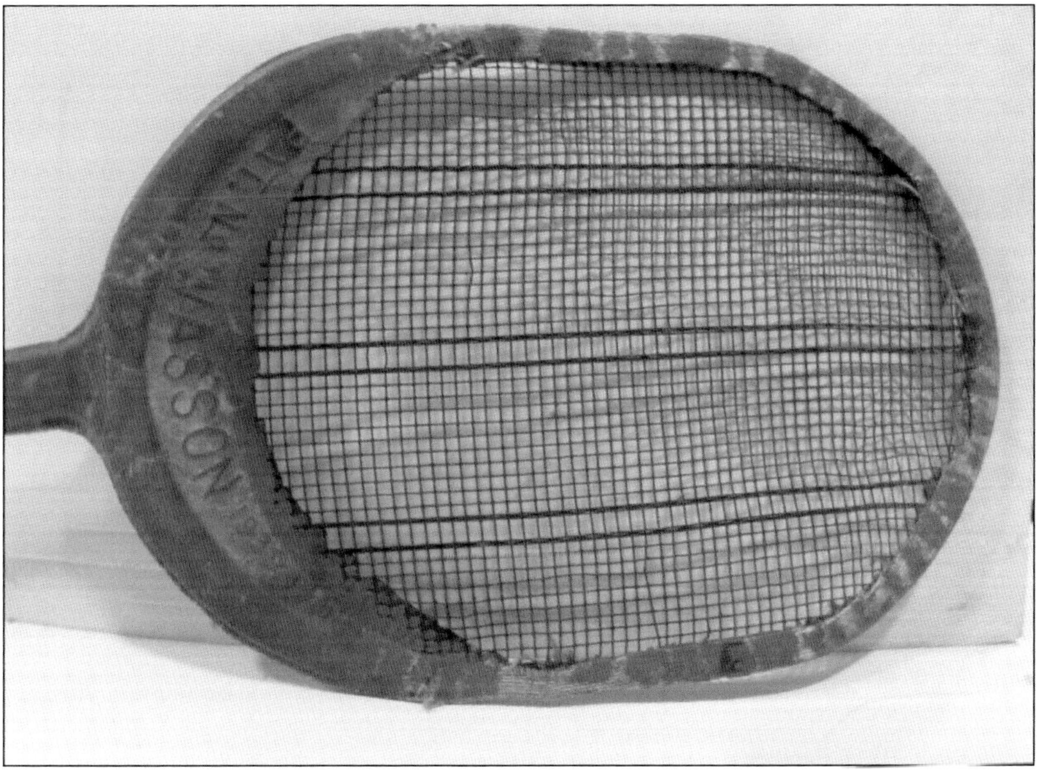

This old flyswatter is probably from the 1930s. Without air-conditioning, open doors and windows were common. Just as common were flies and the swatters used to ward off the unwanted guests. The leather wrapping and wire is in stark contrast to the plastic flyswatters usually seen today. (Photograph by David Schmittinger.)

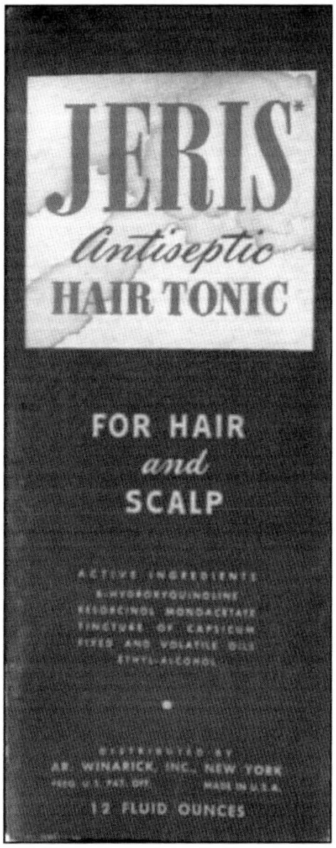

This empty container of hair tonic is likely from the 1930s or 1940s and was probably used by the stage performers when doing their preshow preparation in the makeup rooms below the stage. (Photograph by David Schmittinger.)

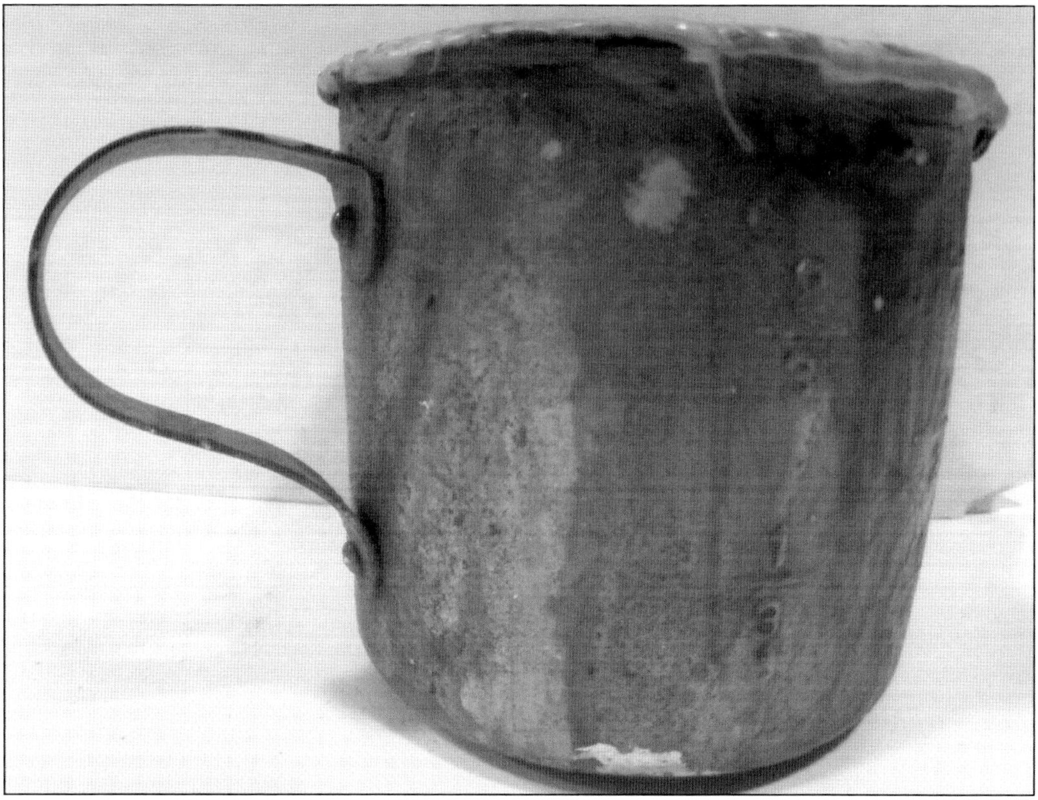

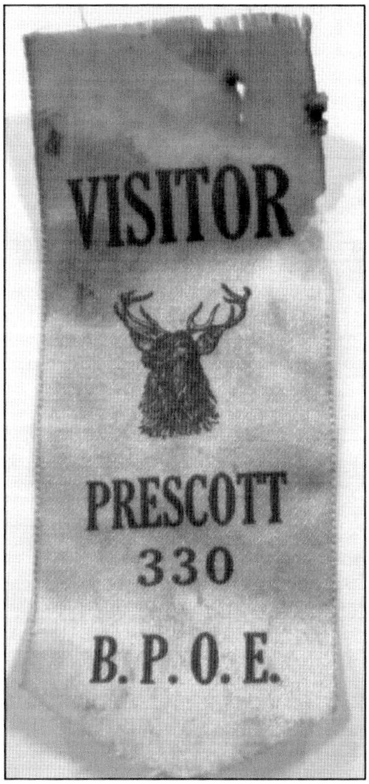

This cup was perhaps used to measure popcorn at the concession stand. Charles T. Manley is credited with developing a small electric popcorn maker in the mid-1920s, which allowed movie theater owners to produce an inexpensive snack for sale inside the theater lobby. Patrons found this to be an ideal movie snack, and it remains so to this day. (Photograph by David Schmittinger.)

This lapel ribbon is probably from an Elks Lodge convention of bygone years. (Photograph by David Schmittinger.)

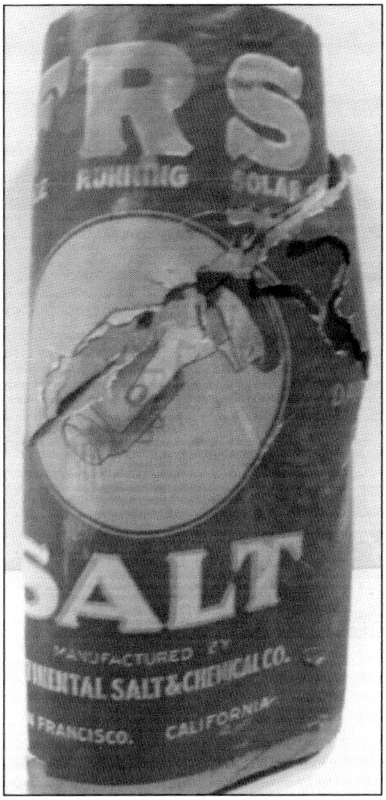

Shown is an empty container of salt, most likely used for flavoring popcorn in the early movie-theater days. (Photograph by David Schmittinger.)

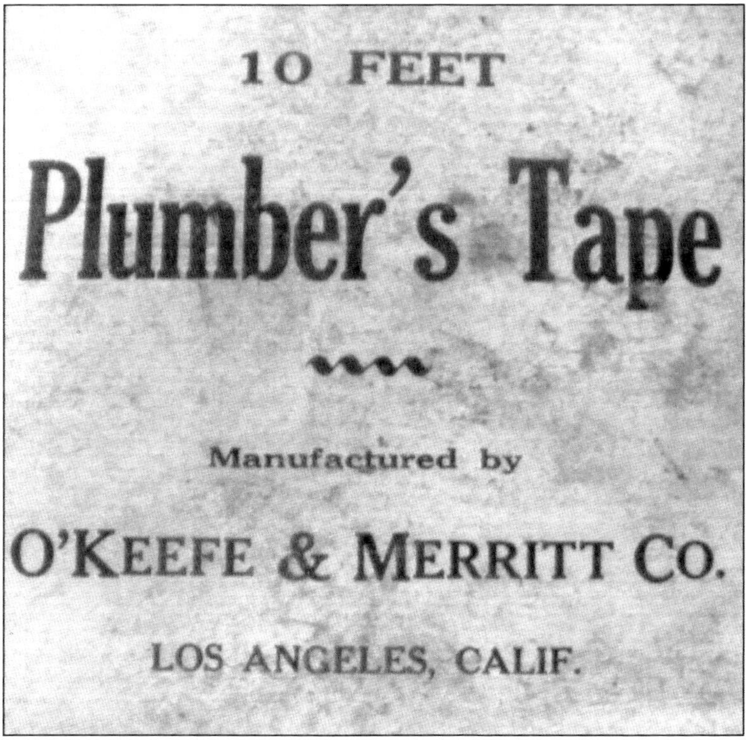

Aging water and steam pipes would spring leaks over time, and the discovery of this empty box of plumber's tape implies that at this stage of the building's existence, the occasional leak would need a plumber to fix it by utilizing the necessary repair materials. (Photograph by David Schmittinger.)

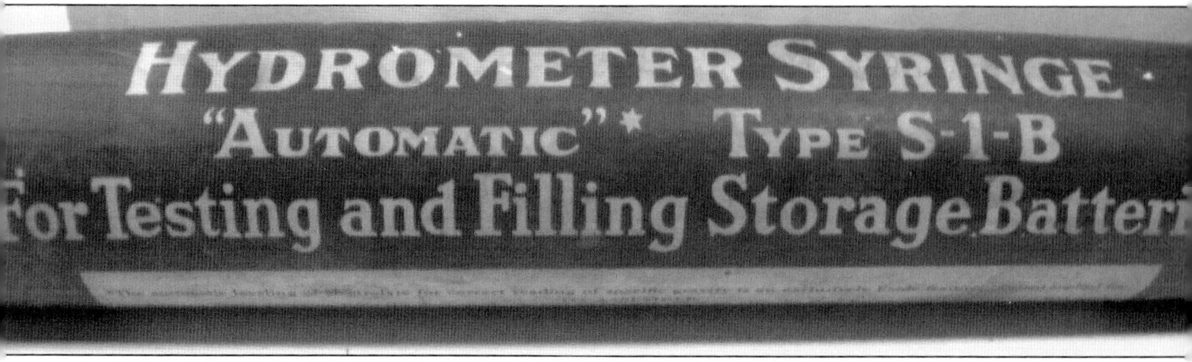

This is an empty container for a hydrometer syringe from the 1940s or 1950s. It was used to measure the specific gravity of fluid for wet-cell batteries. Electric wiring in the building in the early days would have been sporadic, and batteries would have been needed for power in certain locations, most likely in the makeup rooms under the stage. (Photograph by David Schmittinger.)

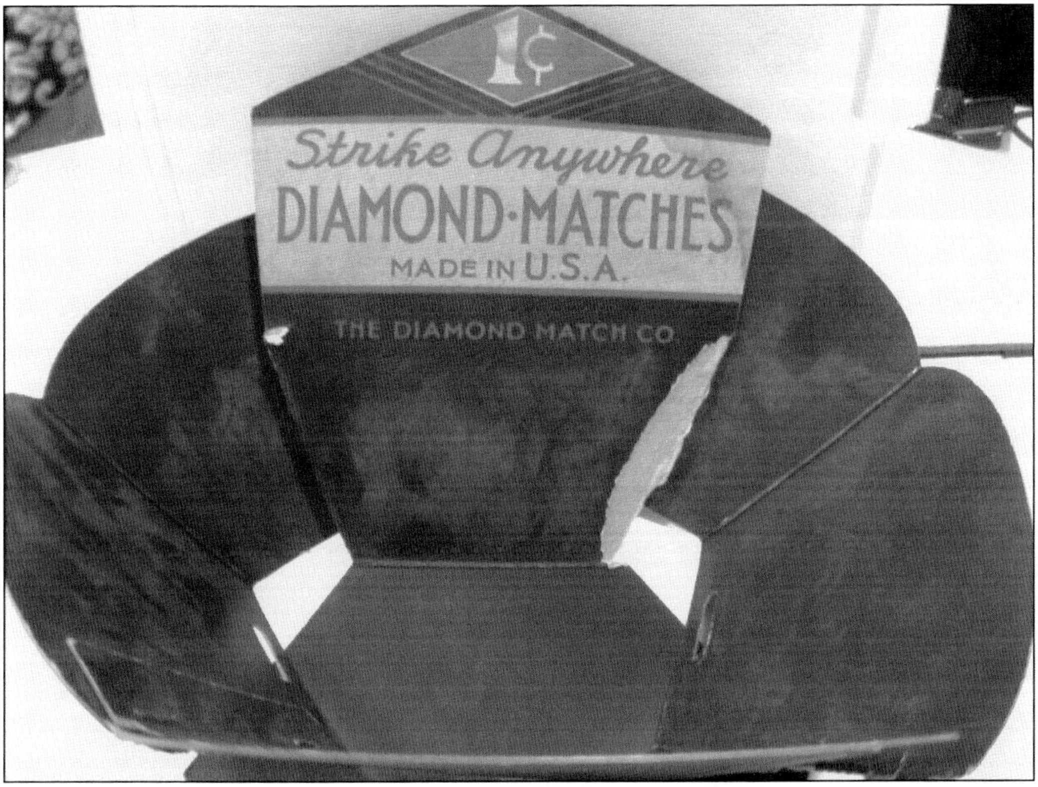

Shown is a display container for matchbooks, which were probably given away with cigarette and cigar purchases at the concession stand in the early movie-theater days at the Elks Theatre. Smoking was allowed in public places during that era and would have been a common occurrence in the theater. (Photograph by David Schmittinger.)

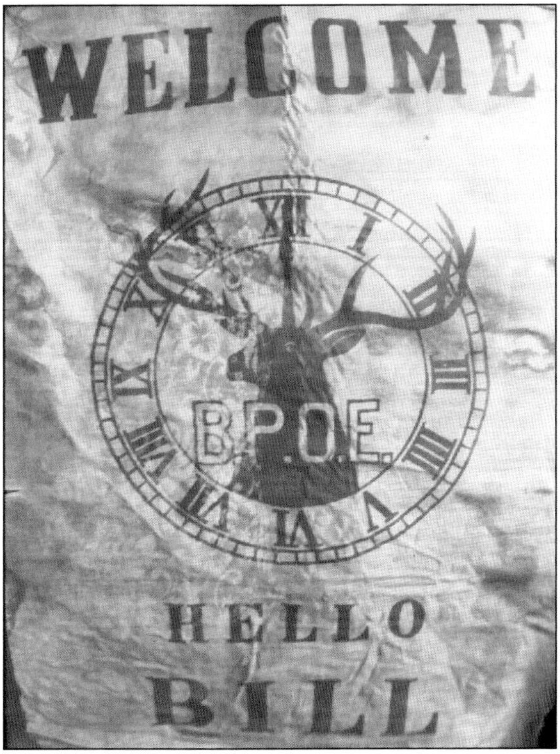

Most interesting of the relics found during construction is this large pennant, which probably dates to an Elks convention in Prescott in 1937. Newspapers of the time reported that Prescott was filled with such pennants during that conference. *Bill* is a term of endearment used by lodge members for their visiting brethren. (Photograph by David Schmittinger.)

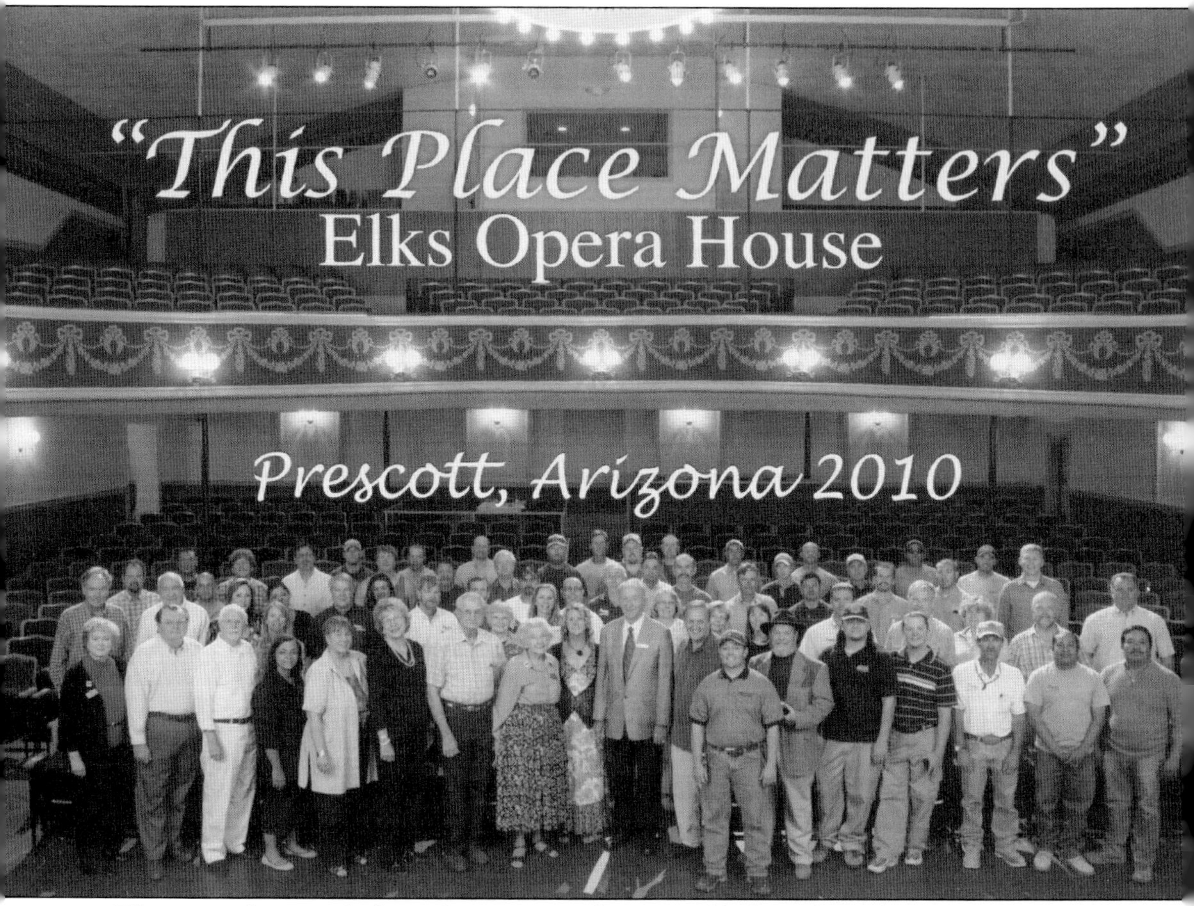

This group photograph shows the many people responsible for making the restoration of the Elks Opera House a reality. (Marchettiphoto.com.)

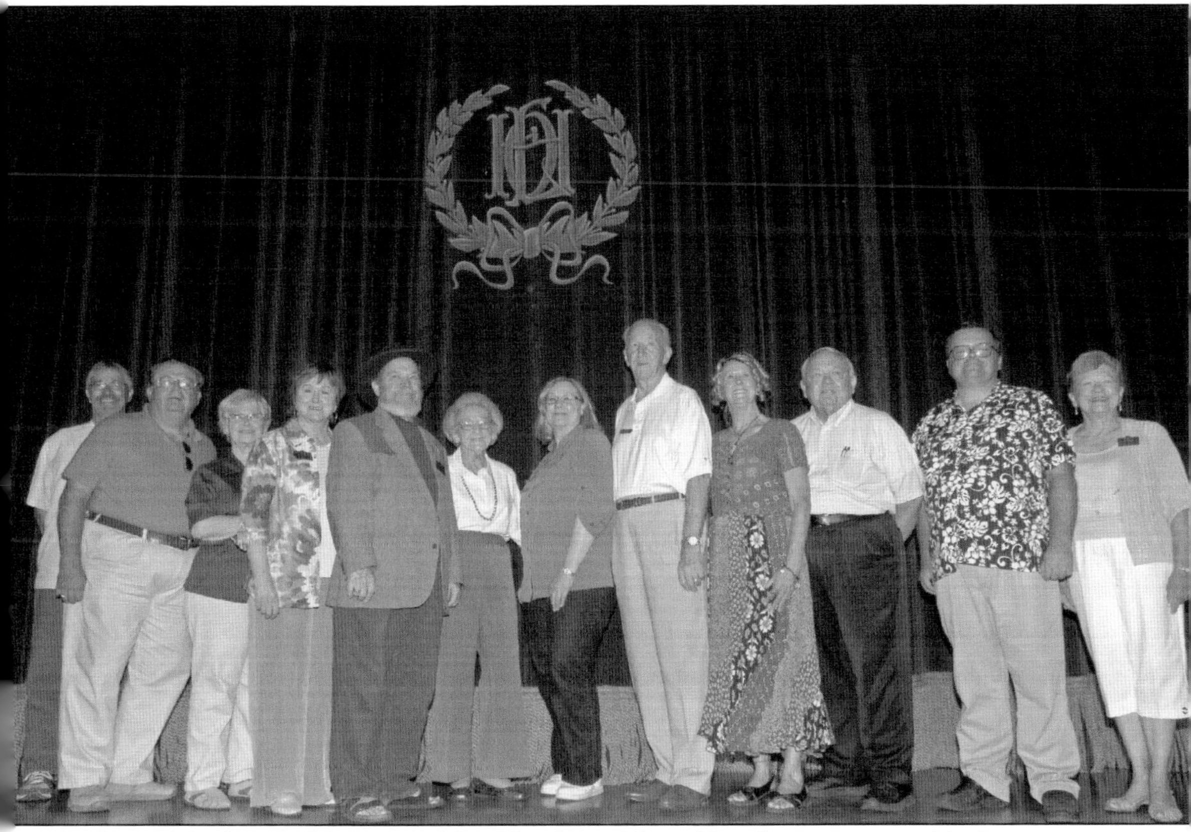

Members of the board of directors of the Elks Opera House Foundation are joined by historian and author Parker Anderson on the Elks Opera House stage. Taken in August 2011, the image shows, from left to right, Terry Berrett, Frank Sente, Maxine Dillahunty, Barbara Watkins, Russell Parker, Elisabeth Ruffner, Cathy Church, Ralph Weiger, Debra Mathews, J.C.T. Pool, Parker Anderson, and Marilyn Henze. (Photograph by Terry Berrett.)

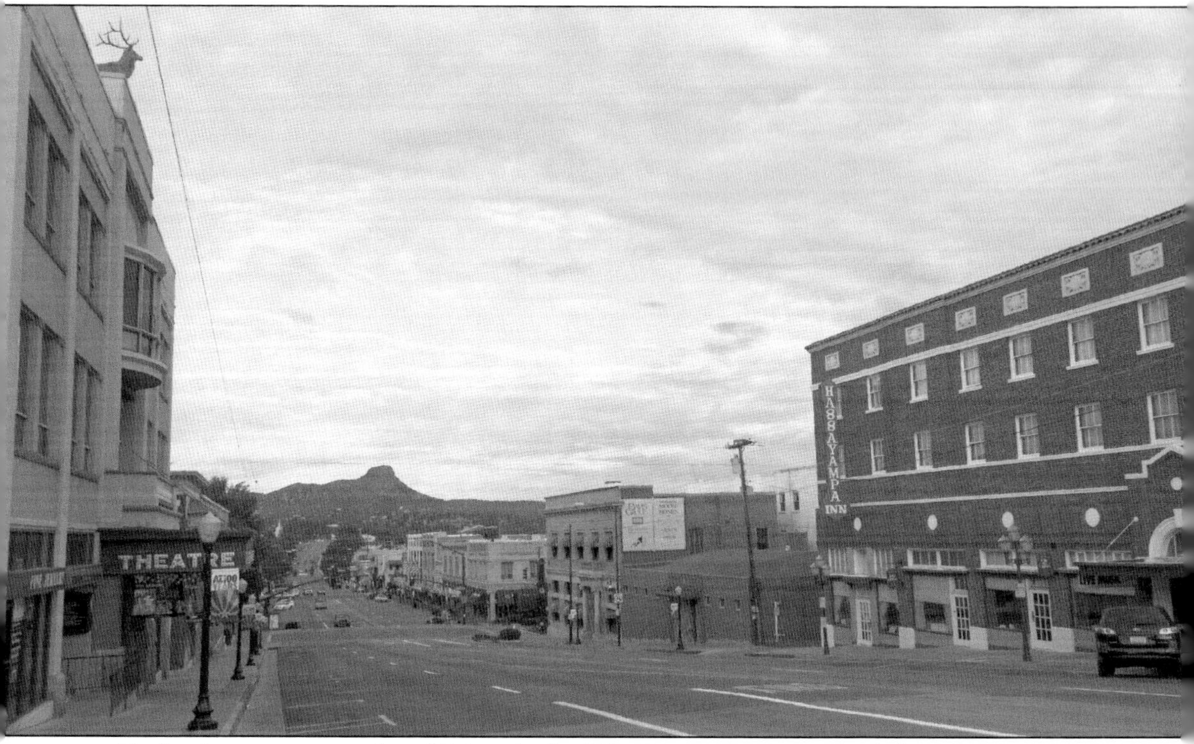

Gurley Street is pictured in 2011 with the Elks Opera House on the left and the Hassayampa Inn on the right. It is interesting to contrast this photograph with earlier-era images in previous chapters of this book to see how much of the scene has changed and how much has remained the same. (Photograph by Terry Berrett.)

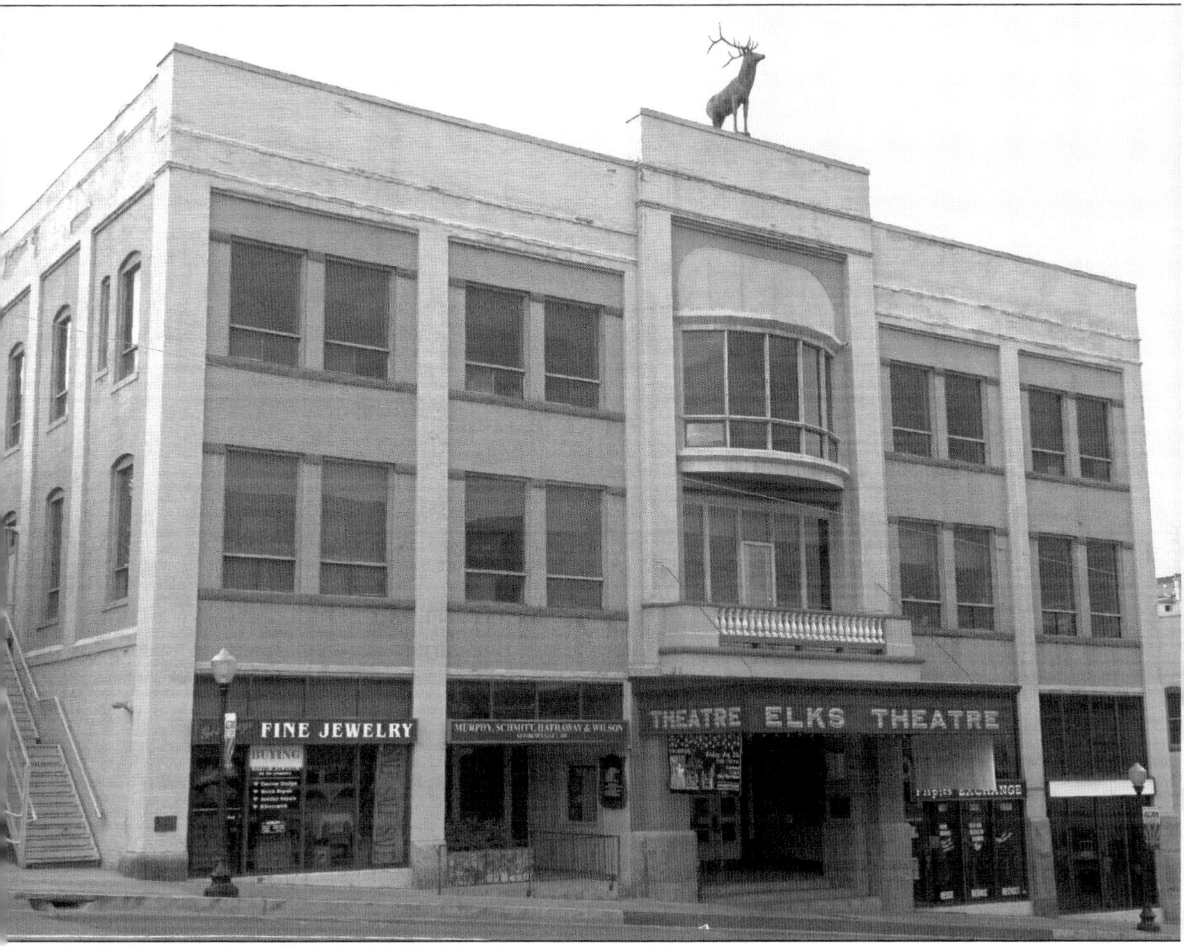

The exterior of the restored Elks Opera House appears in 2011. Despite all the exterior changes over the years, the building today is not materially different from how it stood in 1910. (Photograph by Terry Berrett.)

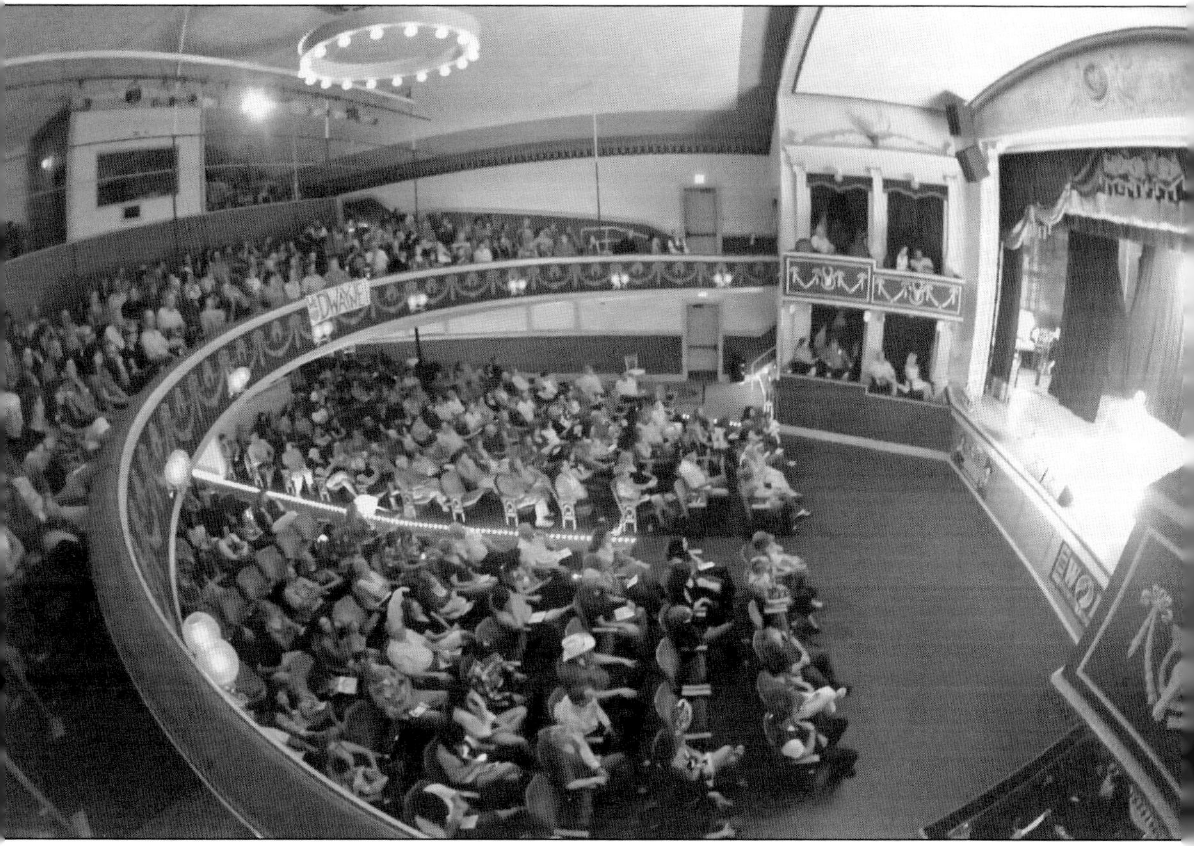

Members of the public fill the Elks Opera House for a performance of the finals of the Prescott Idol competition on September 1, 2011. It is a great example of a dream realized, as the theater is back to its original condition, and the residents of Prescott are once again able to enjoy a wide variety of performing arts in what is arguably the best original period theater between St. Louis and San Francisco. (Photograph by Matt Hinshaw, the *Daily Courier*.)

The Elks Opera House Foundation

The Elks Opera House Foundation was organized in 2002 as an Arizona nonprofit corporation, tax exempt under IRS 501 (c)(3) Internal Revenue Service regulation. Among the initial purposes of the foundation was the restoration of the theater space within the Elks Building at 117 East Gurley Street, Prescott, Arizona. Upon completion of infrastructure and code work by the City of Prescott, owner of the theater, the foundation invested $1.75 million in restoration of the opera house to its 1905 appearance. Renovation of the marquee, foyer, and first and inner lobbies were completed to reflect varying eras to bring the opera house back as close as possible to its original condition. The foundation remains today to invest in productions of all varieties to ensure that the opera house continues into the next century, reflecting the brilliance of the past.